Vance Astro is a psionically-enhanced warrior and sentinel of liberty! Yondu is a master of all weapons! Martinex has control over extremes of heat! Charlie-27 is super-strong and super-fast! Starhawk sees the future with his mystical precognition! In the war-torn world of 3014 A.D., these freedom fighters stand together to overthrow the invasion of the alien Badoon...and to face far darker threats! They are...

GUARDIANS 3000

TIME AFTER TIME

WRITER: **DAN ABNETT**

ARTIST: **GERARDO SANDOVAL**

COLOR ARTISTS: **EDGAR DELGADO**

WITH **RACHELLE ROSENBERG** ("FIGHT FOR THE FUTURE")

LETTERERS: **VC'S CLAYTON COWLES** (#1-2 & #4-5) & **TRAVIS LANHAM** (#3)

WITH **RACHELLE ROSENBERG** ("FIGHT FOR THE FUTURE")

COVER ART: **ALEX ROSS**

EDITOR: **KATIE KUBERT**

EXECUTIVE EDITOR: **MIKE MARTS**

D1517252

COLLECTION EDITOR: **JENNIFER GRÜNWALD**   ASSISTANT EDITOR: **SARAH BRUNSTAD**
ASSOCIATE MANAGING EDITOR: **ALEX STARBUCK**   EDITOR, SPECIAL PROJECTS: **MARK D. BEAZLEY**
SENIOR EDITOR, SPECIAL PROJECTS: **JEFF YOUNGQUIST**   SVP PRINT, SALES & MARKETING: **DAVID GABRIEL**

EDITOR IN CHIEF: **AXEL ALONSO**   CHIEF CREATIVE OFFICER: **JOE QUESADA**
PUBLISHER: **DAN BUCKLEY**   EXECUTIVE PRODUCER: **ALAN FINE**

GUARDIANS 3000 VOL. 1: TIME AFTER TIME. Contains material originally published in magazine form as GUARDIANS OF THE GALAXY #14 and GUARDIANS 3000 #1-5. First printing 2015. ISBN# 978-0-7851-9312-8. Published by MARVEL WORLDWIDE, INC., a subsidiary of MARVEL ENTERTAINMENT, LLC. OFFICE OF PUBLICATION: 135 West 50th Street, New York, NY 10020. Copyright © 2015 MARVEL. No similarity between any of the names, characters, persons, and/or institutions in this magazine with those of any living or dead person or institution is intended, and any such similarity which may exist is purely coincidental. **Printed in Canada.** ALAN FINE, President, Marvel Entertainment; DAN BUCKLEY, President, TV, Publishing and Brand Management; JOE QUESADA, Chief Creative Officer; TOM BREVOORT, SVP of Publishing; DAVID BOGART, SVP of Operations & Procurement, Publishing; C.B. CEBULSKI, VP of International Development & Brand Management; DAVID GABRIEL, SVP Print, Sales & Marketing; JIM O'KEEFE, VP of Operations & Logistics; DAN CARR, Executive Director of Publishing Technology; SUSAN CRESPI, Editorial Operations Manager; ALEX MORALES, Publishing Operations Manager; STAN LEE, Chairman Emeritus. For information regarding advertising in Marvel Comics or on Marvel.com, please contact Jonathan Rheingold, VP of Custom Solutions & Ad Sales, at jrheingold@marvel.com. For Marvel subscription inquiries, please call 800-217-9158. **Manufactured between 4/3/2015 and 5/11/2015 by SOLISCO PRINTERS, SCOTT, QC, CANADA.**

10 9 8 7 6 5 4 3 2 1

EARTH, 3014 A.D.

THE FUTURE USED TO LOOK BRIGHT...

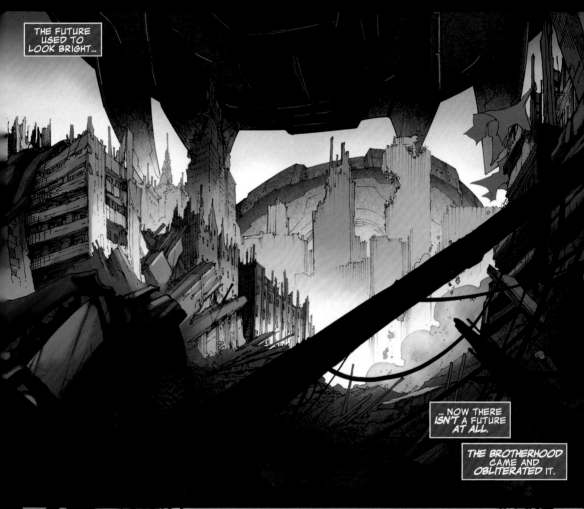

... NOW THERE ISN'T A FUTURE AT ALL.

THE BROTHERHOOD CAME AND OBLITERATED IT.

EARTH BURNED. SO DID THE OTHER PEACEFUL WORLDS OF THE UNITED SYSTEM.

HUMAN CULTURE COLLAPSED OVERNIGHT.

MY NAME IS GEENA DRAKE. I WILL BE DEAD IN THREE DAYS.

I ARRIVED AT LABOR CAMP 347 LAST NIGHT. THEY TELL ME THREE DAYS IS THE TYPICAL LIFE EXPECTANCY FOR A SLAVE WORKER.

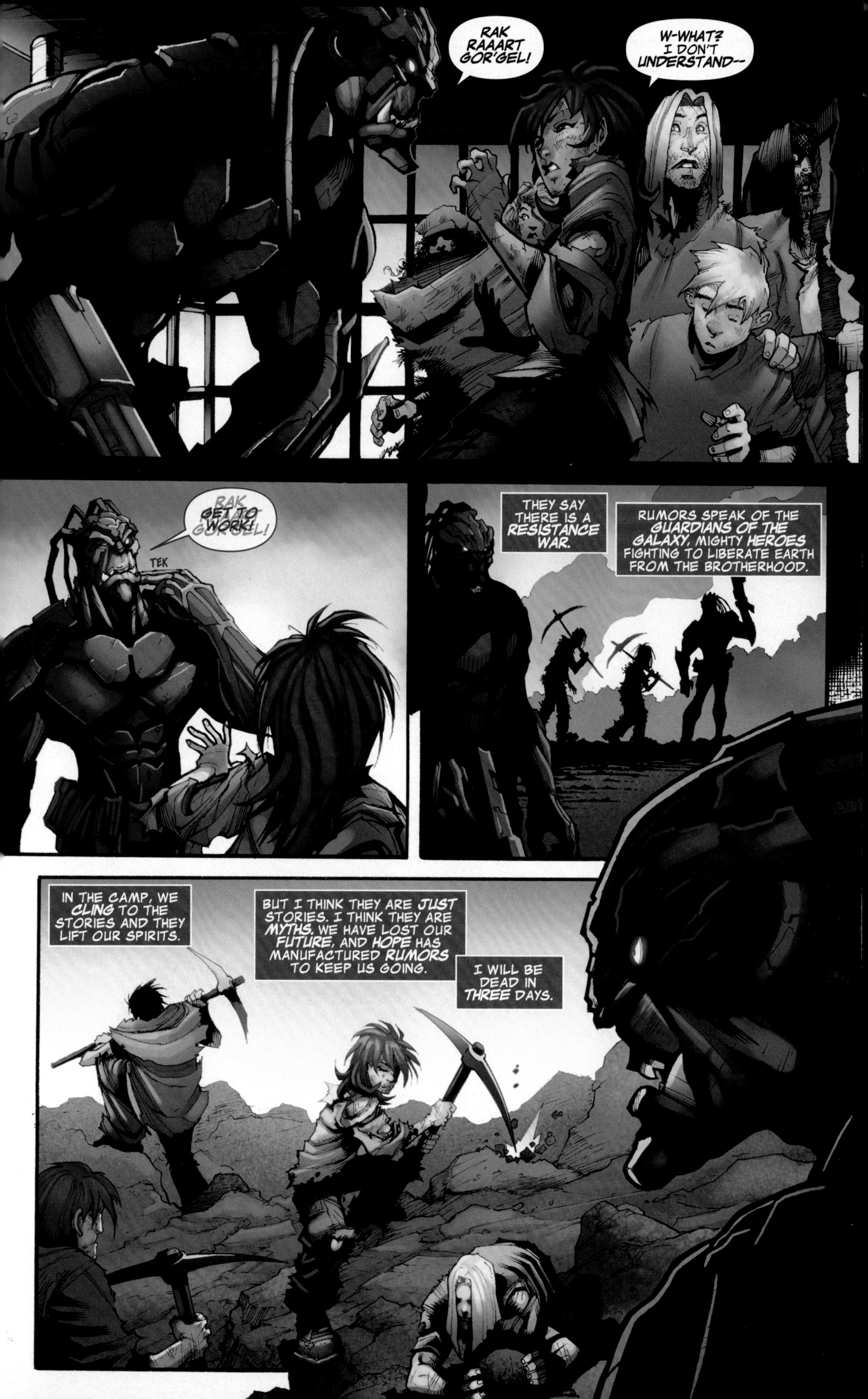
RAK RAAART GOR'GEL!
W-WHAT? I DON'T UNDERSTAND--
RAK RAAART GOR'GEL!
GET TO WORK!
TEK
THEY SAY THERE IS A RESISTANCE WAR.
RUMORS SPEAK OF THE GUARDIANS OF THE GALAXY, MIGHTY HEROES FIGHTING TO LIBERATE EARTH FROM THE BROTHERHOOD.
IN THE CAMP, WE CLING TO THE STORIES AND THEY LIFT OUR SPIRITS.
BUT I THINK THEY ARE JUST STORIES. I THINK THEY ARE MYTHS. WE HAVE LOST OUR FUTURE, AND HOPE HAS MANUFACTURED RUMORS TO KEEP US GOING.
I WILL BE DEAD IN THREE DAYS.

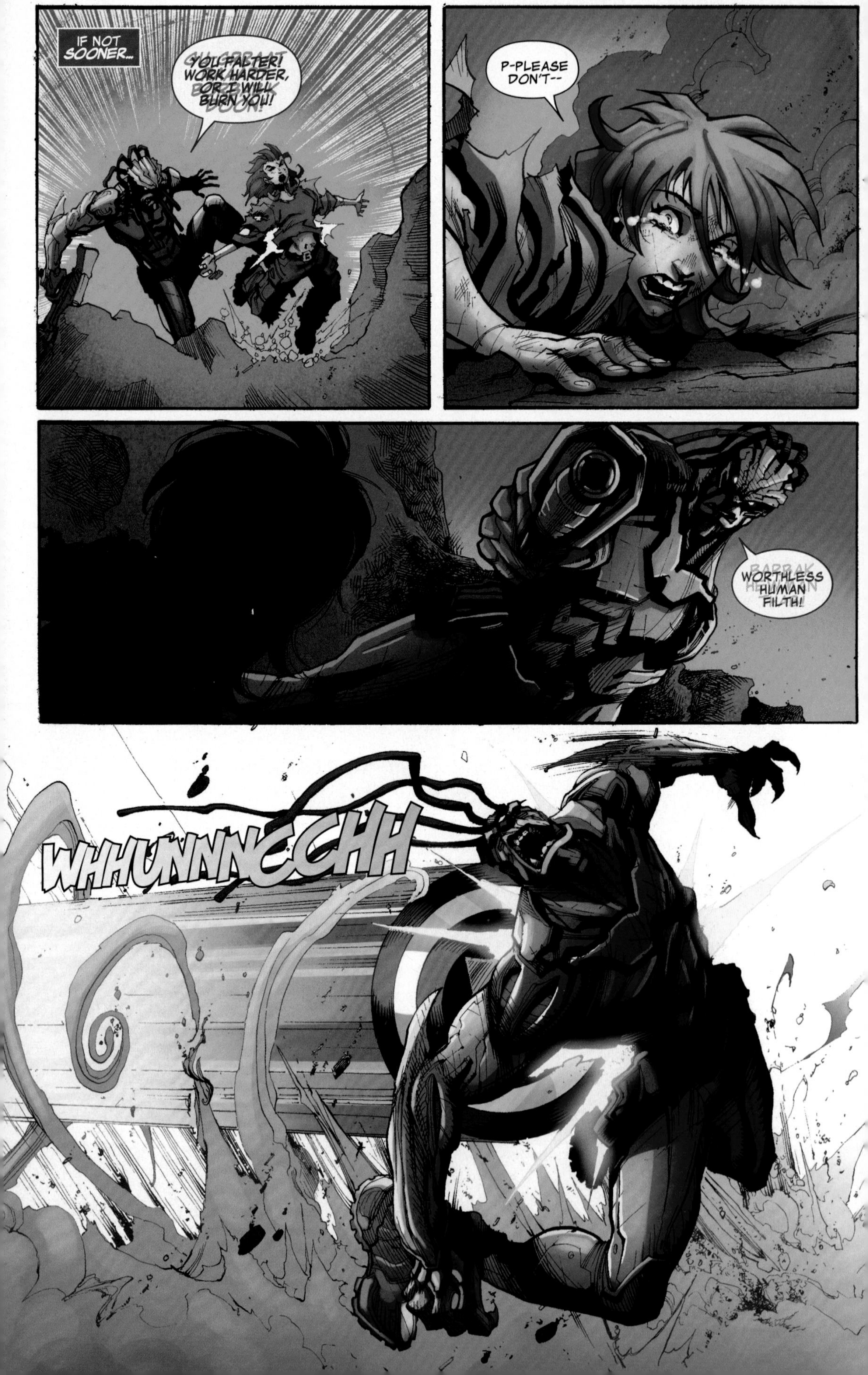
IF NOT SOONER...
YOU FALTER! WORK HARDER, OR I WILL BURN YOU!
P-PLEASE DON'T--
WORTHLESS HUMAN FILTH!
WHHUNNNCCHH

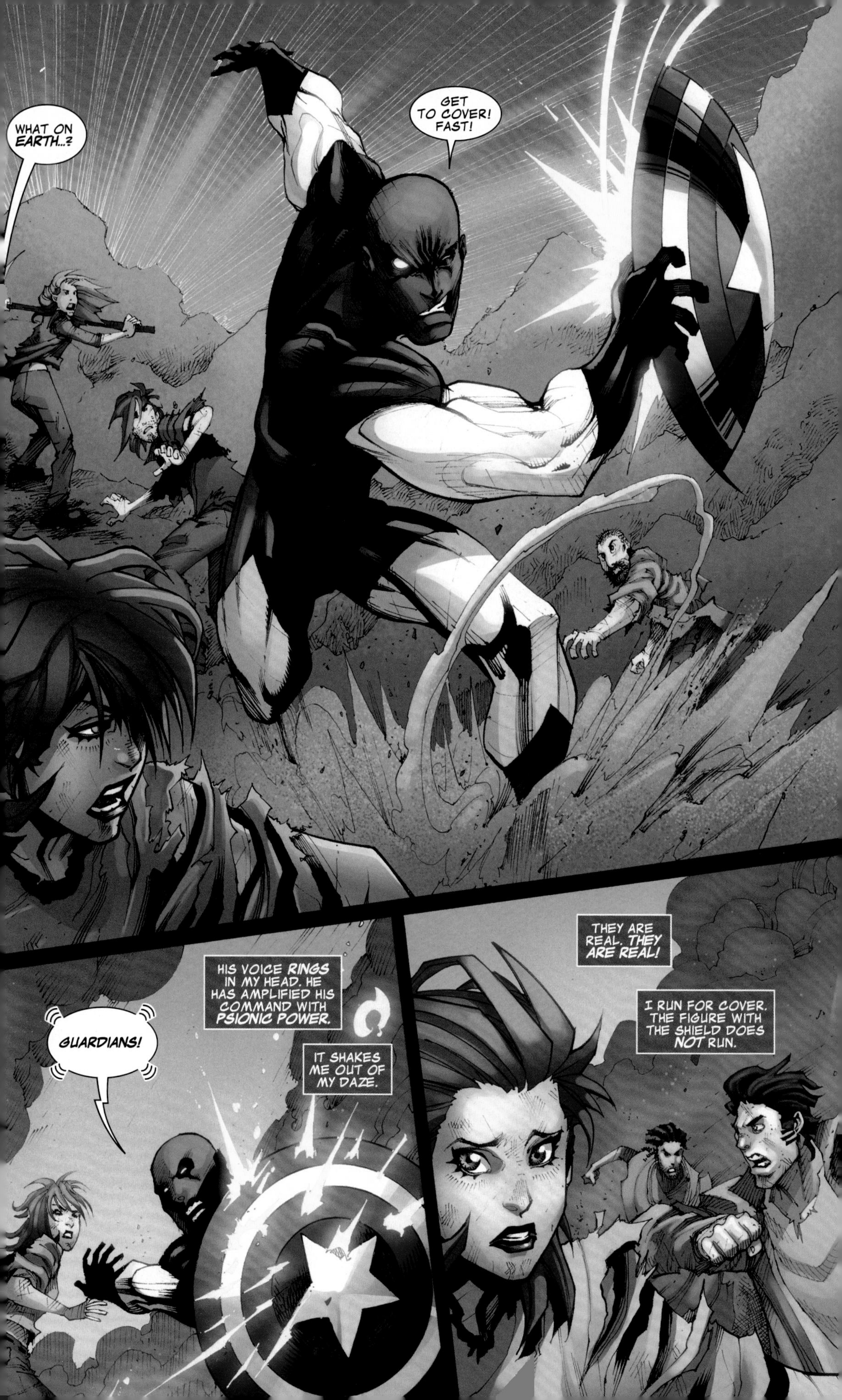
WHAT ON EARTH...?
GET TO COVER! FAST!
GUARDIANS!
HIS VOICE RINGS IN MY HEAD. HE HAS AMPLIFIED HIS COMMAND WITH PSIONIC POWER.
IT SHAKES ME OUT OF MY DAZE.
THEY ARE REAL. THEY ARE REAL!
I RUN FOR COVER. THE FIGURE WITH THE SHIELD DOES NOT RUN.

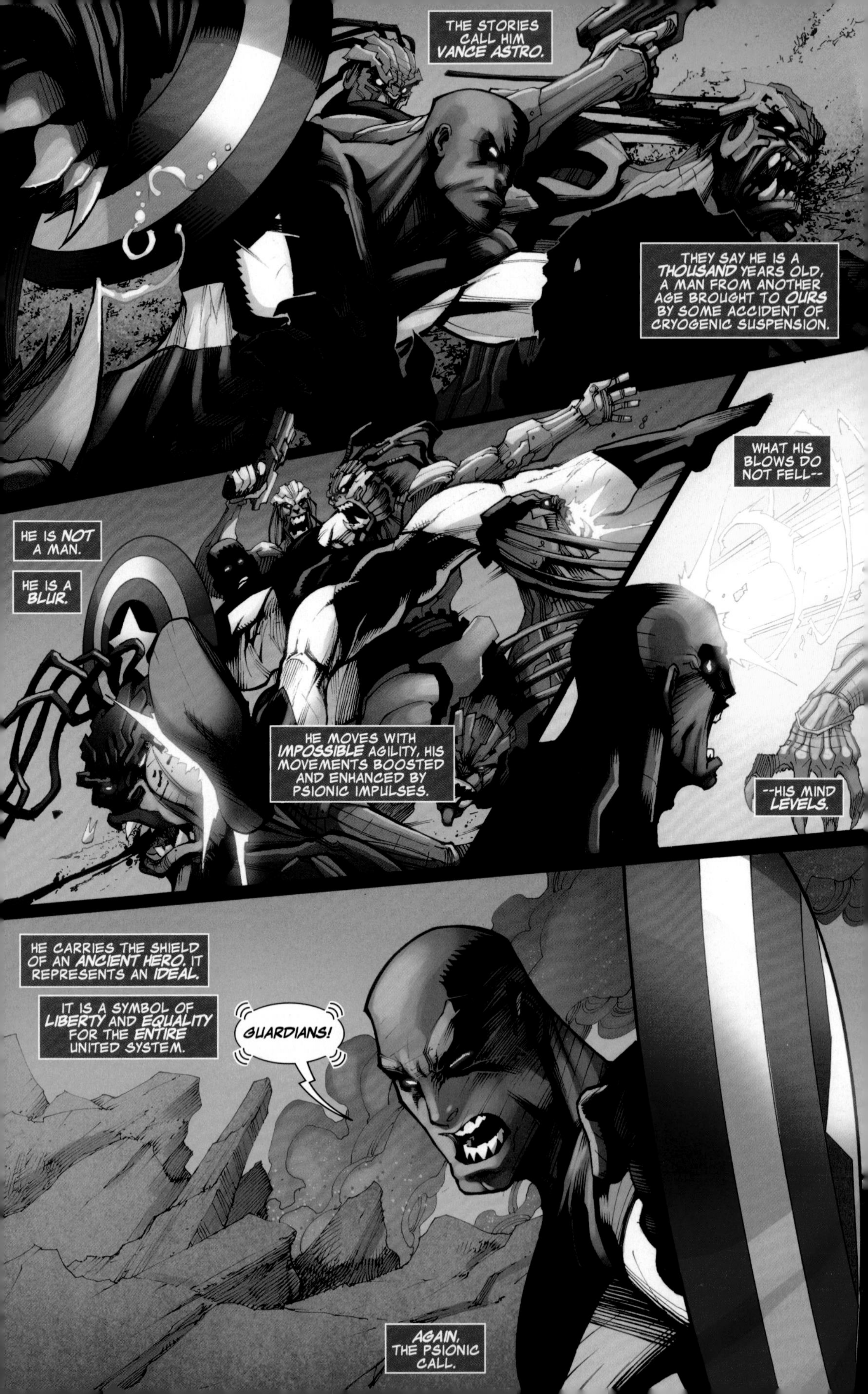
THE STORIES CALL HIM VANCE ASTRO.
THEY SAY HE IS A THOUSAND YEARS OLD, A MAN FROM ANOTHER AGE BROUGHT TO OURS BY SOME ACCIDENT OF CRYOGENIC SUSPENSION.
HE IS NOT A MAN.
HE IS A BLUR.
HE MOVES WITH IMPOSSIBLE AGILITY, HIS MOVEMENTS BOOSTED AND ENHANCED BY PSIONIC IMPULSES.
WHAT HIS BLOWS DO NOT FELL--
--HIS MIND LEVELS.
HE CARRIES THE SHIELD OF AN ANCIENT HERO. IT REPRESENTS AN IDEAL.
IT IS A SYMBOL OF LIBERTY AND EQUALITY FOR THE ENTIRE UNITED SYSTEM.
GUARDIANS!
AGAIN, THE PSIONIC CALL.

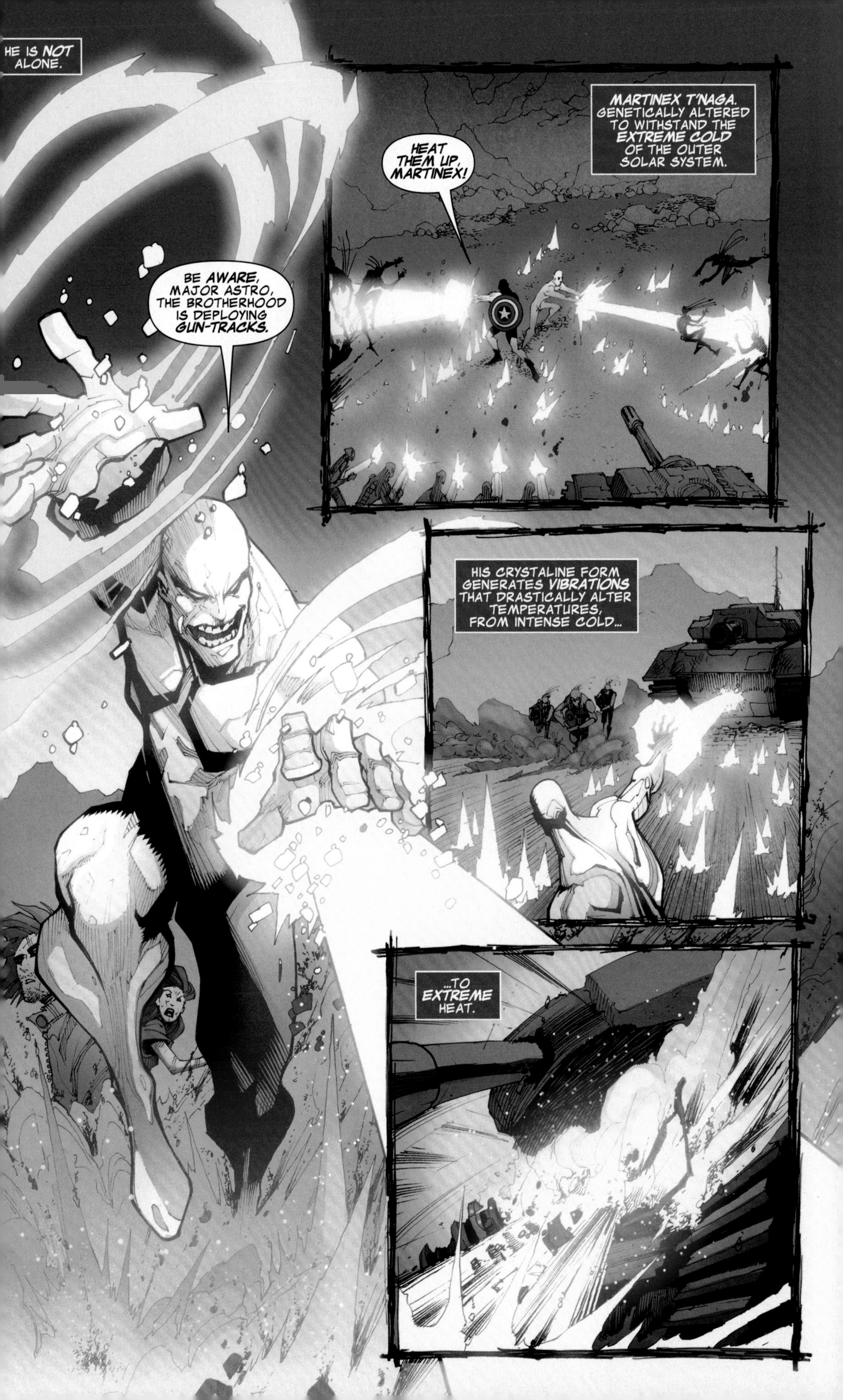

HE IS NOT ALONE.
MARTINEX T'NAGA. GENETICALLY ALTERED TO WITHSTAND THE EXTREME COLD OF THE OUTER SOLAR SYSTEM.
HEAT THEM UP, MARTINEX!
BE AWARE, MAJOR ASTRO, THE BROTHERHOOD IS DEPLOYING GUN-TRACKS.
HIS CRYSTALINE FORM GENERATES VIBRATIONS THAT DRASTICALLY ALTER TEMPERATURES, FROM INTENSE COLD...
...TO EXTREME HEAT.

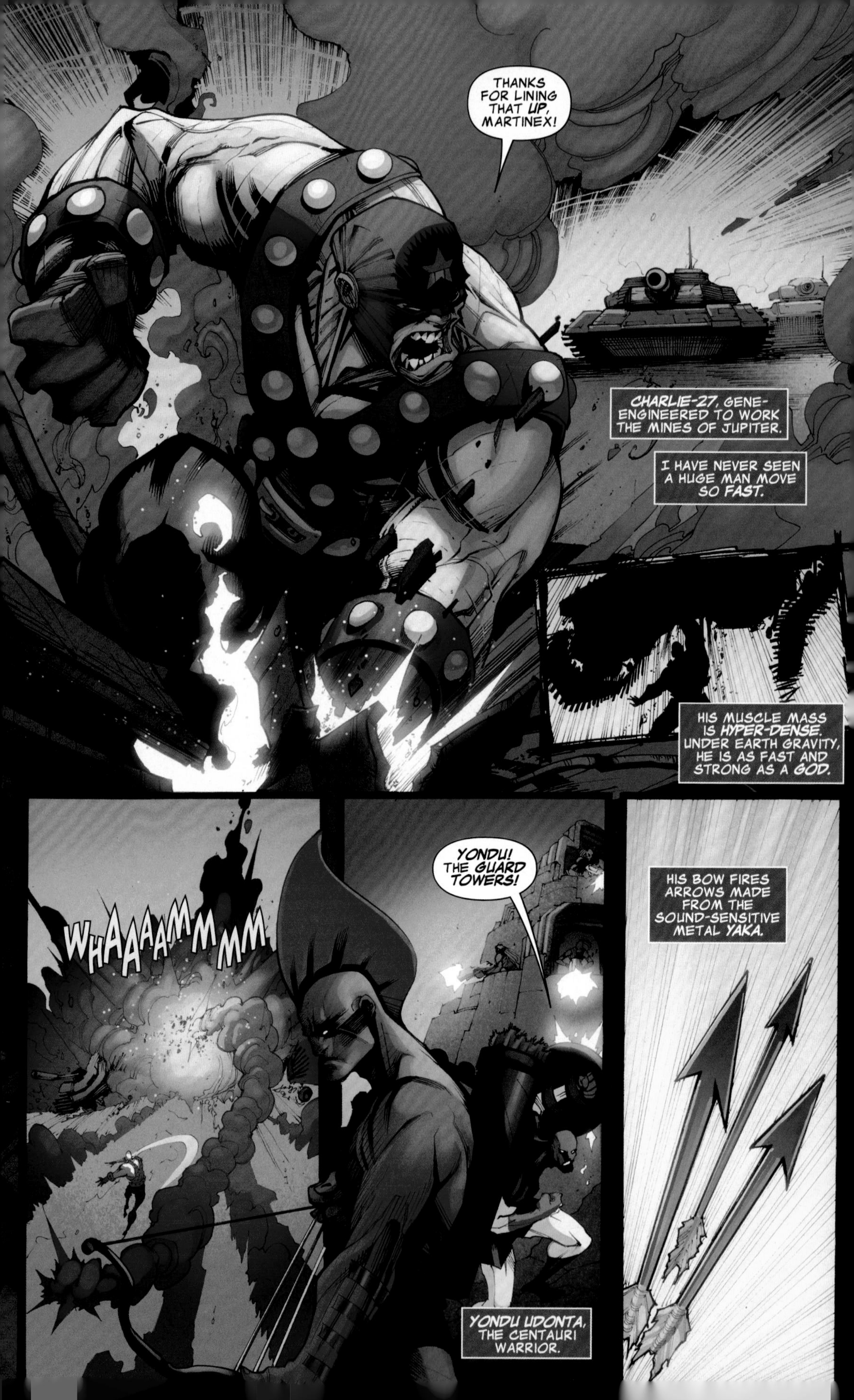

THANKS FOR LINING THAT UP, MARTINEX!
CHARLIE-27, GENE-ENGINEERED TO WORK THE MINES OF JUPITER.
I HAVE NEVER SEEN A HUGE MAN MOVE SO FAST.
HIS MUSCLE MASS IS HYPER-DENSE. UNDER EARTH GRAVITY, HE IS AS FAST AND STRONG AS A GOD.
WHAAAAMMMMM
YONDU! THE GUARD TOWERS!
YONDU UDONTA, THE CENTAURI WARRIOR.
HIS BOW FIRES ARROWS MADE FROM THE SOUND-SENSITIVE METAL YAKA.

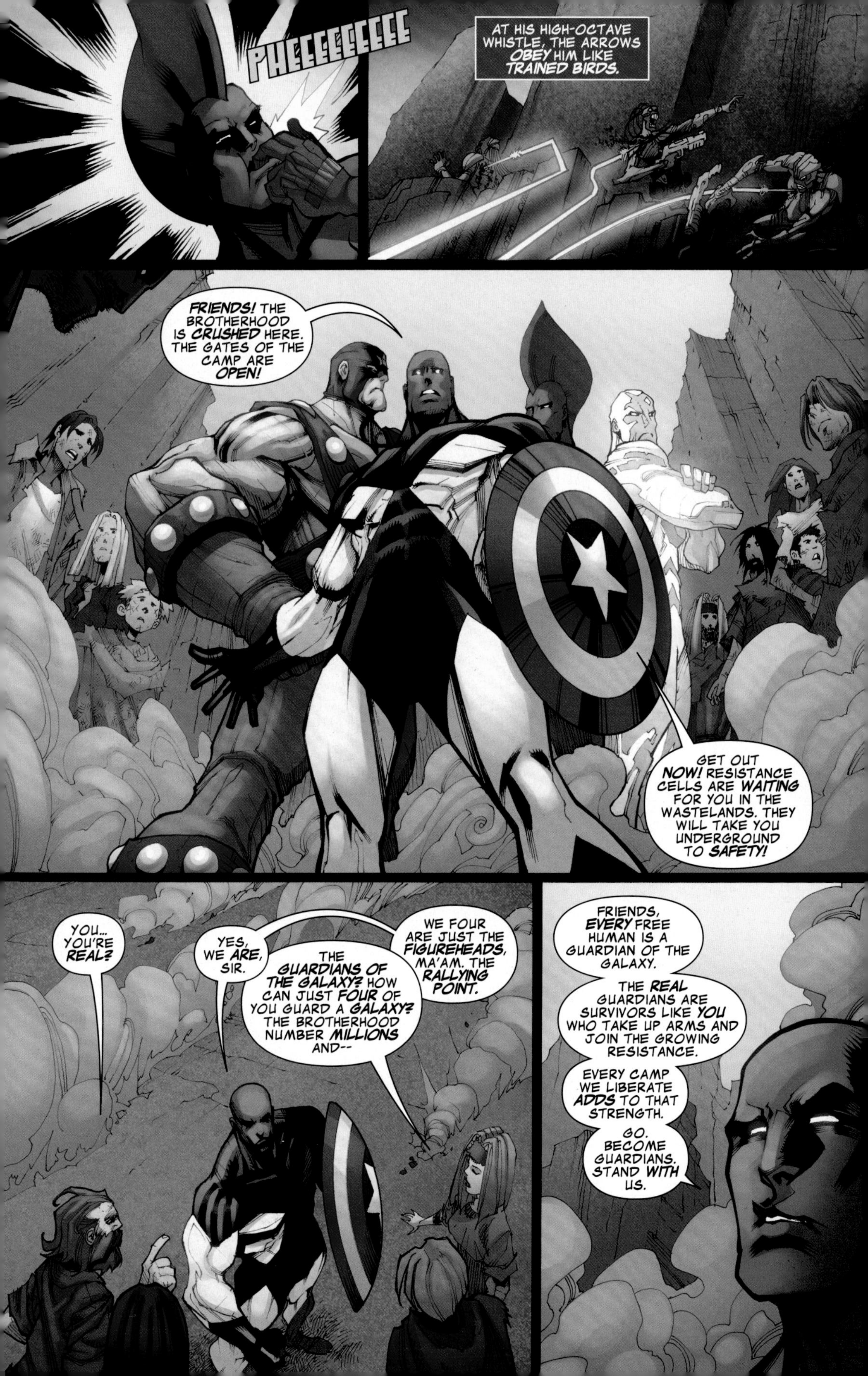
PHEEEEEEEEEE
AT HIS HIGH-OCTAVE WHISTLE, THE ARROWS OBEY HIM LIKE TRAINED BIRDS.
FRIENDS! THE BROTHERHOOD IS CRUSHED HERE. THE GATES OF THE CAMP ARE OPEN!
GET OUT NOW! RESISTANCE CELLS ARE WAITING FOR YOU IN THE WASTELANDS. THEY WILL TAKE YOU UNDERGROUND TO SAFETY!
YOU... YOU'RE REAL?
YES, WE ARE, SIR.
THE GUARDIANS OF THE GALAXY? HOW CAN JUST FOUR OF YOU GUARD A GALAXY? THE BROTHERHOOD NUMBER MILLIONS AND--
WE FOUR ARE JUST THE FIGUREHEADS, MA'AM. THE RALLYING POINT.
FRIENDS, EVERY FREE HUMAN IS A GUARDIAN OF THE GALAXY.
THE REAL GUARDIANS ARE SURVIVORS LIKE YOU WHO TAKE UP ARMS AND JOIN THE GROWING RESISTANCE.
EVERY CAMP WE LIBERATE ADDS TO THAT STRENGTH.
GO. BECOME GUARDIANS. STAND WITH US.

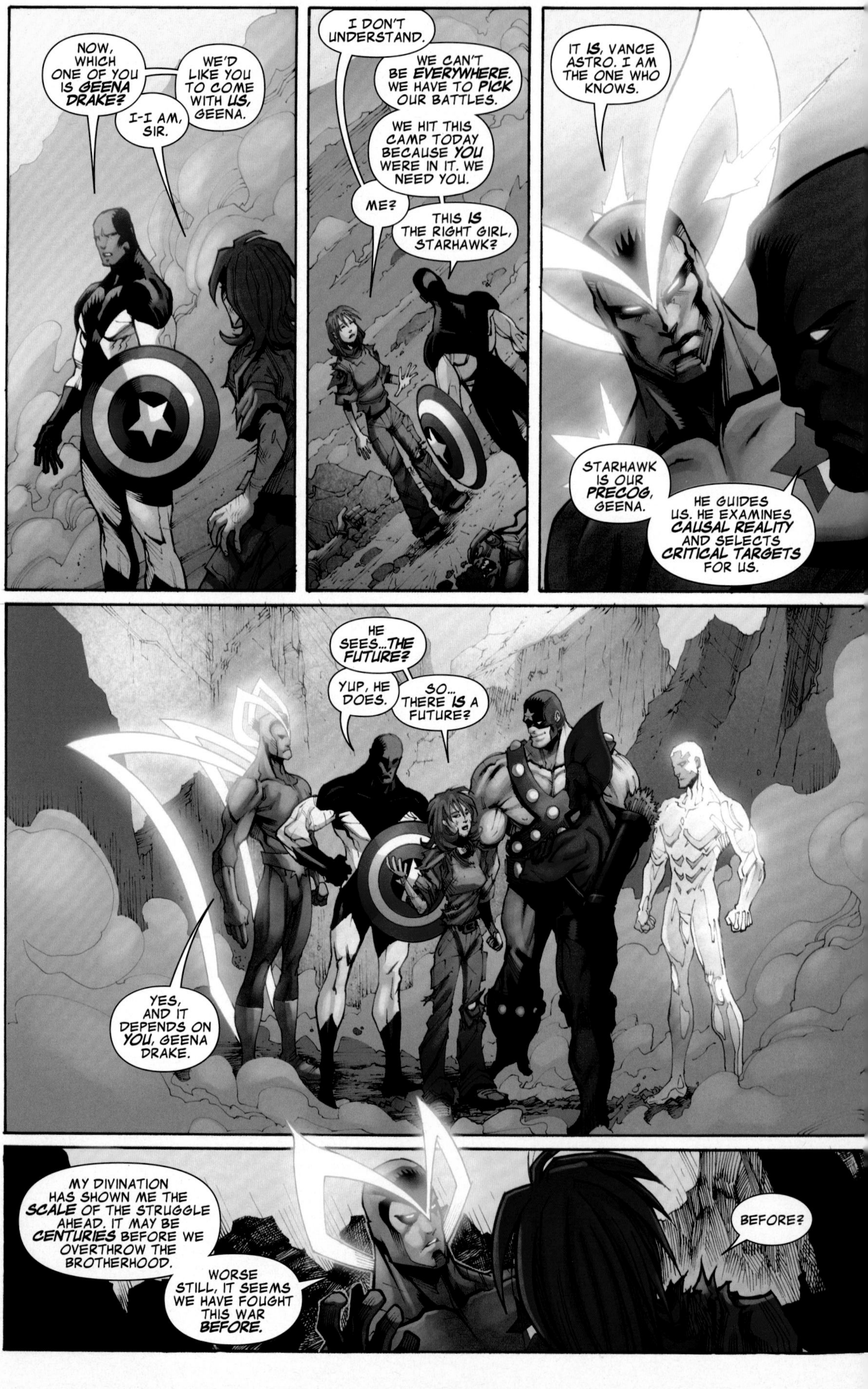
NOW, WHICH ONE OF YOU IS GEENA DRAKE?
WE'D LIKE YOU TO COME WITH US, GEENA.
I-I AM, SIR.
I DON'T UNDERSTAND.
WE CAN'T BE EVERYWHERE. WE HAVE TO PICK OUR BATTLES.
WE HIT THIS CAMP TODAY BECAUSE YOU WERE IN IT. WE NEED YOU.
ME?
THIS IS THE RIGHT GIRL, STARHAWK?
IT IS, VANCE ASTRO. I AM THE ONE WHO KNOWS.
STARHAWK IS OUR PRECOG, GEENA.
HE GUIDES US. HE EXAMINES CAUSAL REALITY AND SELECTS CRITICAL TARGETS FOR US.
HE SEES...THE FUTURE?
YUP, HE DOES.
SO... THERE IS A FUTURE?
YES, AND IT DEPENDS ON YOU, GEENA DRAKE.
MY DIVINATION HAS SHOWN ME THE SCALE OF THE STRUGGLE AHEAD. IT MAY BE CENTURIES BEFORE WE OVERTHROW THE BROTHERHOOD.
WORSE STILL, IT SEEMS WE HAVE FOUGHT THIS WAR BEFORE.
BEFORE?

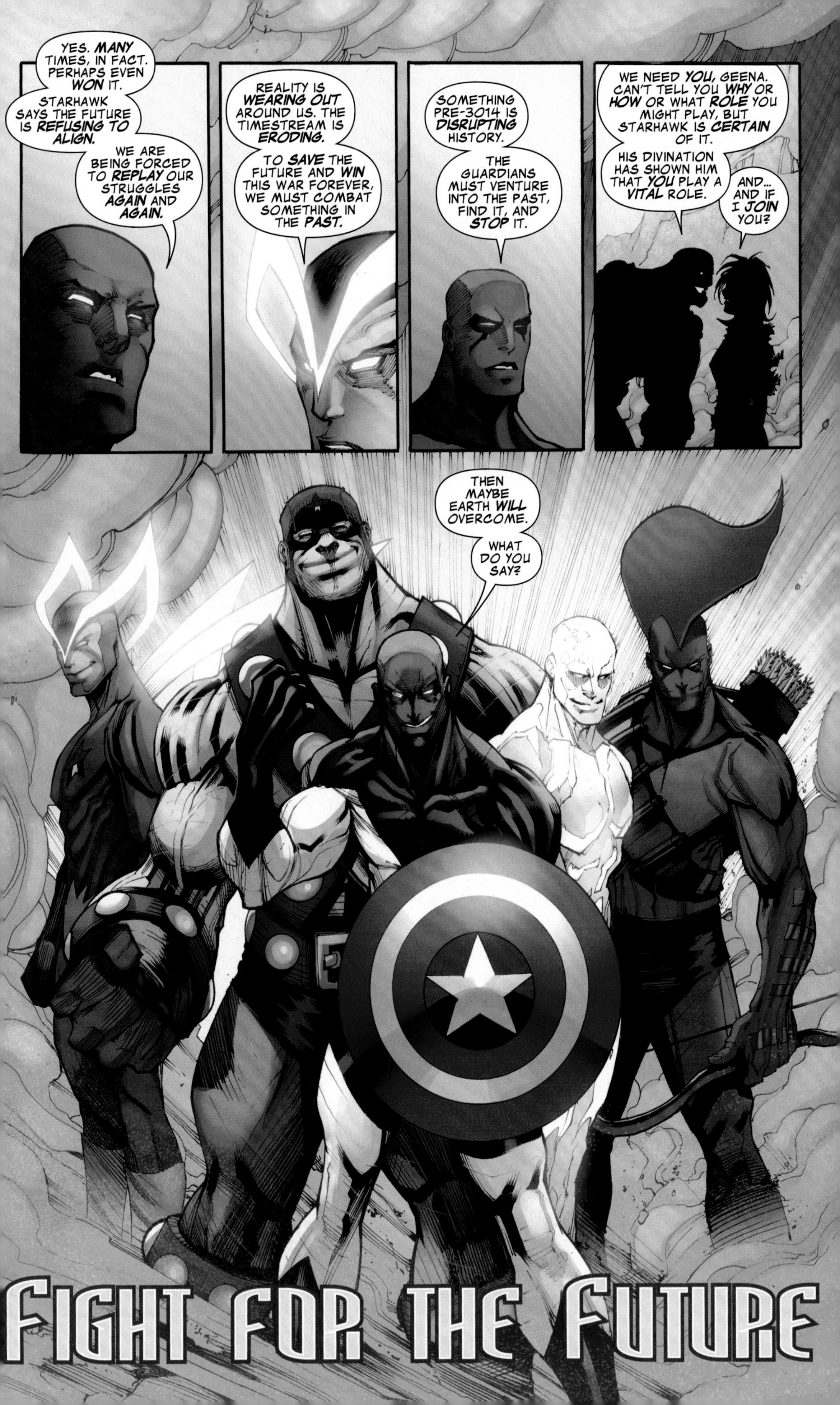

YES. MANY TIMES, IN FACT. PERHAPS EVEN WON IT.
STARHAWK SAYS THE FUTURE IS REFUSING TO ALIGN.
WE ARE BEING FORCED TO REPLAY OUR STRUGGLES AGAIN AND AGAIN.
REALITY IS WEARING OUT AROUND US. THE TIMESTREAM IS ERODING.
TO SAVE THE FUTURE AND WIN THIS WAR FOREVER, WE MUST COMBAT SOMETHING IN THE PAST.
SOMETHING PRE-3014 IS DISRUPTING HISTORY.
THE GUARDIANS MUST VENTURE INTO THE PAST, FIND IT, AND STOP IT.
WE NEED YOU, GEENA. CAN'T TELL YOU WHY OR HOW OR WHAT ROLE YOU MIGHT PLAY, BUT STARHAWK IS CERTAIN OF IT.
HIS DIVINATION HAS SHOWN HIM THAT YOU PLAY A VITAL ROLE.
AND... AND IF I JOIN YOU?
THEN MAYBE EARTH WILL OVERCOME.
WHAT DO YOU SAY?
FIGHT FOR THE FUTURE

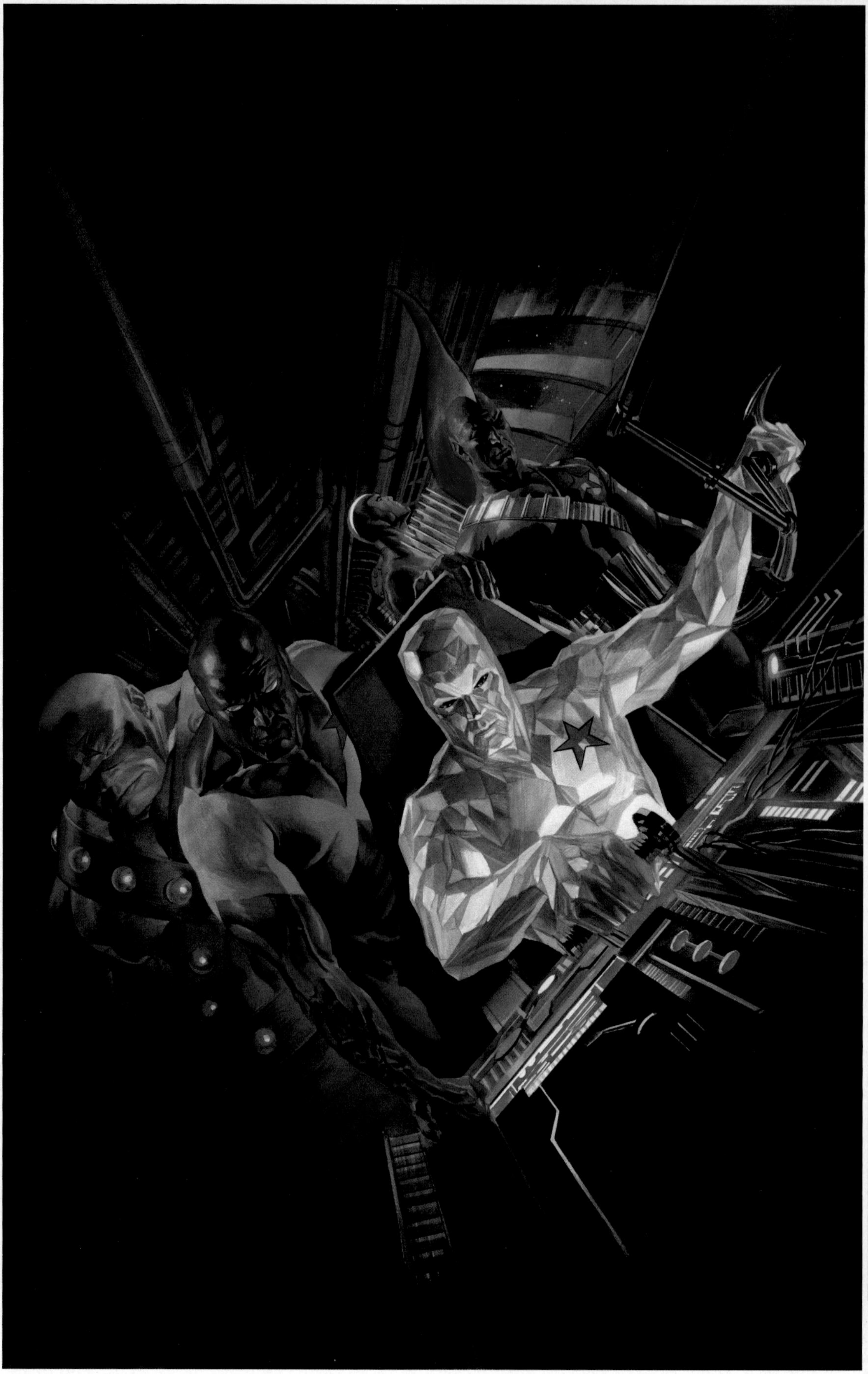

1

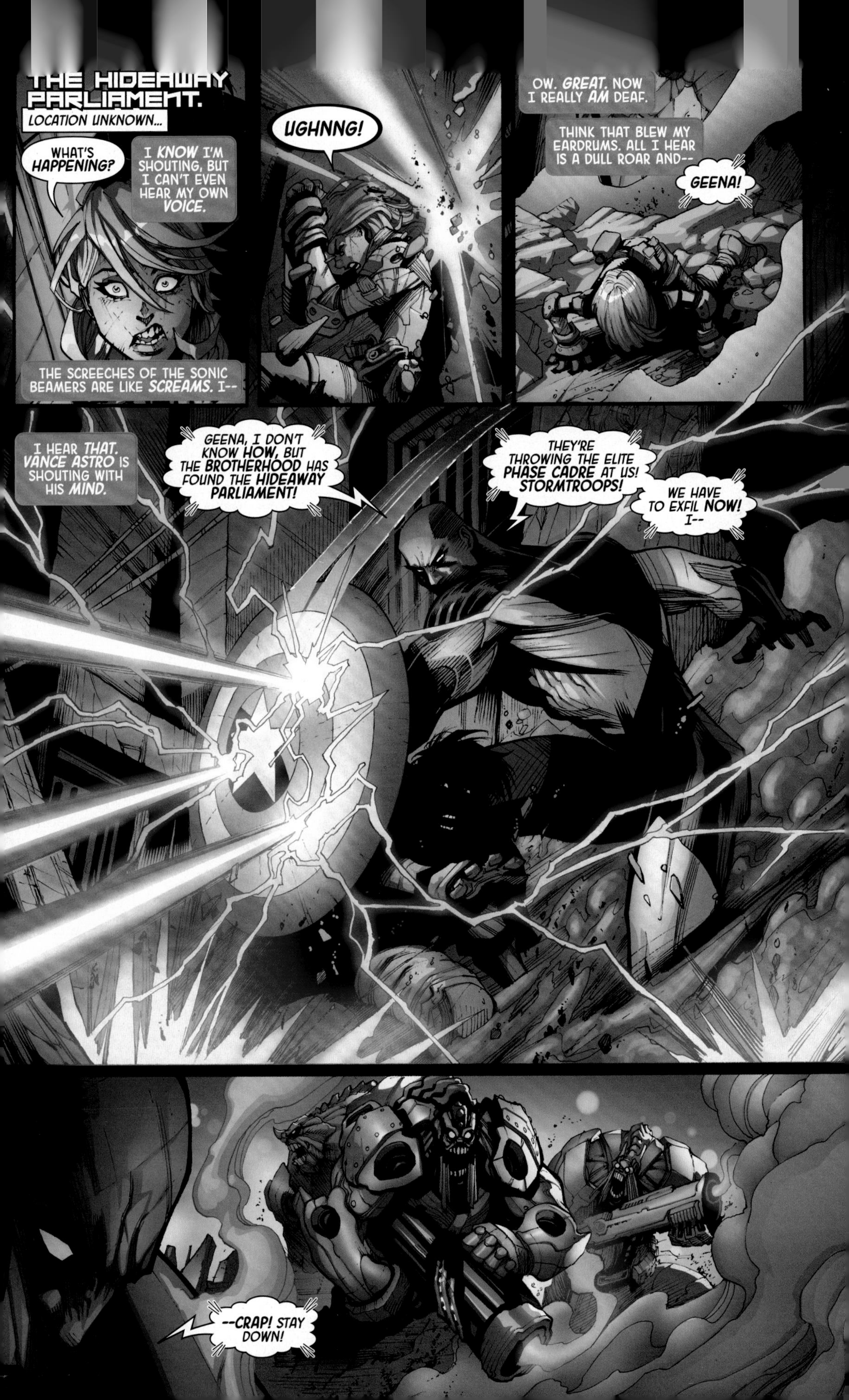
THE HIDEAWAY PARLIAMENT.
LOCATION UNKNOWN...
WHAT'S HAPPENING?
I KNOW I'M SHOUTING, BUT I CAN'T EVEN HEAR MY OWN VOICE.
THE SCREECHES OF THE SONIC BEAMERS ARE LIKE SCREAMS. I--
UGHNNG!
OW. GREAT. NOW I REALLY AM DEAF.
THINK THAT BLEW MY EARDRUMS. ALL I HEAR IS A DULL ROAR AND--
GEENA!
I HEAR THAT. VANCE ASTRO IS SHOUTING WITH HIS MIND.
GEENA, I DON'T KNOW HOW, BUT THE BROTHERHOOD HAS FOUND THE HIDEAWAY PARLIAMENT!
THEY'RE THROWING THE ELITE PHASE CADRE AT US! STORMTROOPS!
WE HAVE TO EXFIL NOW! I--
--CRAP! STAY DOWN!

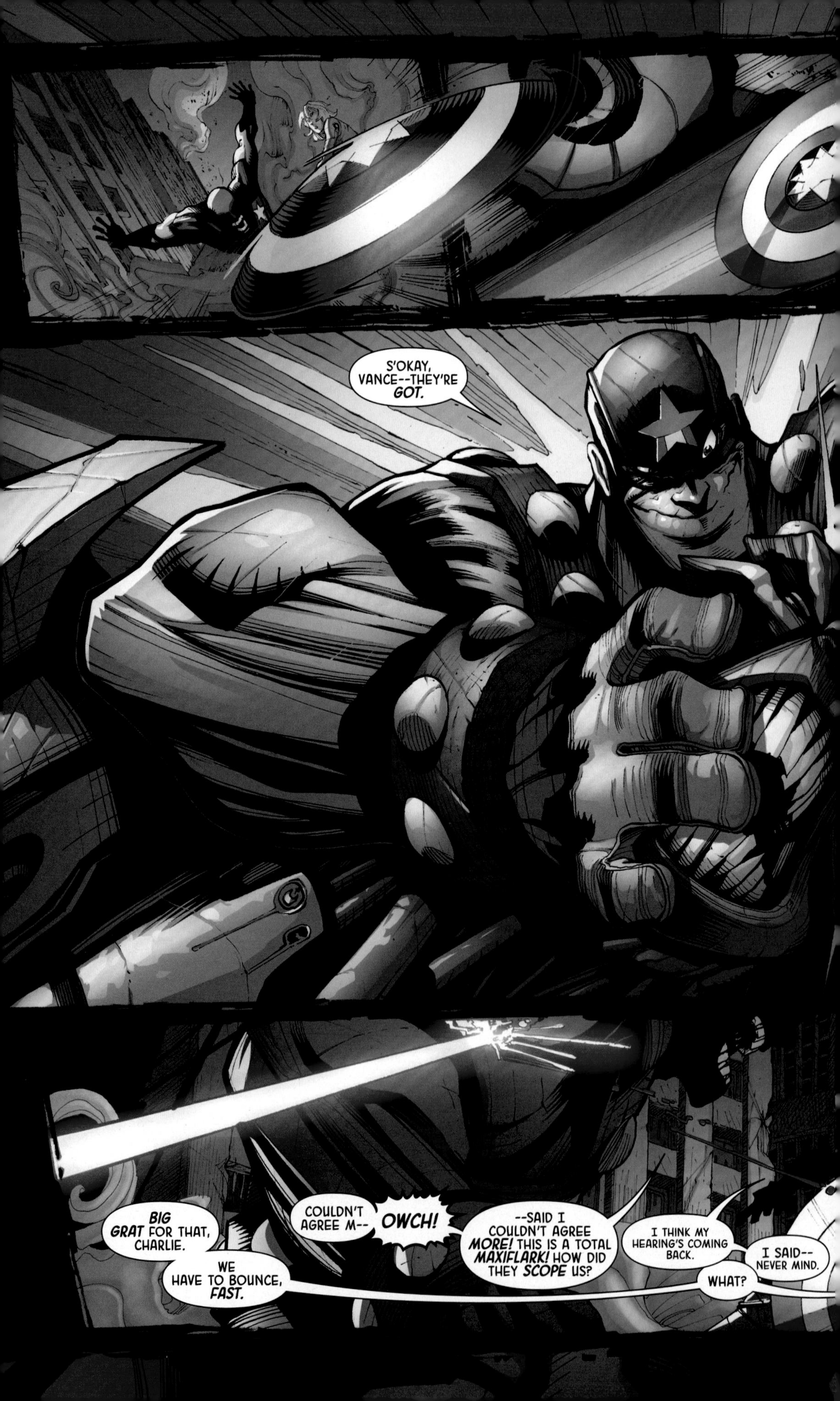
S'OKAY, VANCE--THEY'RE GOT.
BIG GRAT FOR THAT, CHARLIE.
WE HAVE TO BOUNCE, FAST.
COULDN'T AGREE M--
OWCH!
--SAID I COULDN'T AGREE MORE! THIS IS A TOTAL MAXIFLARK! HOW DID THEY SCOPE US?
I THINK MY HEARING'S COMING BACK.
WHAT?
I SAID-- NEVER MIND.

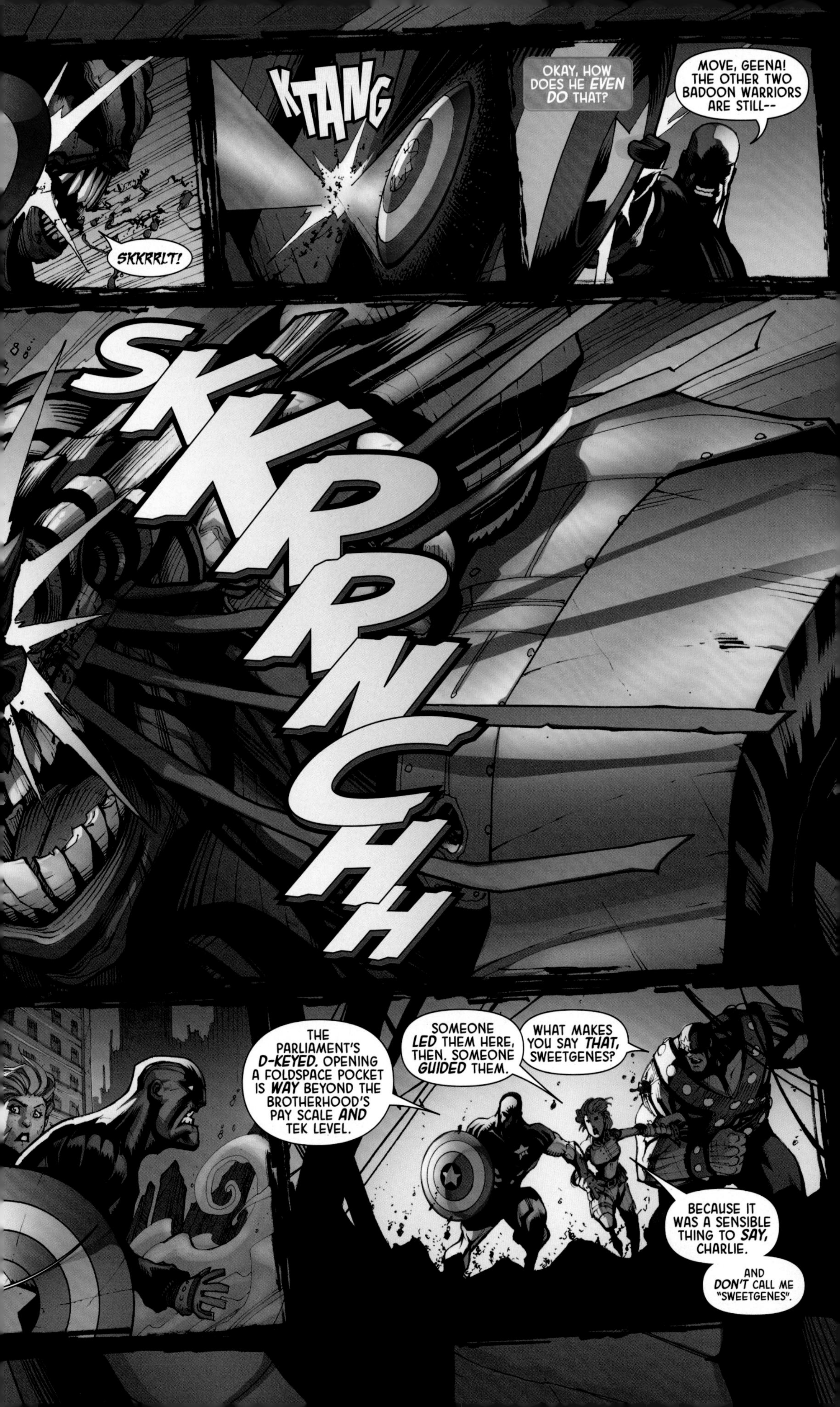
SKKRRLT!
KTANG
OKAY, HOW DOES HE EVEN DO THAT?
MOVE, GEENA! THE OTHER TWO BADOON WARRIORS ARE STILL--
SKKRRNCHH
THE PARLIAMENT'S D-KEYED. OPENING A FOLDSPACE POCKET IS WAY BEYOND THE BROTHERHOOD'S PAY SCALE AND TEK LEVEL.
SOMEONE LED THEM HERE, THEN. SOMEONE GUIDED THEM.
WHAT MAKES YOU SAY THAT, SWEETGENES?
BECAUSE IT WAS A SENSIBLE THING TO SAY, CHARLIE.
AND DON'T CALL ME "SWEETGENES".

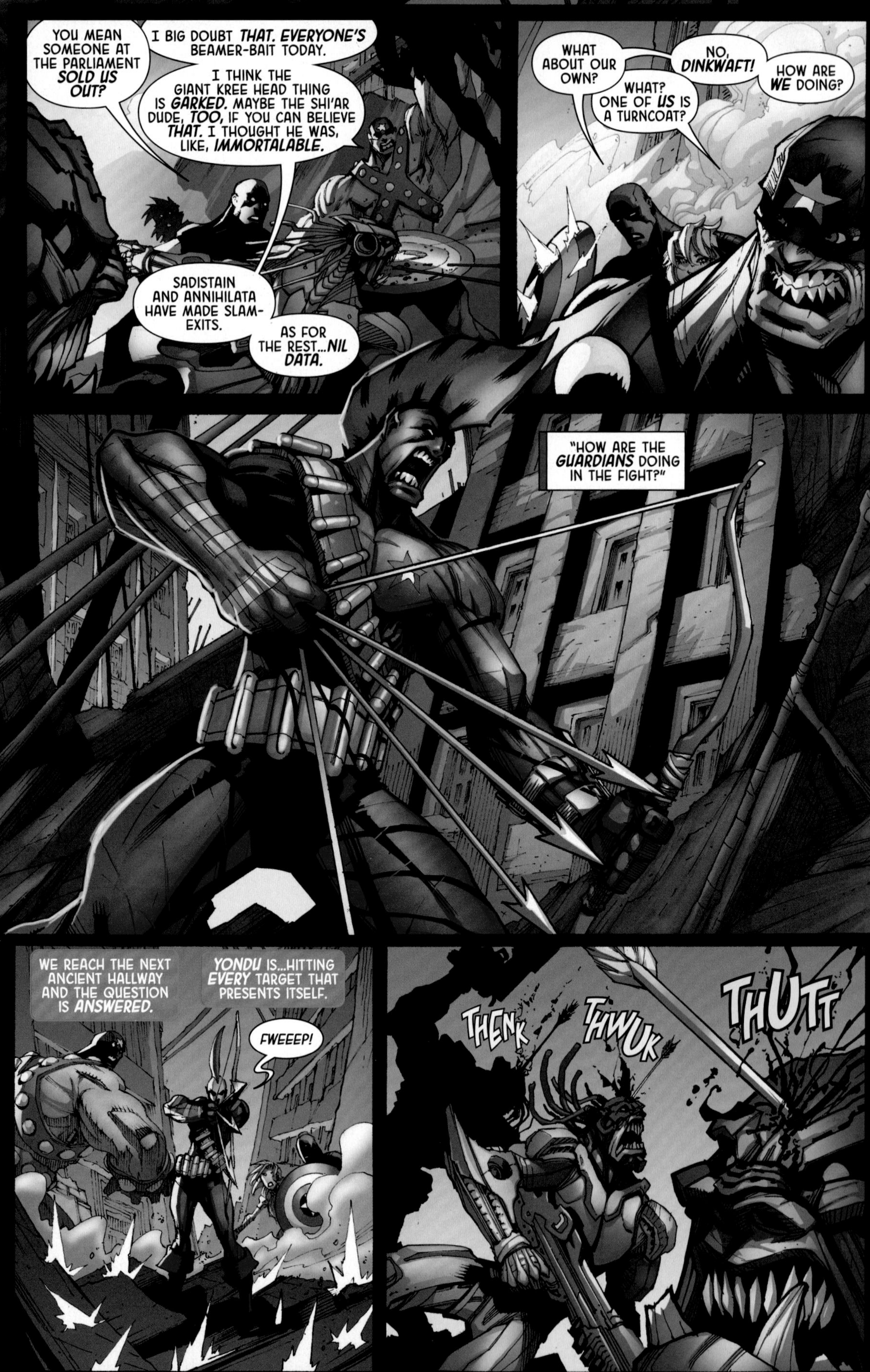
YOU MEAN SOMEONE AT THE PARLIAMENT SOLD US OUT?
I BIG DOUBT THAT. EVERYONE'S BEAMER-BAIT TODAY.
I THINK THE GIANT KREE HEAD THING IS GARKED. MAYBE THE SHI'AR DUDE, TOO, IF YOU CAN BELIEVE THAT. I THOUGHT HE WAS, LIKE, IMMORTALABLE.
SADISTAIN AND ANNIHILATA HAVE MADE SLAM-EXITS.
AS FOR THE REST...NIL DATA.
WHAT ABOUT OUR OWN?
WHAT? ONE OF US IS A TURNCOAT?
NO, DINKWAFT!
HOW ARE WE DOING?
"HOW ARE THE GUARDIANS DOING IN THE FIGHT?"
WE REACH THE NEXT ANCIENT HALLWAY AND THE QUESTION IS ANSWERED.
YONDU IS...HITTING EVERY TARGET THAT PRESENTS ITSELF.
FWEEEP!
THENK
THWUK
THUTTT

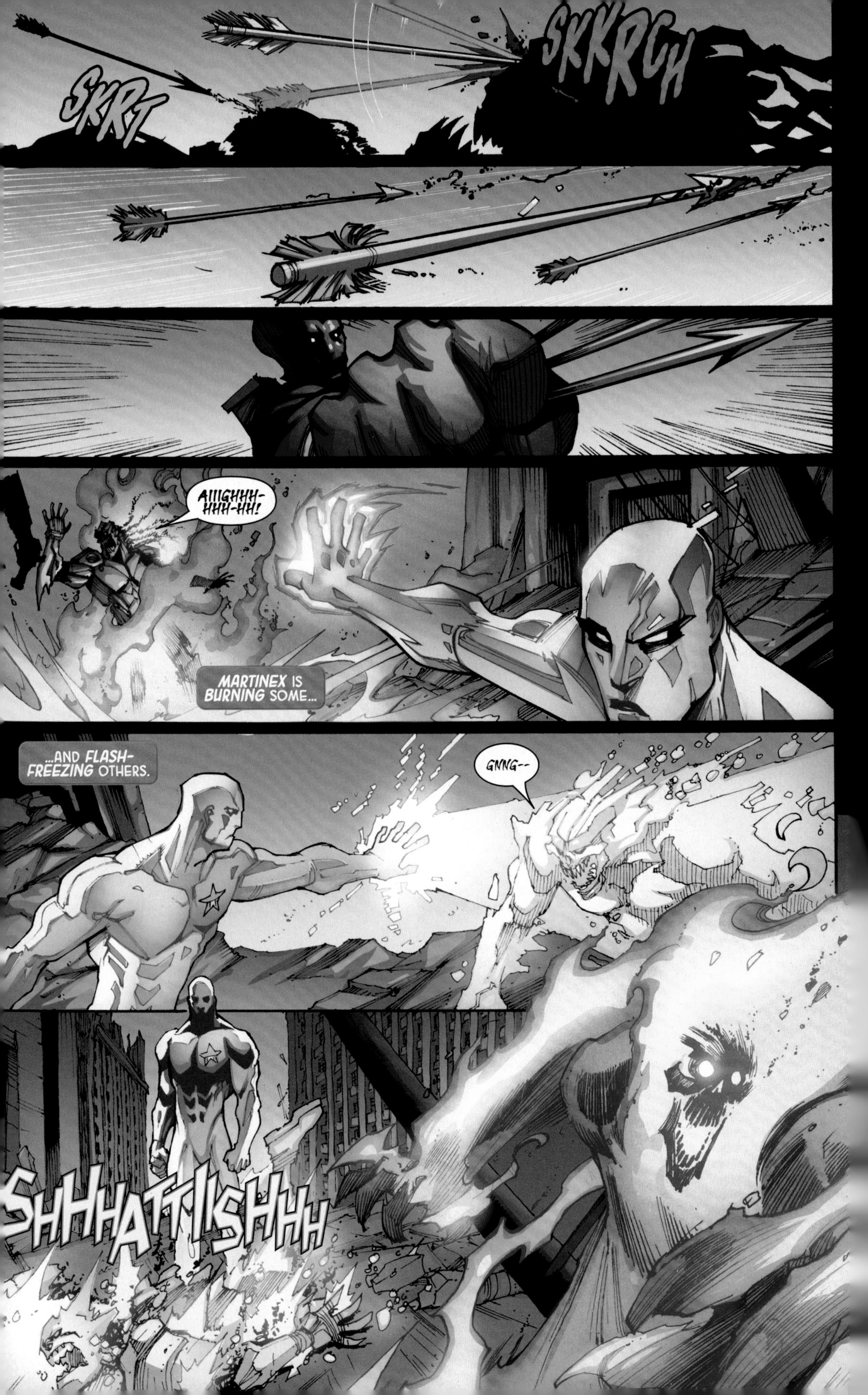
SKRT
SKKRCH
AIIIGHHH-HHH-HH!
MARTINEX IS BURNING SOME...
...AND FLASH-FREEZING OTHERS.
GNNG--
SHHATTIISHHH

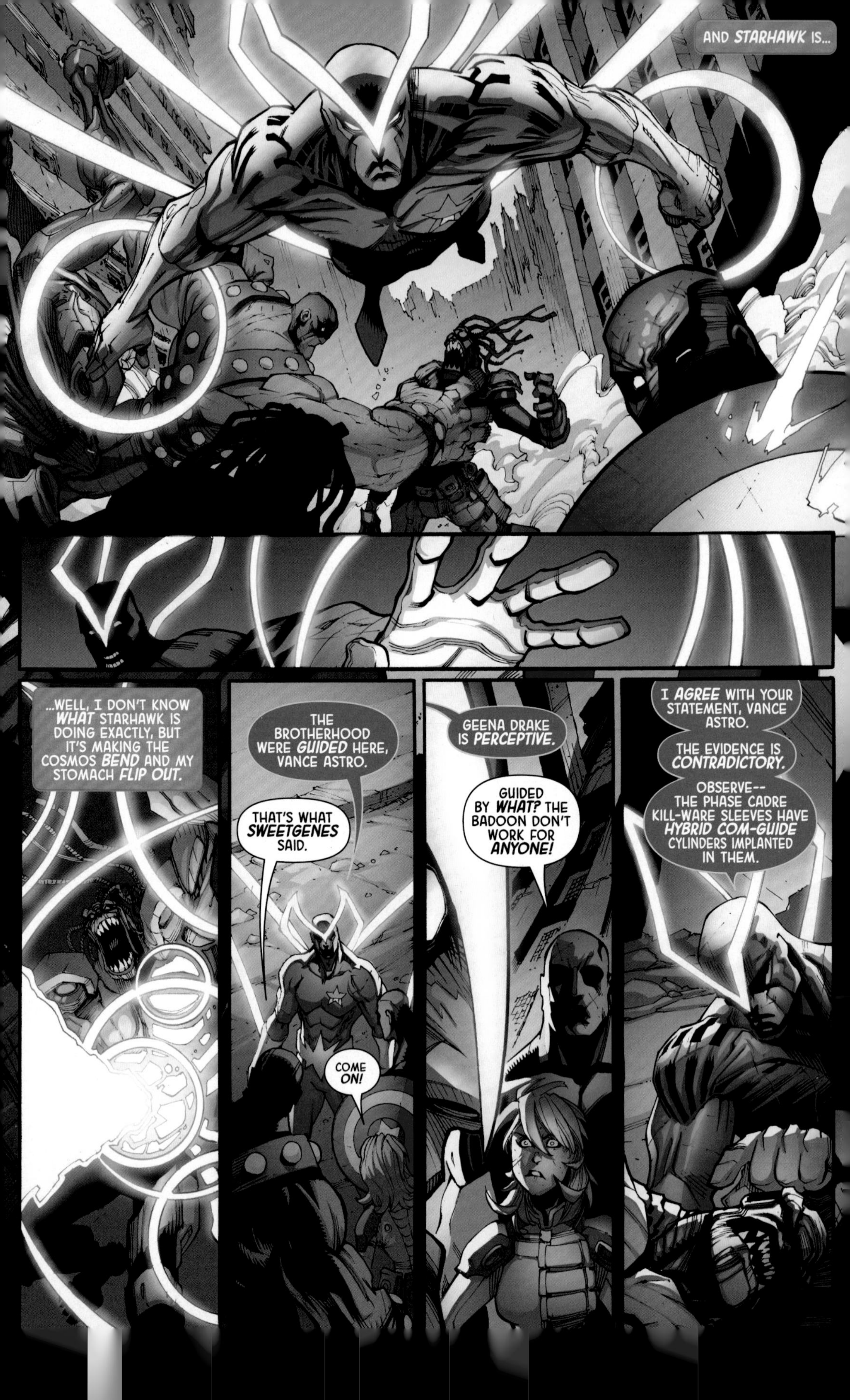
AND STARHAWK IS...
...WELL, I DON'T KNOW WHAT STARHAWK IS DOING EXACTLY, BUT IT'S MAKING THE COSMOS BEND AND MY STOMACH FLIP OUT.
THE BROTHERHOOD WERE GUIDED HERE, VANCE ASTRO.
THAT'S WHAT SWEETGENES SAID.
COME ON!
GEENA DRAKE IS PERCEPTIVE.
GUIDED BY WHAT? THE BADOON DON'T WORK FOR ANYONE!
I AGREE WITH YOUR STATEMENT, VANCE ASTRO.
THE EVIDENCE IS CONTRADICTORY.
OBSERVE-- THE PHASE CADRE KILL-WARE SLEEVES HAVE HYBRID COM-GUIDE CYLINDERS IMPLANTED IN THEM.

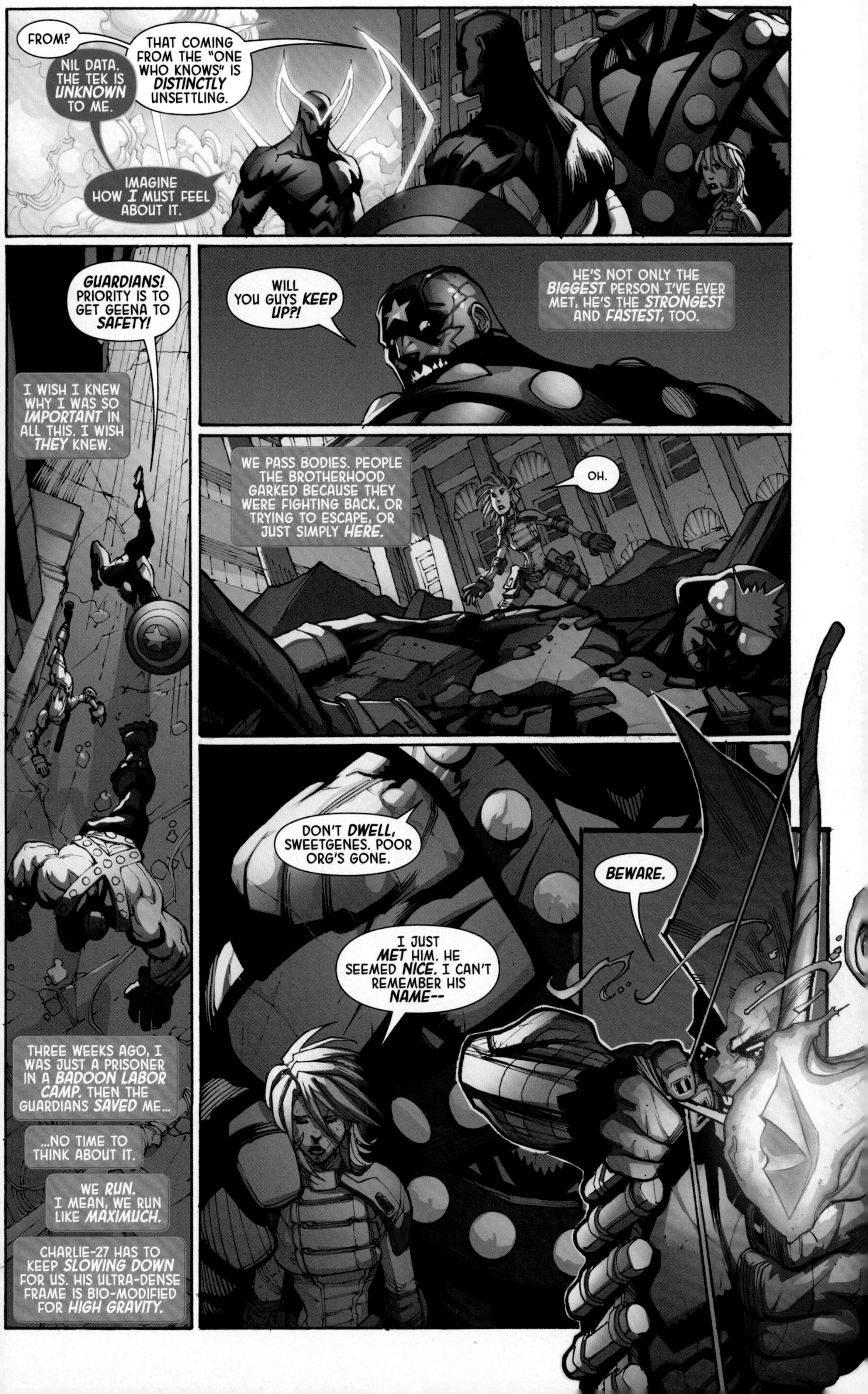
FROM?
NIL DATA. THE TEK IS UNKNOWN TO ME.
THAT COMING FROM THE "ONE WHO KNOWS" IS DISTINCTLY UNSETTLING.
IMAGINE HOW I MUST FEEL ABOUT IT.
GUARDIANS! PRIORITY IS TO GET GEENA TO SAFETY!
WILL YOU GUYS KEEP UP?!
HE'S NOT ONLY THE BIGGEST PERSON I'VE EVER MET, HE'S THE STRONGEST AND FASTEST, TOO.
I WISH I KNEW WHY I WAS SO IMPORTANT IN ALL THIS. I WISH THEY KNEW.
WE PASS BODIES. PEOPLE THE BROTHERHOOD GARKED BECAUSE THEY WERE FIGHTING BACK, OR TRYING TO ESCAPE, OR JUST SIMPLY HERE.
OH.
DON'T DWELL, SWEETGENES. POOR ORG'S GONE.
BEWARE.
I JUST MET HIM. HE SEEMED NICE. I CAN'T REMEMBER HIS NAME--
THREE WEEKS AGO, I WAS JUST A PRISONER IN A BADOON LABOR CAMP. THEN THE GUARDIANS SAVED ME...
...NO TIME TO THINK ABOUT IT.
WE RUN. I MEAN, WE RUN LIKE MAXIMUCH.
CHARLIE-27 HAS TO KEEP SLOWING DOWN FOR US. HIS ULTRA-DENSE FRAME IS BIO-MODIFIED FOR HIGH GRAVITY.

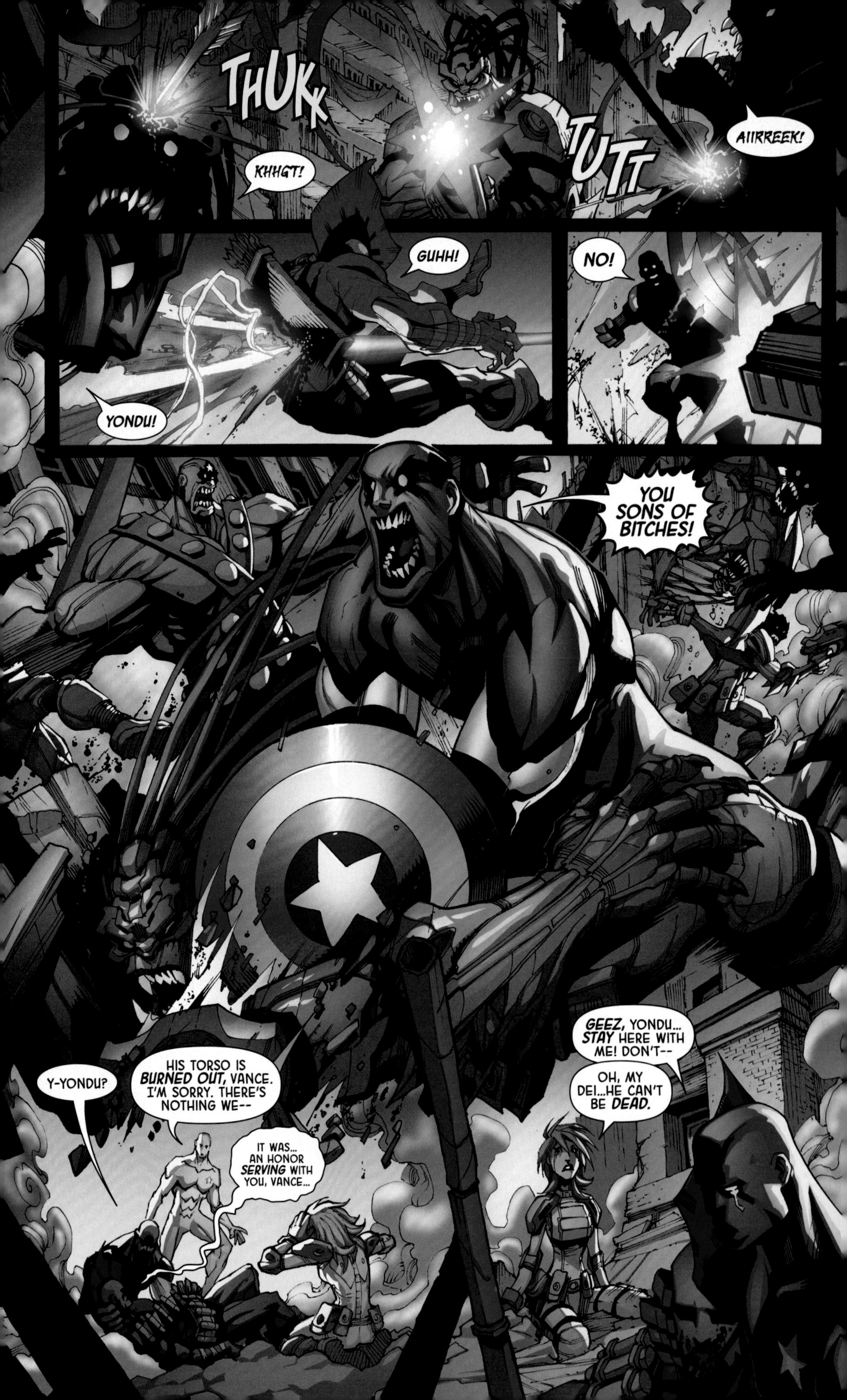
THUKK
KHHGT!
TUTT
AIIRREEK!
GUHH!
YONDU!
NO!
YOU SONS OF BITCHES!
Y-YONDU?
HIS TORSO IS BURNED OUT, VANCE. I'M SORRY. THERE'S NOTHING WE--
IT WAS... AN HONOR SERVING WITH YOU, VANCE...
GEEZ, YONDU... STAY HERE WITH ME! DON'T--
OH, MY DEI...HE CAN'T BE DEAD.

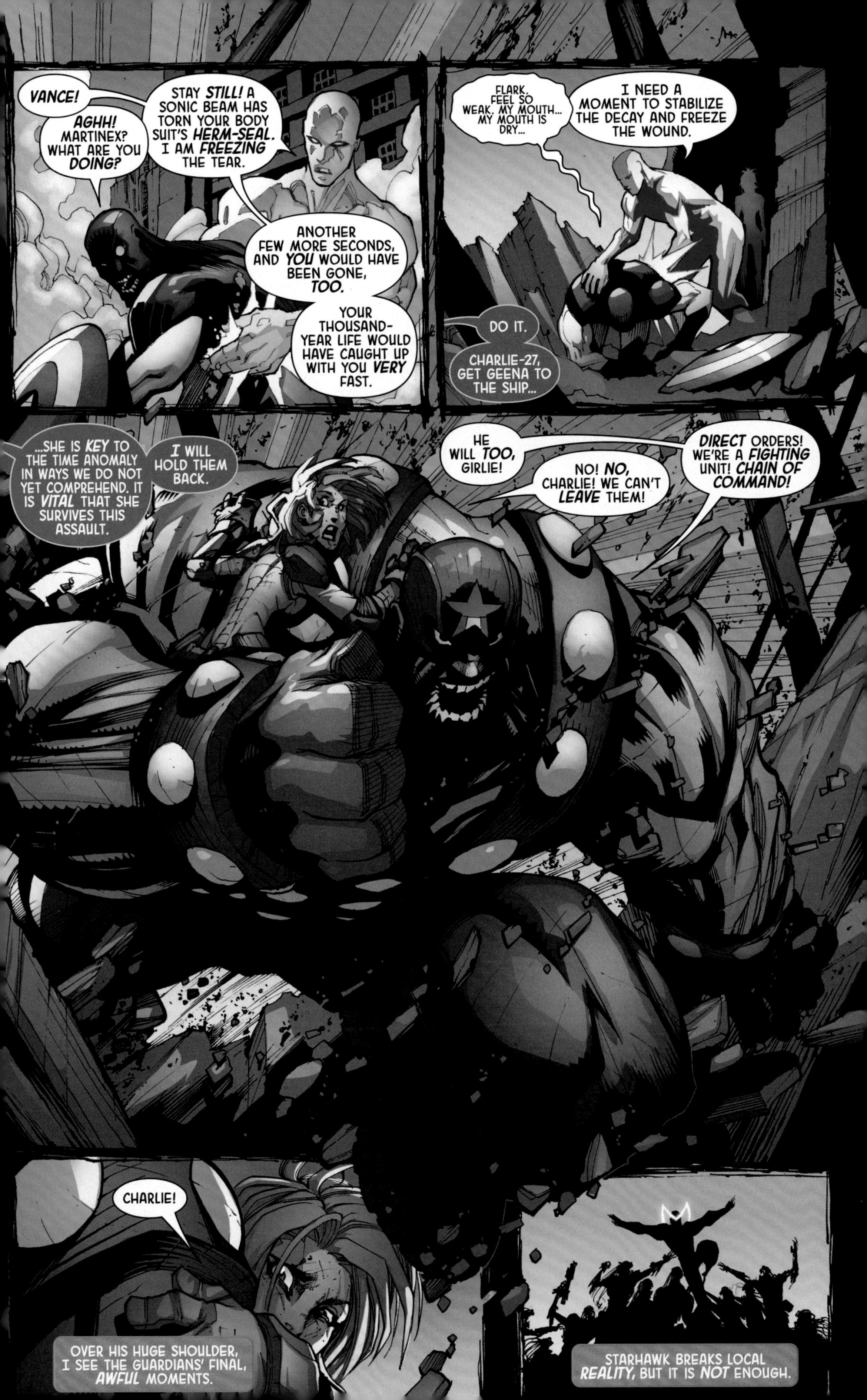

VANCE!
AGHH! MARTINEX? WHAT ARE YOU DOING?
STAY STILL! A SONIC BEAM HAS TORN YOUR BODY SUIT'S HERM-SEAL. I AM FREEZING THE TEAR.
ANOTHER FEW MORE SECONDS, AND YOU WOULD HAVE BEEN GONE, TOO.
YOUR THOUSAND-YEAR LIFE WOULD HAVE CAUGHT UP WITH YOU VERY FAST.
FLARK. FEEL SO WEAK. MY MOUTH... MY MOUTH IS DRY...
I NEED A MOMENT TO STABILIZE THE DECAY AND FREEZE THE WOUND.
DO IT.
CHARLIE-27, GET GEENA TO THE SHIP...
...SHE IS KEY TO THE TIME ANOMALY IN WAYS WE DO NOT YET COMPREHEND. IT IS VITAL THAT SHE SURVIVES THIS ASSAULT.
I WILL HOLD THEM BACK.
HE WILL TOO, GIRLIE!
NO! NO, CHARLIE! WE CAN'T LEAVE THEM!
DIRECT ORDERS! WE'RE A FIGHTING UNIT! CHAIN OF COMMAND!
CHARLIE!
OVER HIS HUGE SHOULDER, I SEE THE GUARDIANS' FINAL, AWFUL MOMENTS.
STARHAWK BREAKS LOCAL REALITY, BUT IT IS NOT ENOUGH.

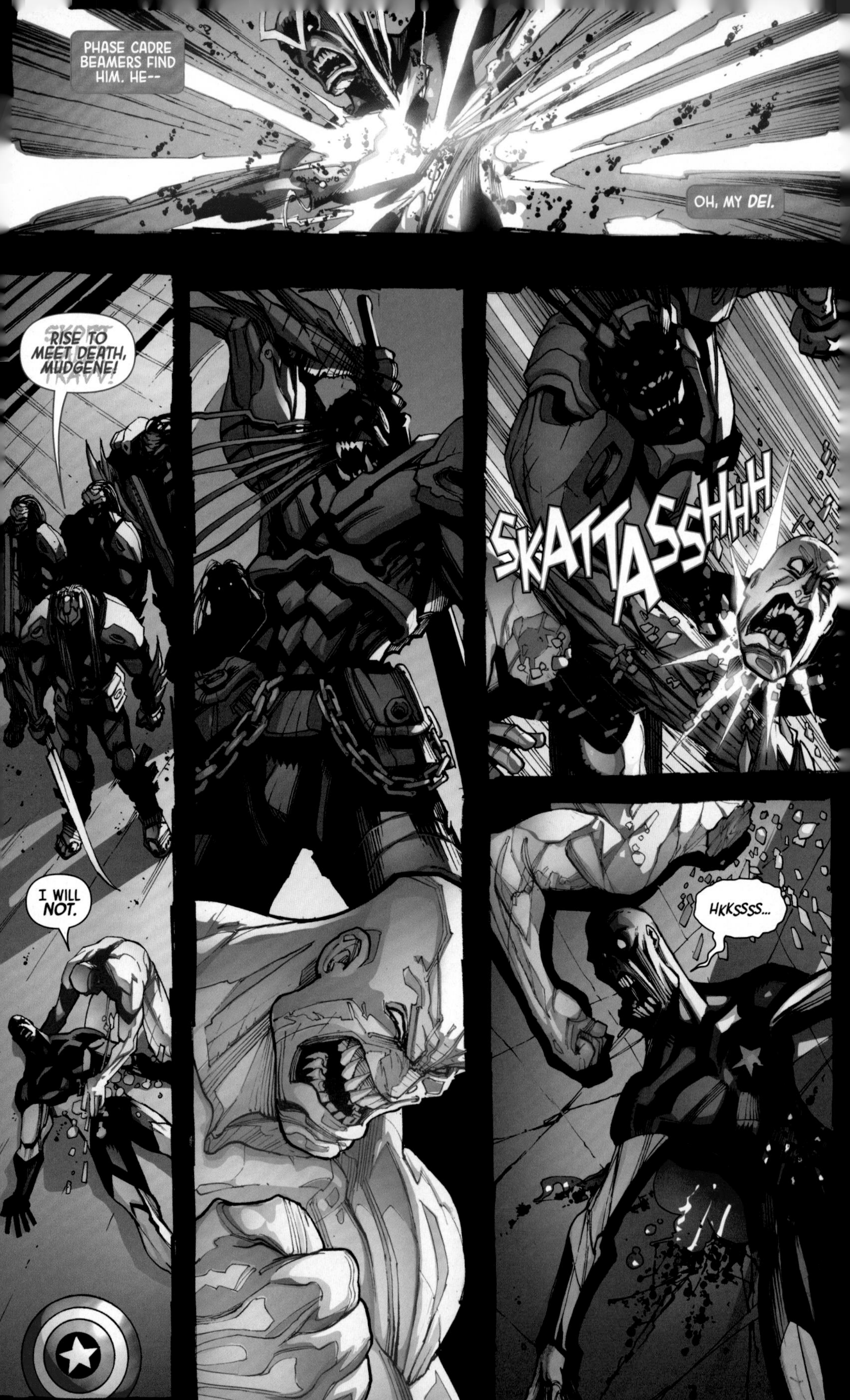
PHASE CADRE BEAMERS FIND HIM. HE--
OH, MY DEI.
RISE TO MEET DEATH, MUDGENE!
I WILL NOT.
SKATTASSHHH
HKKSSSS...

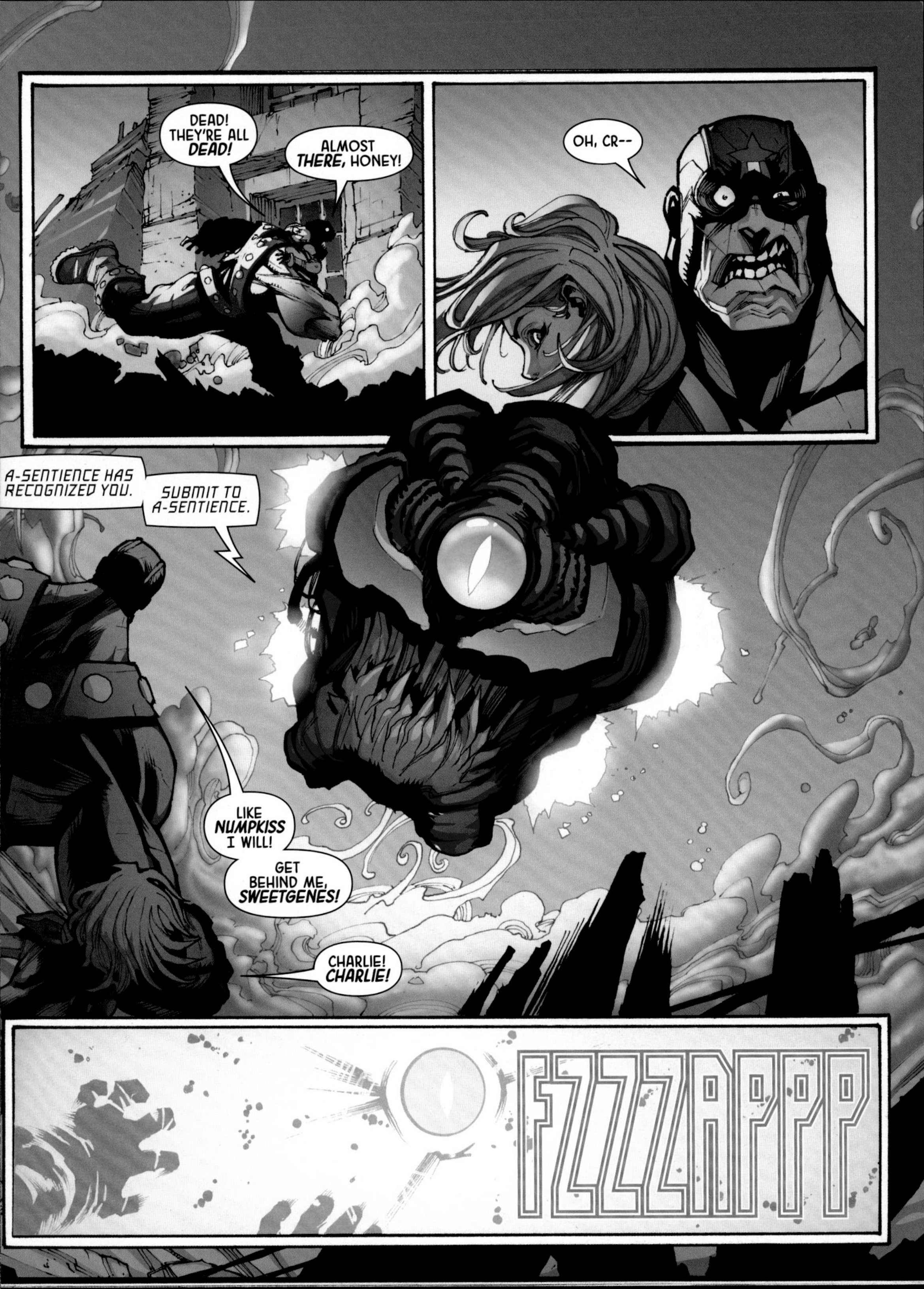
DEAD! THEY'RE ALL DEAD!
ALMOST THERE, HONEY!
OH, CR--
A-SENTIENCE HAS RECOGNIZED YOU.
SUBMIT TO A-SENTIENCE.
LIKE NUMPKISS I WILL!
GET BEHIND ME, SWEETGENES!
CHARLIE! CHARLIE!
FZZZAPPP

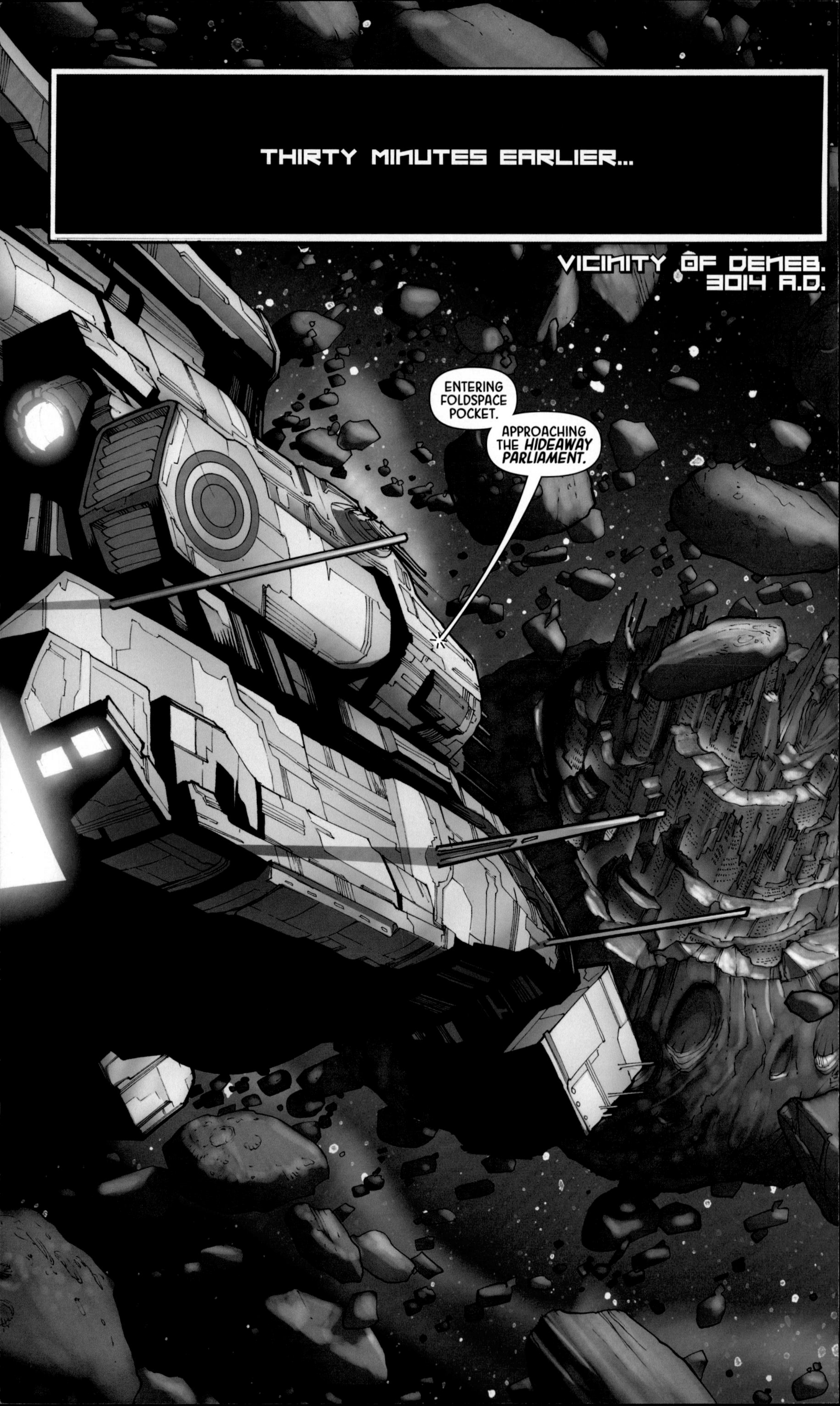
THIRTY MINUTES EARLIER...
VICINITY OF DENEB.
3014 A.D.
ENTERING FOLDSPACE POCKET.
APPROACHING THE HIDEAWAY PARLIAMENT.

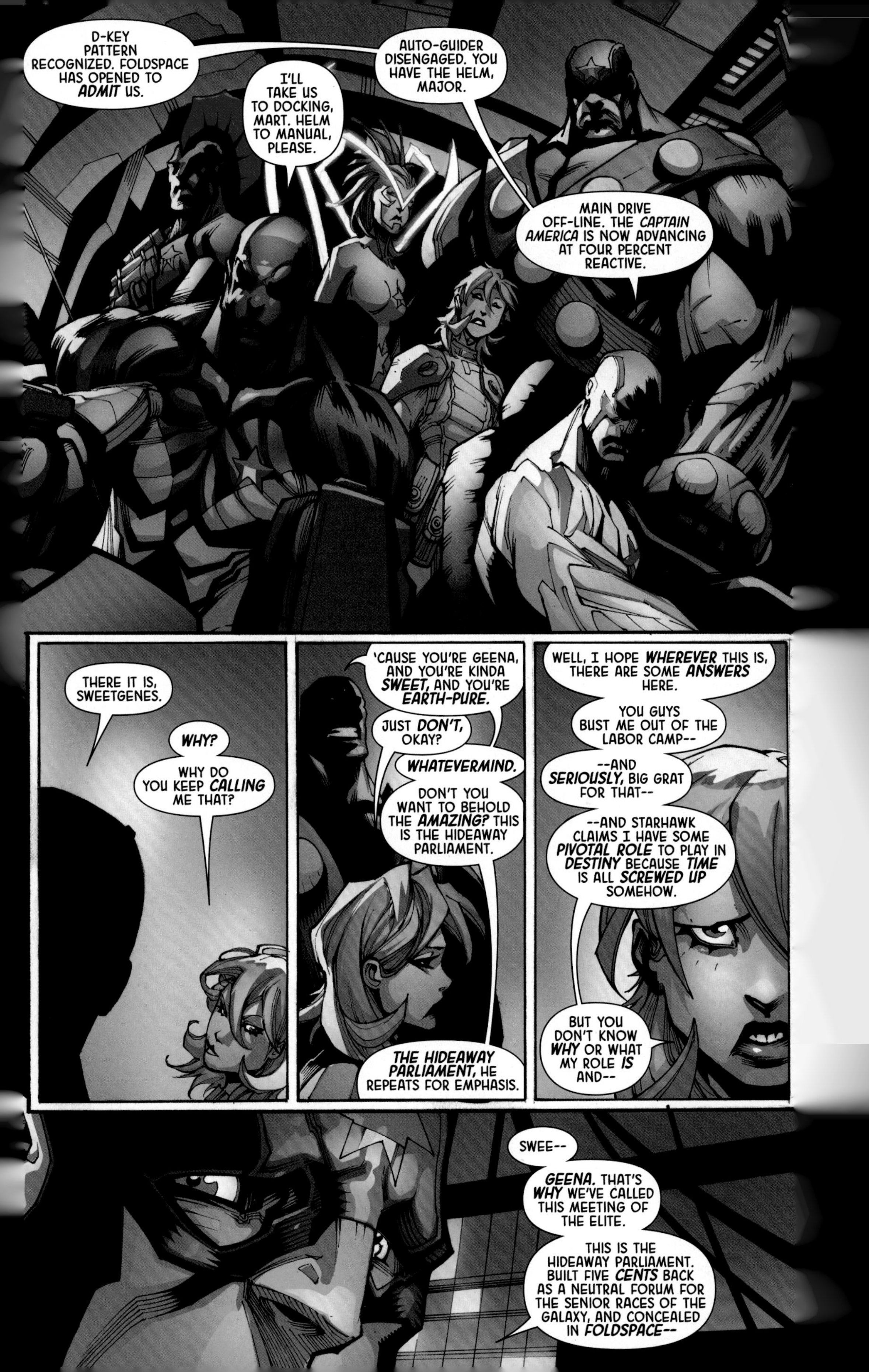

D-KEY PATTERN RECOGNIZED. FOLDSPACE HAS OPENED TO *ADMIT* US.
I'LL TAKE US TO DOCKING, MART. HELM TO MANUAL, PLEASE.
AUTO-GUIDER DISENGAGED. YOU HAVE THE HELM, MAJOR.
MAIN DRIVE OFF-LINE. THE *CAPTAIN AMERICA* IS NOW ADVANCING AT FOUR PERCENT REACTIVE.
THERE IT IS, SWEETGENES.
WHY?
WHY DO YOU KEEP *CALLING* ME THAT?
'CAUSE YOU'RE GEENA, AND YOU'RE KINDA *SWEET,* AND YOU'RE *EARTH-PURE.*
JUST *DON'T,* OKAY?
WHATEVERMIND.
DON'T YOU WANT TO BEHOLD THE *AMAZING?* THIS IS THE HIDEAWAY PARLIAMENT.
THE HIDEAWAY PARLIAMENT, HE REPEATS FOR EMPHASIS.
WELL, I HOPE *WHEREVER* THIS IS, THERE ARE SOME *ANSWERS* HERE.
YOU GUYS BUST ME OUT OF THE LABOR CAMP--
--AND *SERIOUSLY,* BIG GRAT FOR THAT--
--AND STARHAWK CLAIMS I HAVE SOME *PIVOTAL ROLE* TO PLAY IN *DESTINY* BECAUSE *TIME* IS ALL *SCREWED UP* SOMEHOW.
BUT YOU DON'T KNOW *WHY* OR WHAT MY ROLE *IS* AND--
SWEE--
GEENA. THAT'S *WHY* WE'VE CALLED THIS MEETING OF THE ELITE.
THIS IS THE HIDEAWAY PARLIAMENT. BUILT FIVE *CENTS* BACK AS A NEUTRAL FORUM FOR THE SENIOR RACES OF THE GALAXY, AND CONCEALED IN *FOLDSPACE--*

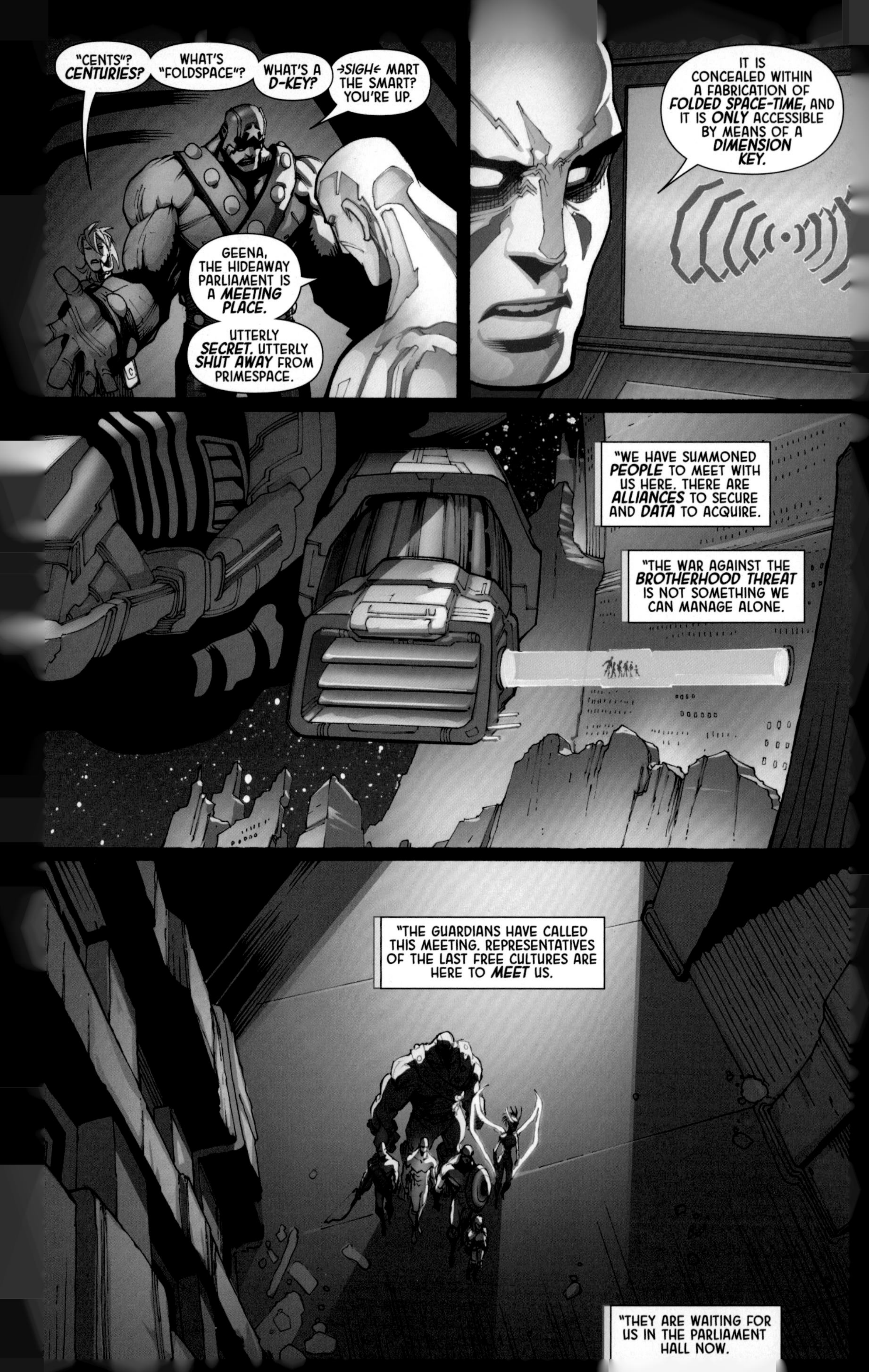
"CENTS"? CENTURIES?
WHAT'S "FOLDSPACE"?
WHAT'S A D-KEY?
→SIGH← MART THE SMART? YOU'RE UP.
GEENA, THE HIDEAWAY PARLIAMENT IS A MEETING PLACE.
UTTERLY SECRET. UTTERLY SHUT AWAY FROM PRIMESPACE.
IT IS CONCEALED WITHIN A FABRICATION OF FOLDED SPACE-TIME, AND IT IS ONLY ACCESSIBLE BY MEANS OF A DIMENSION KEY.
"WE HAVE SUMMONED PEOPLE TO MEET WITH US HERE. THERE ARE ALLIANCES TO SECURE AND DATA TO ACQUIRE.
"THE WAR AGAINST THE BROTHERHOOD THREAT IS NOT SOMETHING WE CAN MANAGE ALONE.
"THE GUARDIANS HAVE CALLED THIS MEETING. REPRESENTATIVES OF THE LAST FREE CULTURES ARE HERE TO MEET US.
"THEY ARE WAITING FOR US IN THE PARLIAMENT HALL NOW.

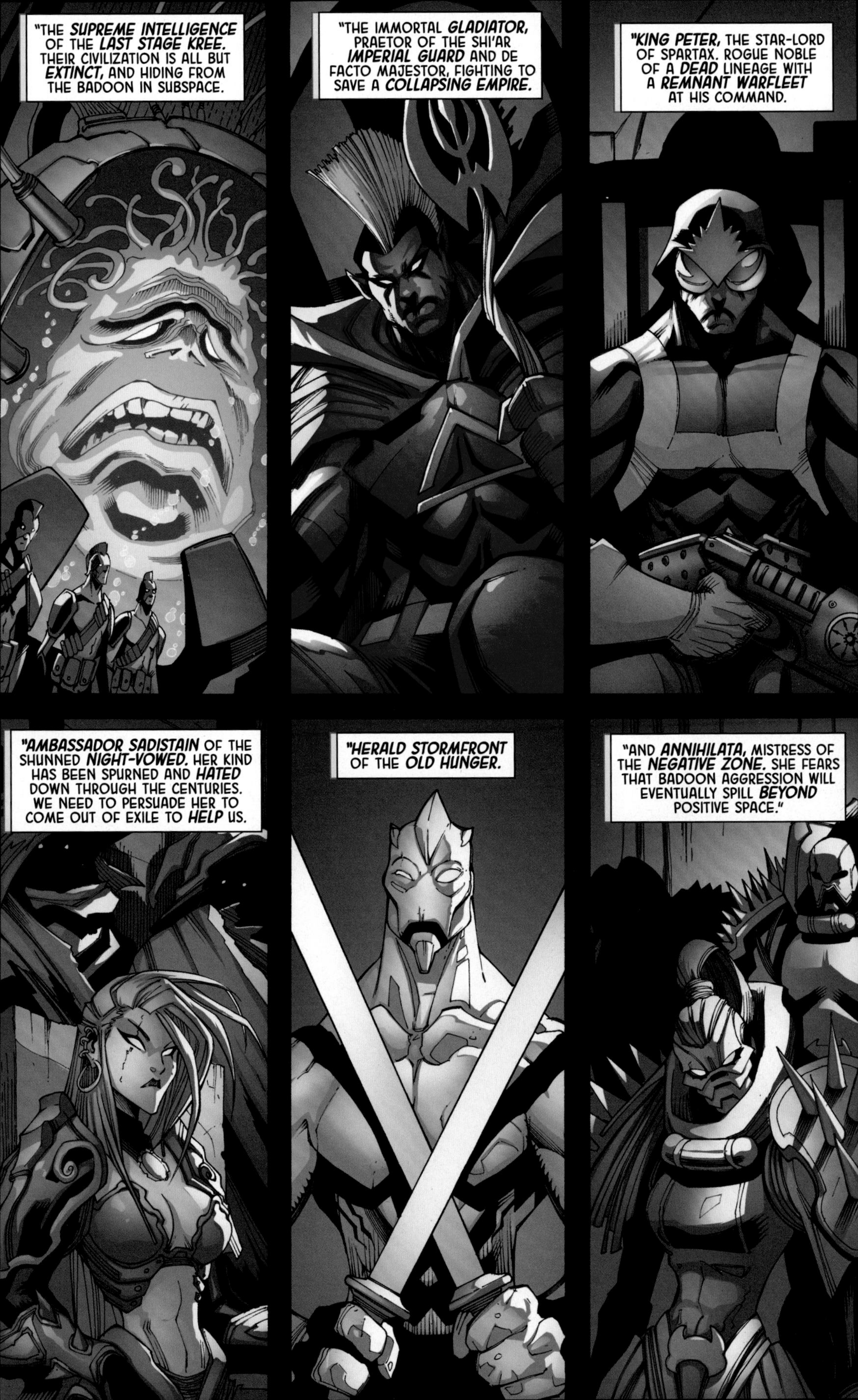
"THE SUPREME INTELLIGENCE OF THE LAST STAGE KREE. THEIR CIVILIZATION IS ALL BUT EXTINCT, AND HIDING FROM THE BADOON IN SUBSPACE.
"THE IMMORTAL GLADIATOR, PRAETOR OF THE SHI'AR IMPERIAL GUARD AND DE FACTO MAJESTOR, FIGHTING TO SAVE A COLLAPSING EMPIRE.
"KING PETER, THE STAR-LORD OF SPARTAX. ROGUE NOBLE OF A DEAD LINEAGE WITH A REMNANT WARFLEET AT HIS COMMAND.
"AMBASSADOR SADISTAIN OF THE SHUNNED NIGHT-VOWED. HER KIND HAS BEEN SPURNED AND HATED DOWN THROUGH THE CENTURIES. WE NEED TO PERSUADE HER TO COME OUT OF EXILE TO HELP US.
"HERALD STORMFRONT OF THE OLD HUNGER.
"AND ANNIHILATA, MISTRESS OF THE NEGATIVE ZONE. SHE FEARS THAT BADOON AGGRESSION WILL EVENTUALLY SPILL BEYOND POSITIVE SPACE."

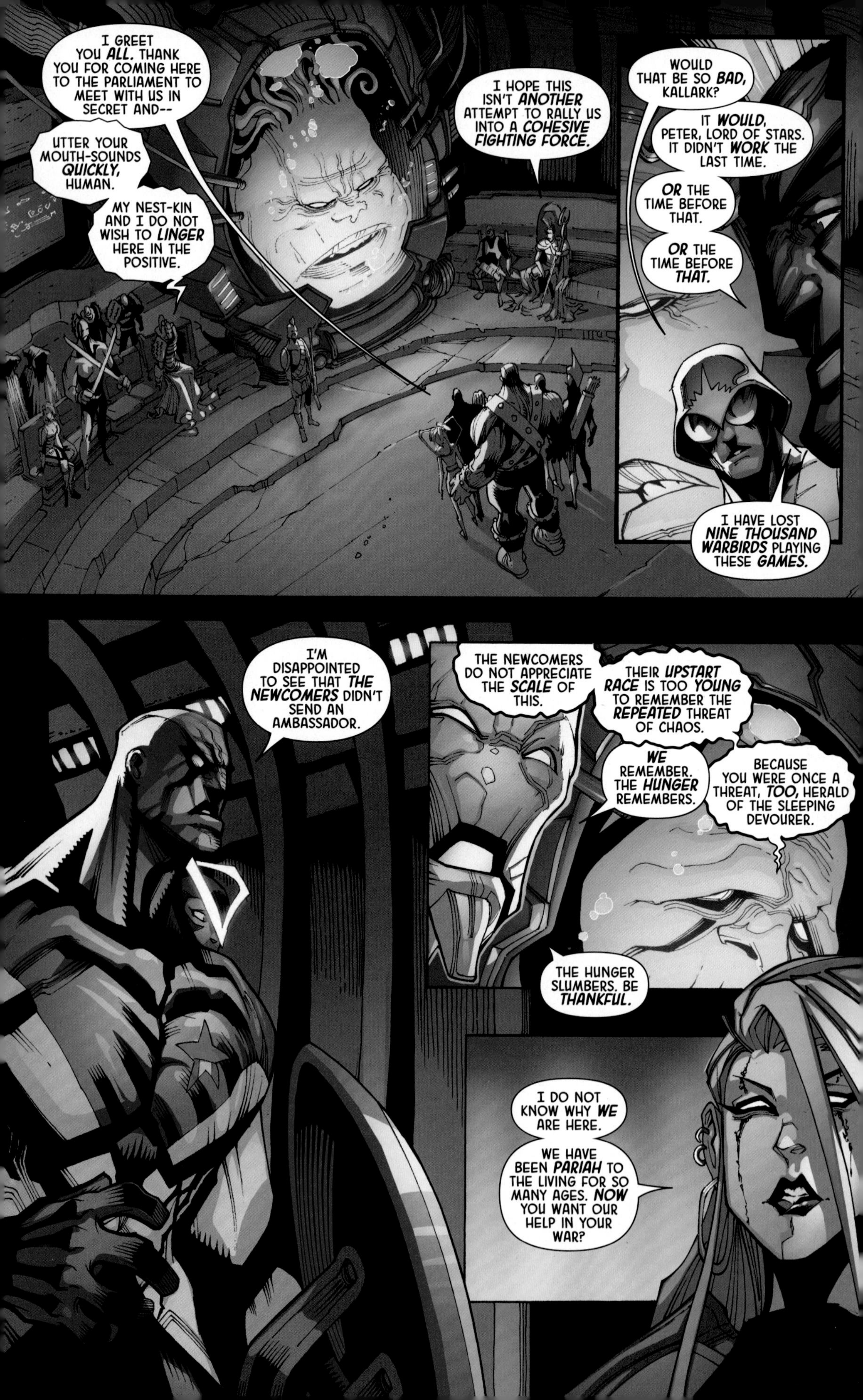
I GREET YOU ALL. THANK YOU FOR COMING HERE TO THE PARLIAMENT TO MEET WITH US IN SECRET AND--
UTTER YOUR MOUTH-SOUNDS QUICKLY, HUMAN.
MY NEST-KIN AND I DO NOT WISH TO LINGER HERE IN THE POSITIVE.
I HOPE THIS ISN'T ANOTHER ATTEMPT TO RALLY US INTO A COHESIVE FIGHTING FORCE.
WOULD THAT BE SO BAD, KALLARK?
IT WOULD, PETER, LORD OF STARS. IT DIDN'T WORK THE LAST TIME.
OR THE TIME BEFORE THAT.
OR THE TIME BEFORE THAT.
I HAVE LOST NINE THOUSAND WARBIRDS PLAYING THESE GAMES.
I'M DISAPPOINTED TO SEE THAT THE NEWCOMERS DIDN'T SEND AN AMBASSADOR.
THE NEWCOMERS DO NOT APPRECIATE THE SCALE OF THIS.
THEIR UPSTART RACE IS TOO YOUNG TO REMEMBER THE REPEATED THREAT OF CHAOS.
WE REMEMBER. THE HUNGER REMEMBERS.
BECAUSE YOU WERE ONCE A THREAT, TOO, HERALD OF THE SLEEPING DEVOURER.
THE HUNGER SLUMBERS. BE THANKFUL.
I DO NOT KNOW WHY WE ARE HERE.
WE HAVE BEEN PARIAH TO THE LIVING FOR SO MANY AGES. NOW YOU WANT OUR HELP IN YOUR WAR?

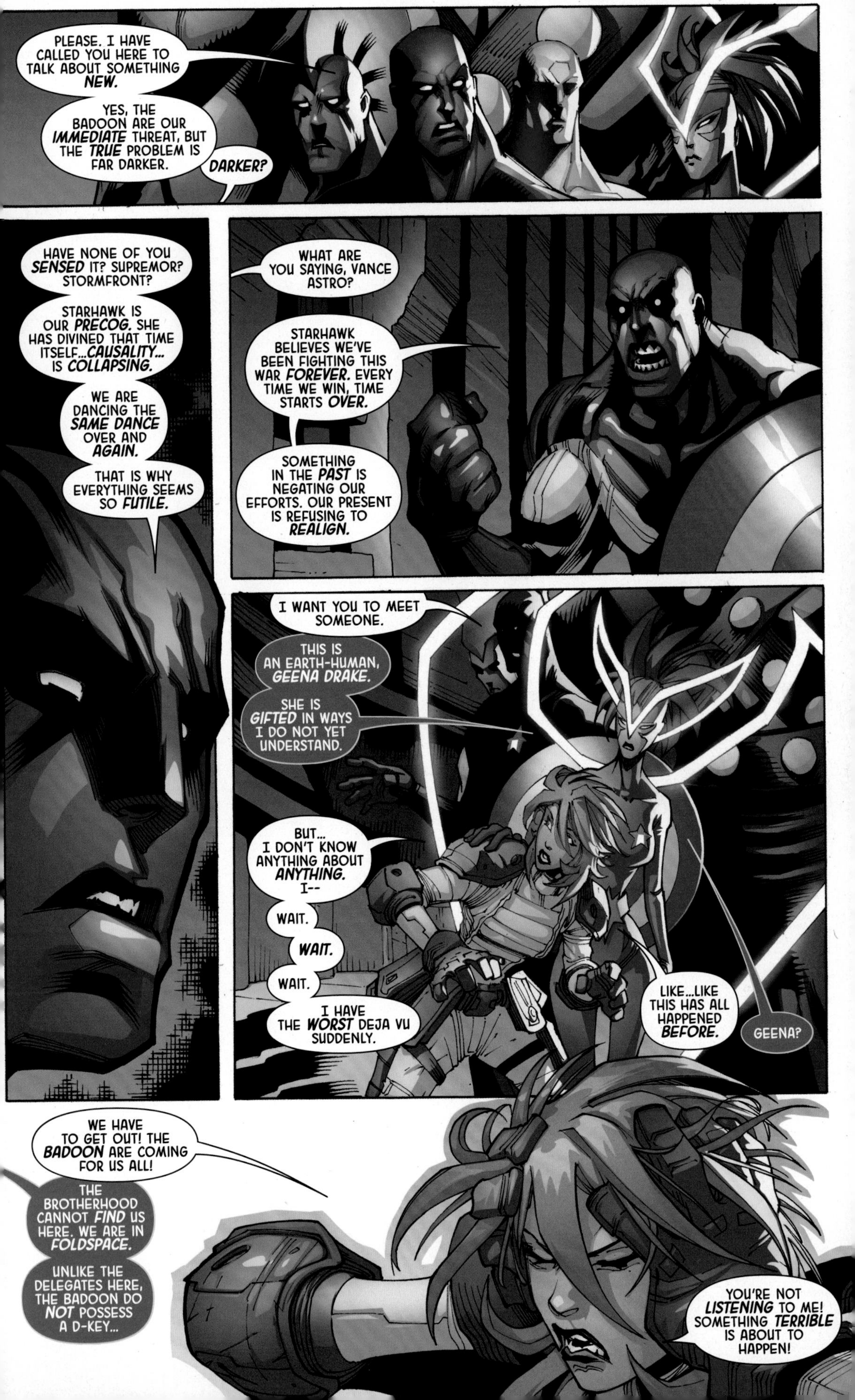
PLEASE. I HAVE CALLED YOU HERE TO TALK ABOUT SOMETHING NEW.
YES, THE BADOON ARE OUR IMMEDIATE THREAT, BUT THE TRUE PROBLEM IS FAR DARKER.
DARKER?
HAVE NONE OF YOU SENSED IT? SUPREMOR? STORMFRONT?
STARHAWK IS OUR PRECOG. SHE HAS DIVINED THAT TIME ITSELF...CAUSALITY... IS COLLAPSING.
WE ARE DANCING THE SAME DANCE OVER AND AGAIN.
THAT IS WHY EVERYTHING SEEMS SO FUTILE.
WHAT ARE YOU SAYING, VANCE ASTRO?
STARHAWK BELIEVES WE'VE BEEN FIGHTING THIS WAR FOREVER. EVERY TIME WE WIN, TIME STARTS OVER.
SOMETHING IN THE PAST IS NEGATING OUR EFFORTS. OUR PRESENT IS REFUSING TO REALIGN.
I WANT YOU TO MEET SOMEONE.
THIS IS AN EARTH-HUMAN, GEENA DRAKE.
SHE IS GIFTED IN WAYS I DO NOT YET UNDERSTAND.
BUT... I DON'T KNOW ANYTHING ABOUT ANYTHING. I--
WAIT.
WAIT.
WAIT.
I HAVE THE WORST DEJA VU SUDDENLY.
LIKE...LIKE THIS HAS ALL HAPPENED BEFORE.
GEENA?
WE HAVE TO GET OUT! THE BADOON ARE COMING FOR US ALL!
THE BROTHERHOOD CANNOT FIND US HERE. WE ARE IN FOLDSPACE.
UNLIKE THE DELEGATES HERE, THE BADOON DO NOT POSSESS A D-KEY...
YOU'RE NOT LISTENING TO ME! SOMETHING TERRIBLE IS ABOUT TO HAPPEN!

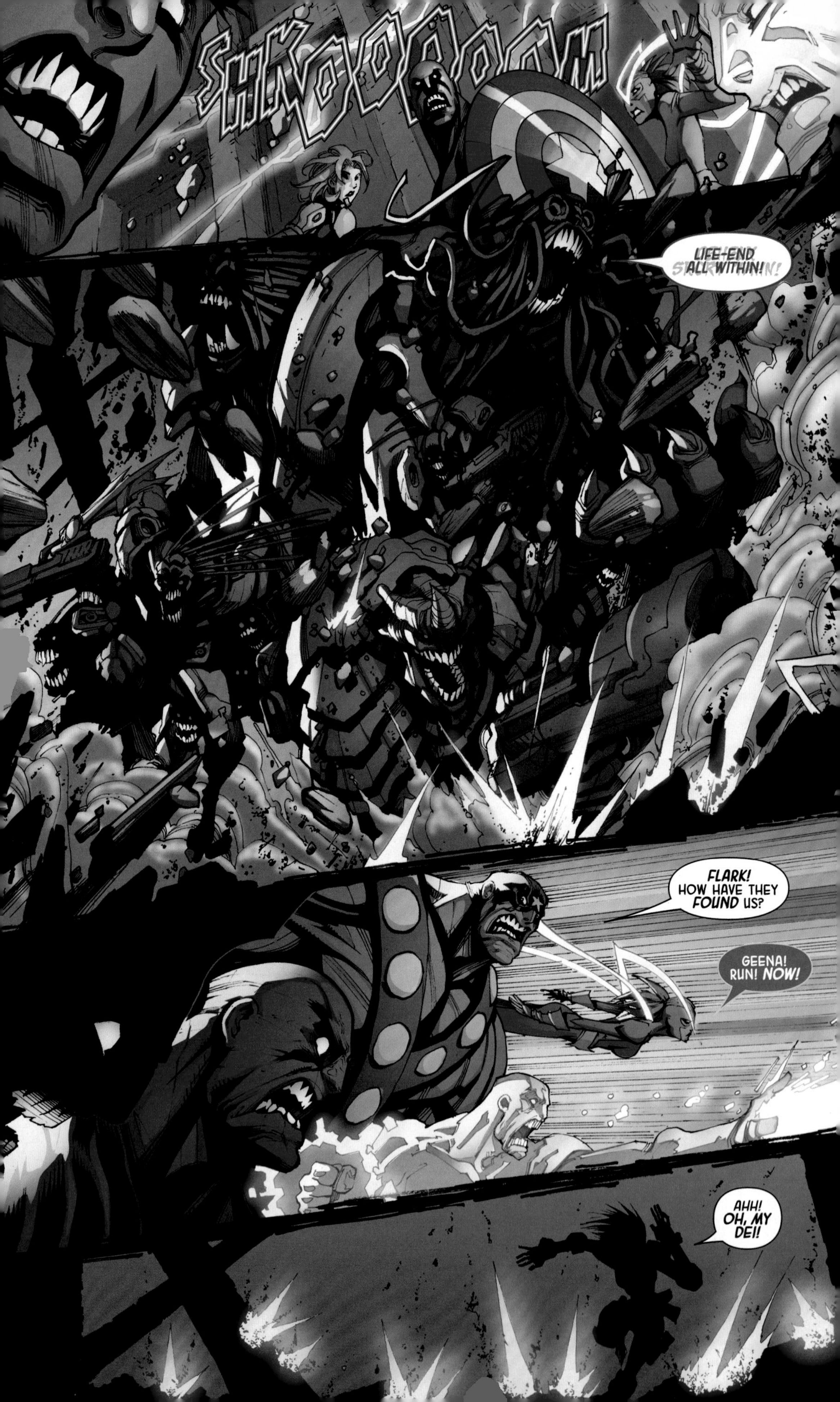
SHKOOOOOOM
LIFE-END ALL WITHIN!
FLARK! HOW HAVE THEY FOUND US?
GEENA! RUN! NOW!
AHH! OH, MY DEI!

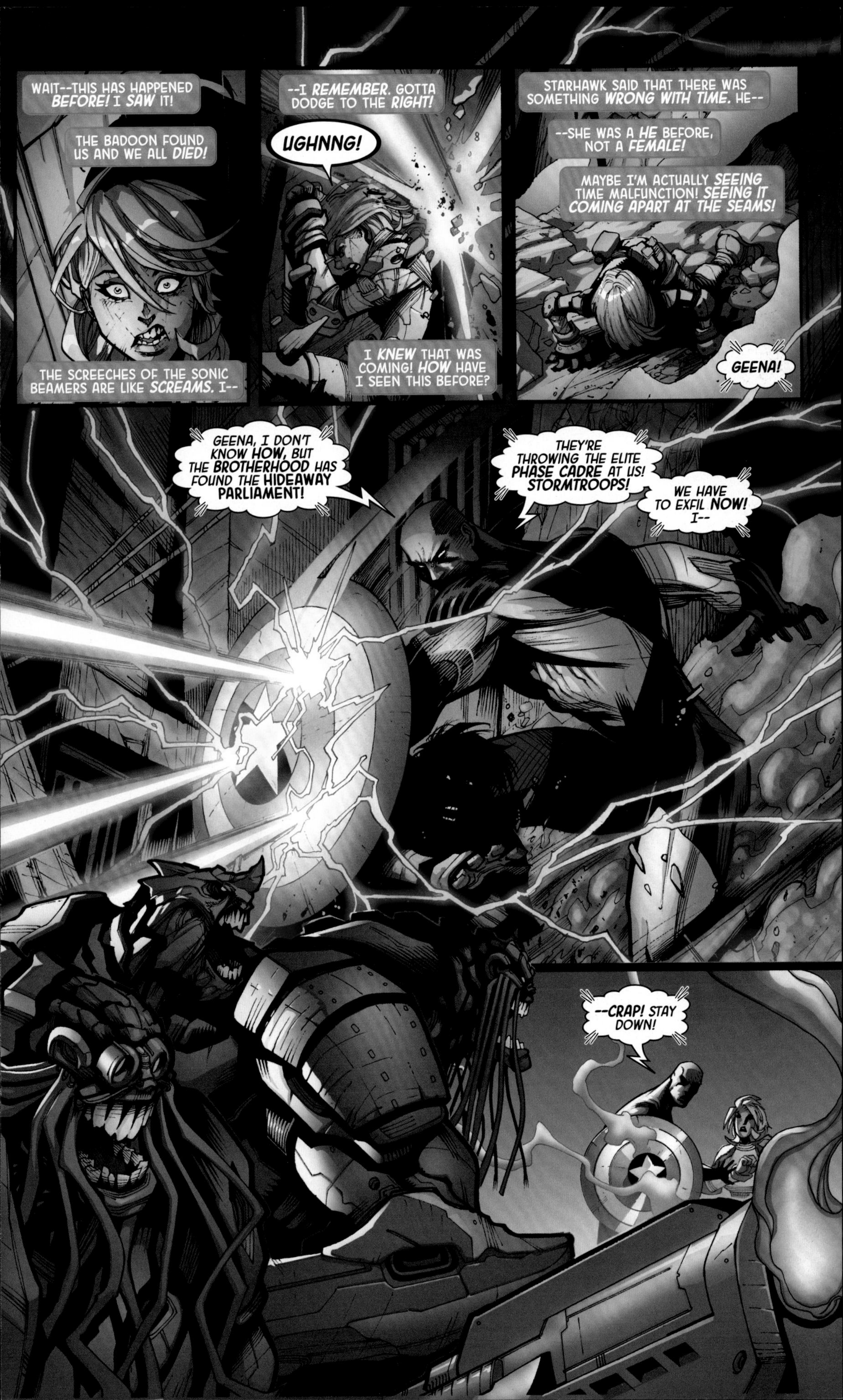

WAIT--THIS HAS HAPPENED BEFORE! I SAW IT!
THE BADOON FOUND US AND WE ALL DIED!
THE SCREECHES OF THE SONIC BEAMERS ARE LIKE SCREAMS. I--
--I REMEMBER. GOTTA DODGE TO THE RIGHT!
UGHNNG!
I KNEW THAT WAS COMING! HOW HAVE I SEEN THIS BEFORE?
STARHAWK SAID THAT THERE WAS SOMETHING WRONG WITH TIME. HE--
--SHE WAS A HE BEFORE, NOT A FEMALE!
MAYBE I'M ACTUALLY SEEING TIME MALFUNCTION! SEEING IT COMING APART AT THE SEAMS!
GEENA!
GEENA, I DON'T KNOW HOW, BUT THE BROTHERHOOD HAS FOUND THE HIDEAWAY PARLIAMENT!
THEY'RE THROWING THE ELITE PHASE CADRE AT US! STORMTROOPS!
WE HAVE TO EXFIL NOW! I--
--CRAP! STAY DOWN!

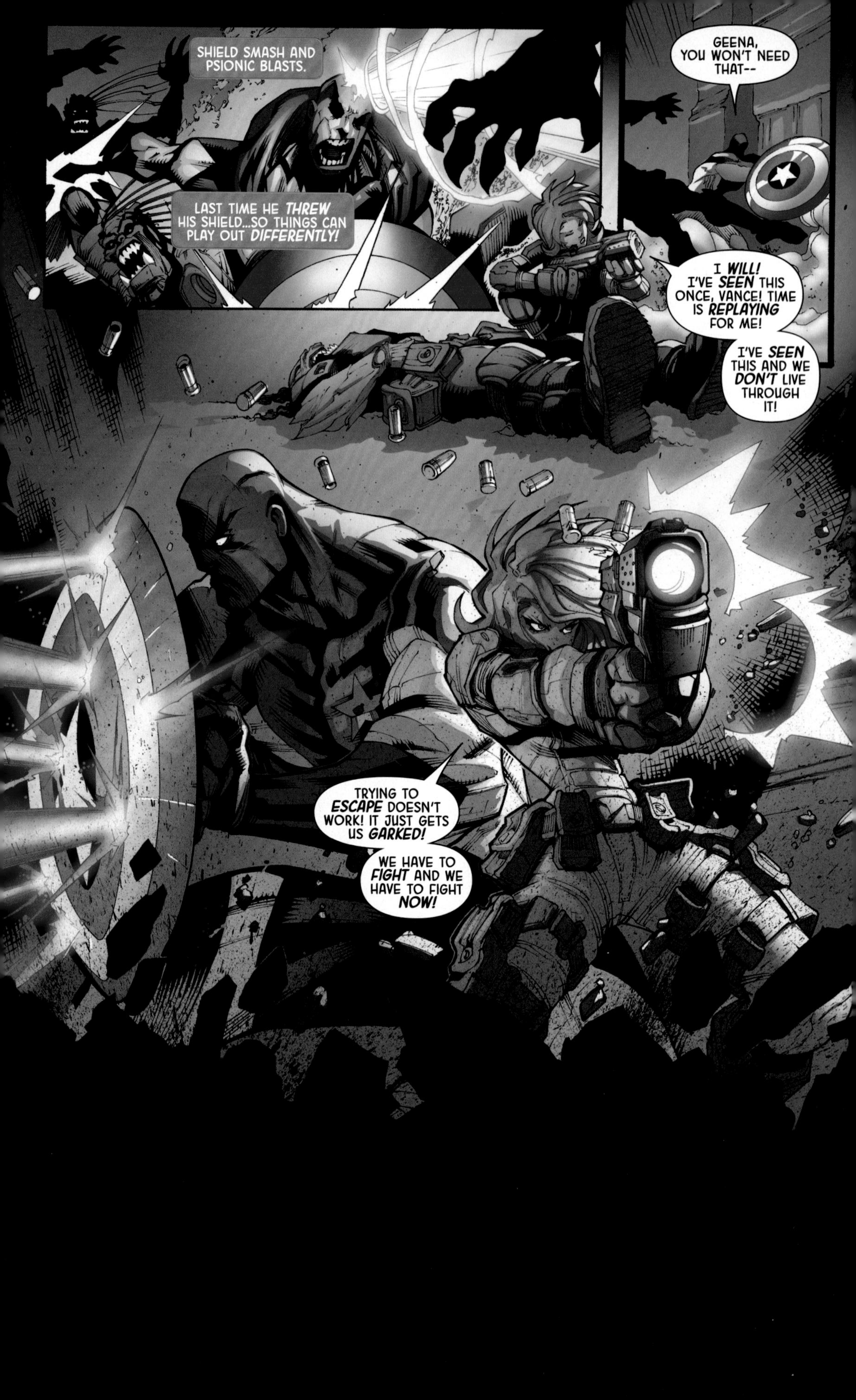
SHIELD SMASH AND PSIONIC BLASTS.
LAST TIME HE THREW HIS SHIELD...SO THINGS CAN PLAY OUT DIFFERENTLY!
GEENA, YOU WON'T NEED THAT--
I WILL! I'VE SEEN THIS ONCE, VANCE! TIME IS REPLAYING FOR ME!
I'VE SEEN THIS AND WE DON'T LIVE THROUGH IT!
TRYING TO ESCAPE DOESN'T WORK! IT JUST GETS US GARKED!
WE HAVE TO FIGHT AND WE HAVE TO FIGHT NOW!

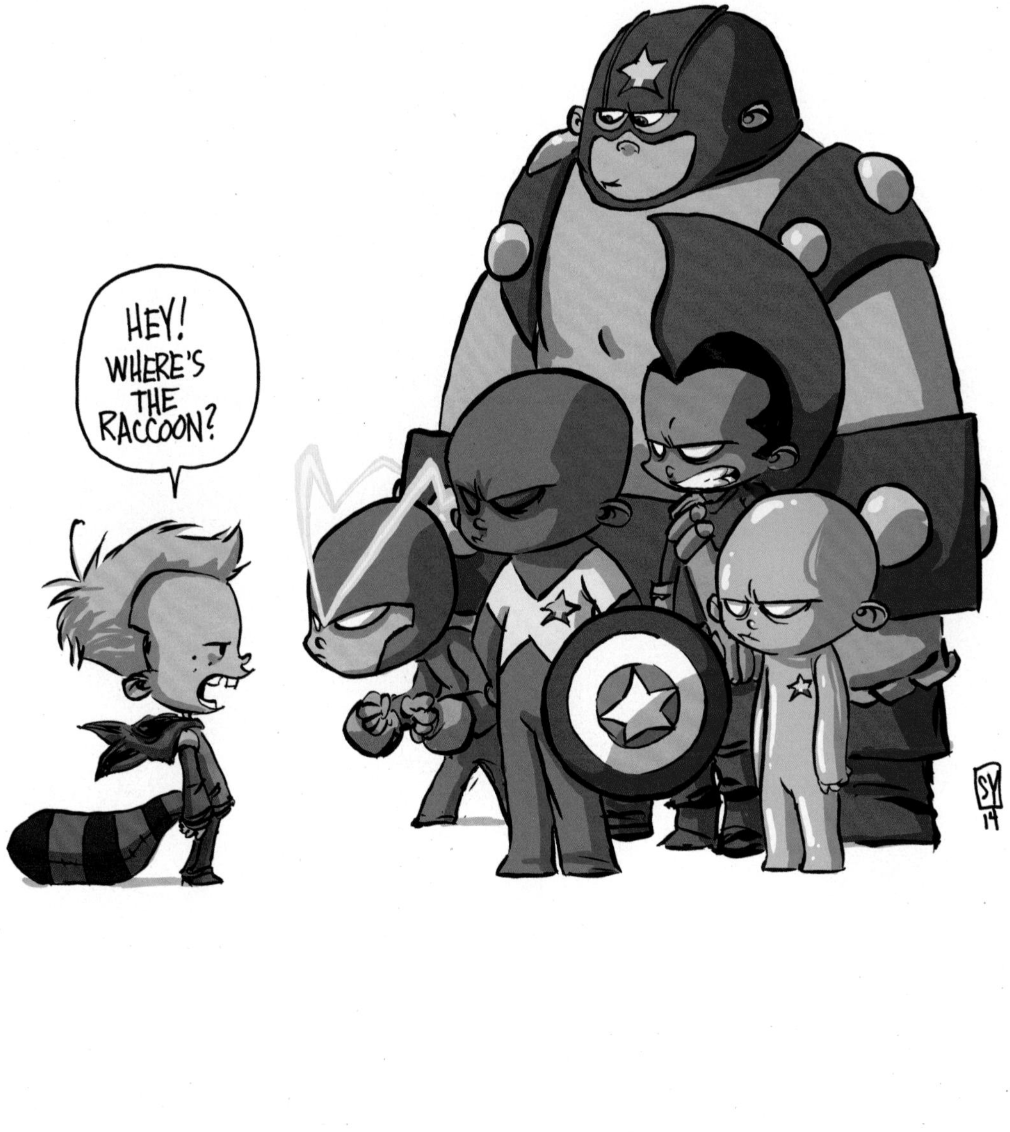
HEY! WHERE'S THE RACCOON?

#1 **VARIANT** BY SKOTTIE YOUNG

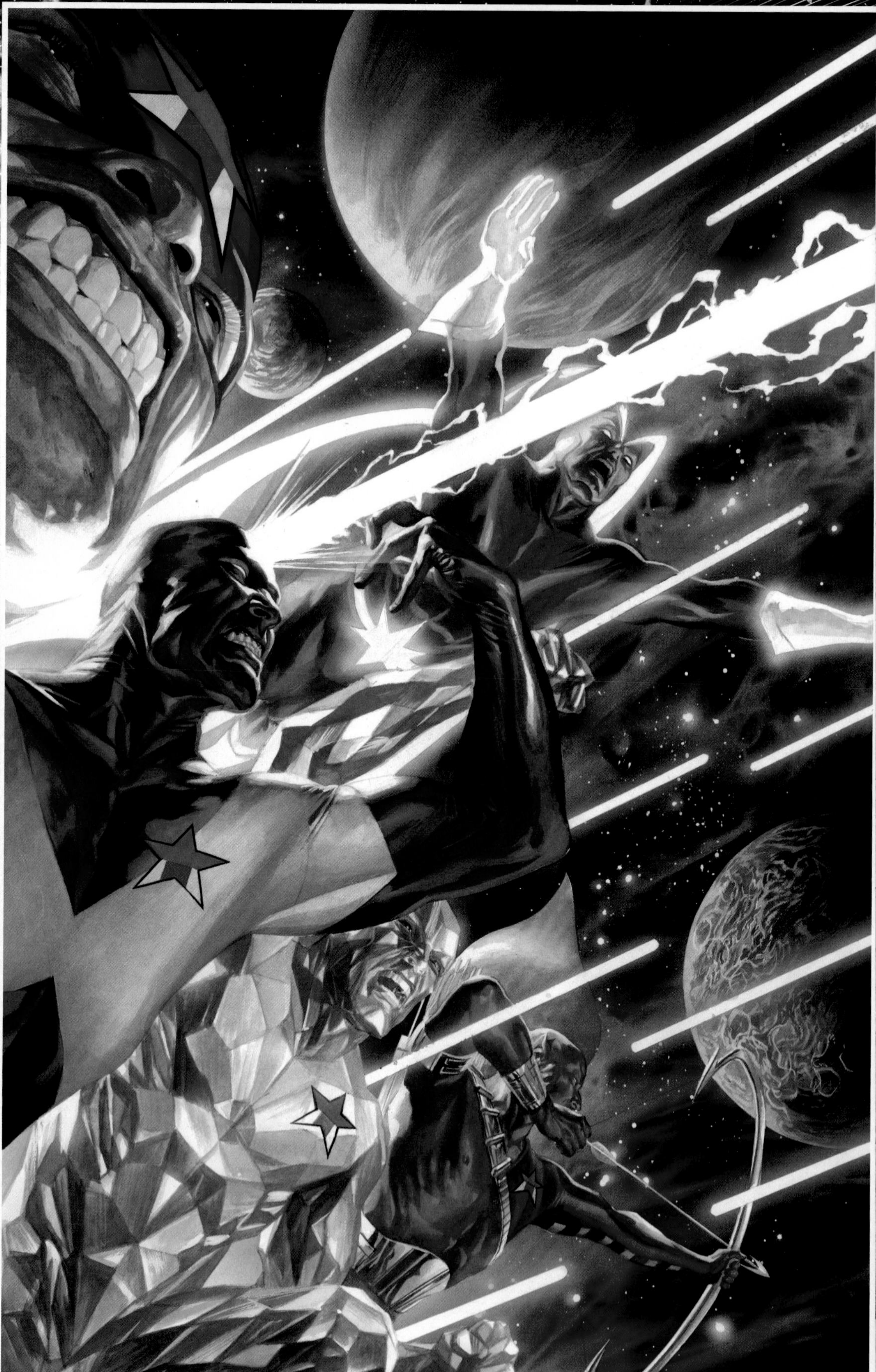

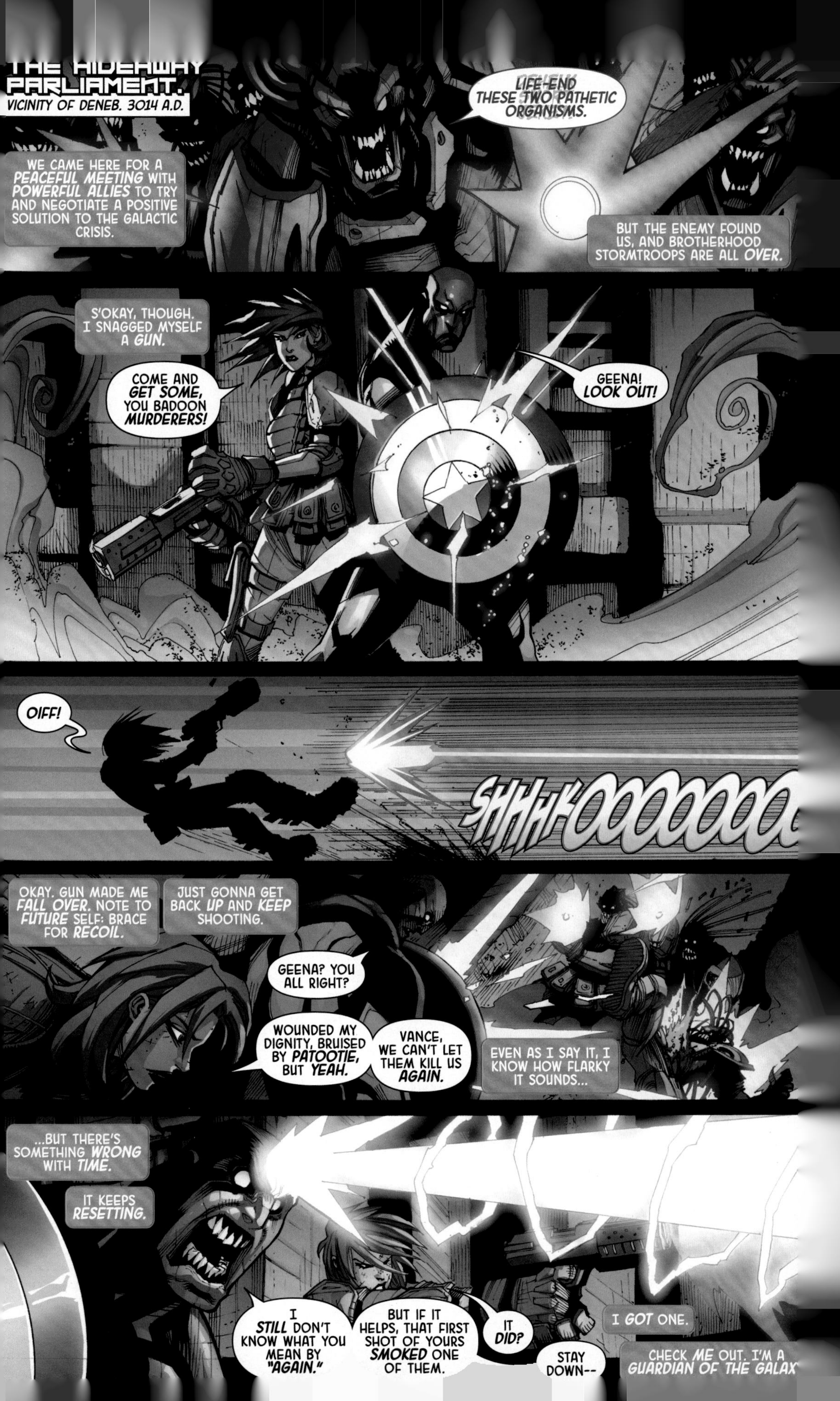

THE HIDEAWAY PARLIAMENT.
VICINITY OF DENEB. 3014 A.D.
LIFE-END THESE TWO PATHETIC ORGANISMS.
WE CAME HERE FOR A PEACEFUL MEETING WITH POWERFUL ALLIES TO TRY AND NEGOTIATE A POSITIVE SOLUTION TO THE GALACTIC CRISIS.
BUT THE ENEMY FOUND US, AND BROTHERHOOD STORMTROOPS ARE ALL OVER.
S'OKAY, THOUGH. I SNAGGED MYSELF A GUN.
COME AND GET SOME, YOU BADOON MURDERERS!
GEENA! LOOK OUT!
OIFF!
SHHK-OOOOOOO
OKAY. GUN MADE ME FALL OVER. NOTE TO FUTURE SELF: BRACE FOR RECOIL.
JUST GONNA GET BACK UP AND KEEP SHOOTING.
GEENA? YOU ALL RIGHT?
WOUNDED MY DIGNITY, BRUISED BY PATOOTIE, BUT YEAH.
VANCE, WE CAN'T LET THEM KILL US AGAIN.
EVEN AS I SAY IT, I KNOW HOW FLARKY IT SOUNDS...
...BUT THERE'S SOMETHING WRONG WITH TIME.
IT KEEPS RESETTING.
I STILL DON'T KNOW WHAT YOU MEAN BY "AGAIN."
BUT IF IT HELPS, THAT FIRST SHOT OF YOURS SMOKED ONE OF THEM.
IT DID?
STAY DOWN--
I GOT ONE.
CHECK ME OUT. I'M A GUARDIAN OF THE GALAX

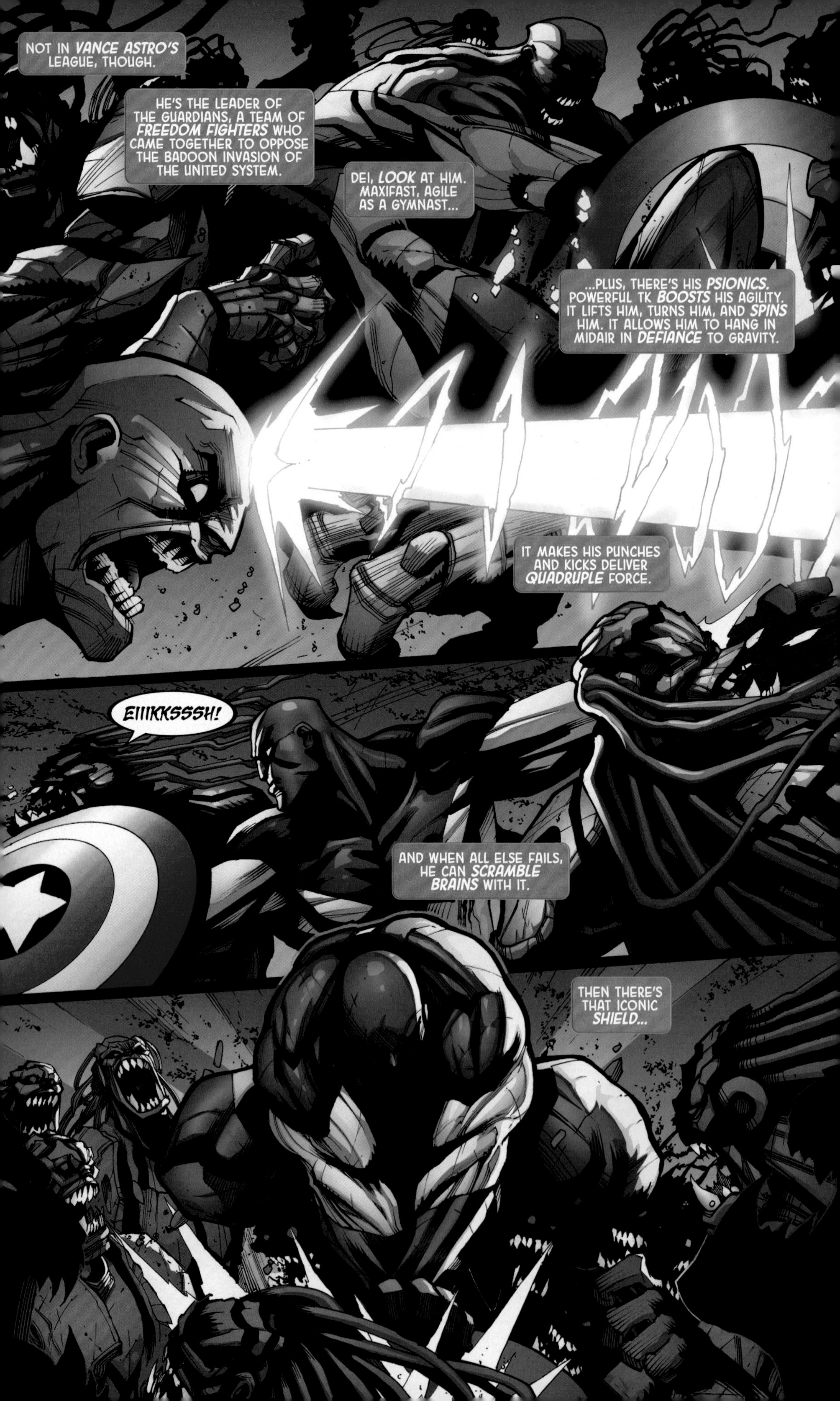
NOT IN VANCE ASTRO'S LEAGUE, THOUGH.
HE'S THE LEADER OF THE GUARDIANS, A TEAM OF FREEDOM FIGHTERS WHO CAME TOGETHER TO OPPOSE THE BADOON INVASION OF THE UNITED SYSTEM.
DEI, LOOK AT HIM. MAXIFAST, AGILE AS A GYMNAST...
...PLUS, THERE'S HIS PSIONICS. POWERFUL TK BOOSTS HIS AGILITY. IT LIFTS HIM, TURNS HIM, AND SPINS HIM. IT ALLOWS HIM TO HANG IN MIDAIR IN DEFIANCE TO GRAVITY.
IT MAKES HIS PUNCHES AND KICKS DELIVER QUADRUPLE FORCE.
EIIIKKSSSH!
AND WHEN ALL ELSE FAILS, HE CAN SCRAMBLE BRAINS WITH IT.
THEN THERE'S THAT ICONIC SHIELD...

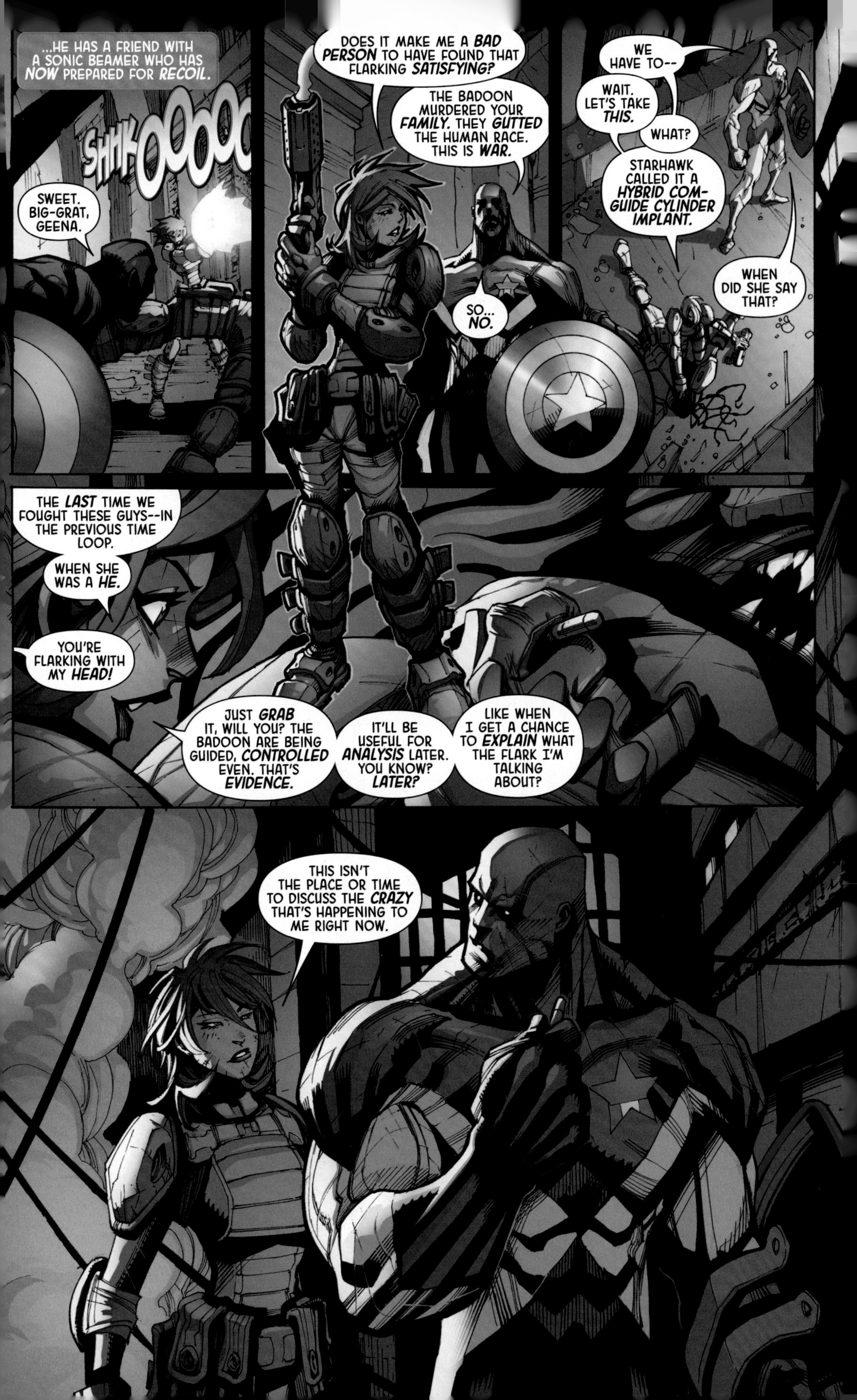

...HE HAS A FRIEND WITH A SONIC BEAMER WHO HAS NOW PREPARED FOR RECOIL.
SHHKOOOOOO
SWEET. BIG-GRAT, GEENA.
DOES IT MAKE ME A BAD PERSON TO HAVE FOUND THAT FLARKING SATISFYING?
THE BADOON MURDERED YOUR FAMILY. THEY GUTTED THE HUMAN RACE. THIS IS WAR.
SO... NO.
WE HAVE TO--
WAIT. LET'S TAKE THIS.
WHAT?
STARHAWK CALLED IT A HYBRID COM-GUIDE CYLINDER IMPLANT.
WHEN DID SHE SAY THAT?
THE LAST TIME WE FOUGHT THESE GUYS--IN THE PREVIOUS TIME LOOP.
WHEN SHE WAS A HE.
YOU'RE FLARKING WITH MY HEAD!
JUST GRAB IT, WILL YOU? THE BADOON ARE BEING GUIDED, CONTROLLED EVEN. THAT'S EVIDENCE.
IT'LL BE USEFUL FOR ANALYSIS LATER. YOU KNOW? LATER?
LIKE WHEN I GET A CHANCE TO EXPLAIN WHAT THE FLARK I'M TALKING ABOUT?
THIS ISN'T THE PLACE OR TIME TO DISCUSS THE CRAZY THAT'S HAPPENING TO ME RIGHT NOW.

WE ALL **DIED**, VANCE.

IS **THAT** WHY TIME RESET? BECAUSE WE **DIED**? I DON'T KNOW. I DON'T **THINK** SO.

AND WHAT HAPPENS **THIS** TIME?

I DON'T **KNOW!** IT HASN'T **HAPPENED** YET!

YOU INSIST THIS HAS HAPPENED **BEFORE**? THAT TIME IS **REPLAYING** ITSELF?

YES.

AND ONLY **YOU** CAN SEE IT?

APPARENTLY I'M **BLESSED** THAT WAY.

WHAT HAPPENED THE **FIRST** TIME?

BUT THIS TIME I WAS ABLE TO **WARN** EVERYONE. JUST BY A **SECOND** OR TWO, BUT MAYBE ENOUGH TO MAKE A **DIFFERENCE**.

YOU THINK?

VANCE, IT'S **ALREADY** DIFFERENT. I THINK WE CAN **CHANGE** THE OUTCOME.

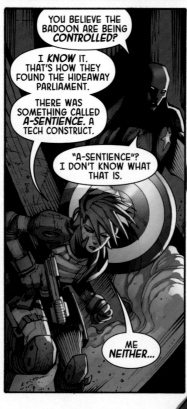

YOU BELIEVE THE BADOON ARE BEING **CONTROLLED**?

I **KNOW** IT. THAT'S HOW THEY FOUND THE HIDEAWAY PARLIAMENT.

THERE WAS SOMETHING CALLED **A-SENTIENCE**. A TECH CONSTRUCT.

"A-SENTIENCE"? I DON'T KNOW WHAT THAT IS.

ME **NEITHER**...

...BUT I KID YOU NOT, IT LOOKED JUST LIKE **THAT**.

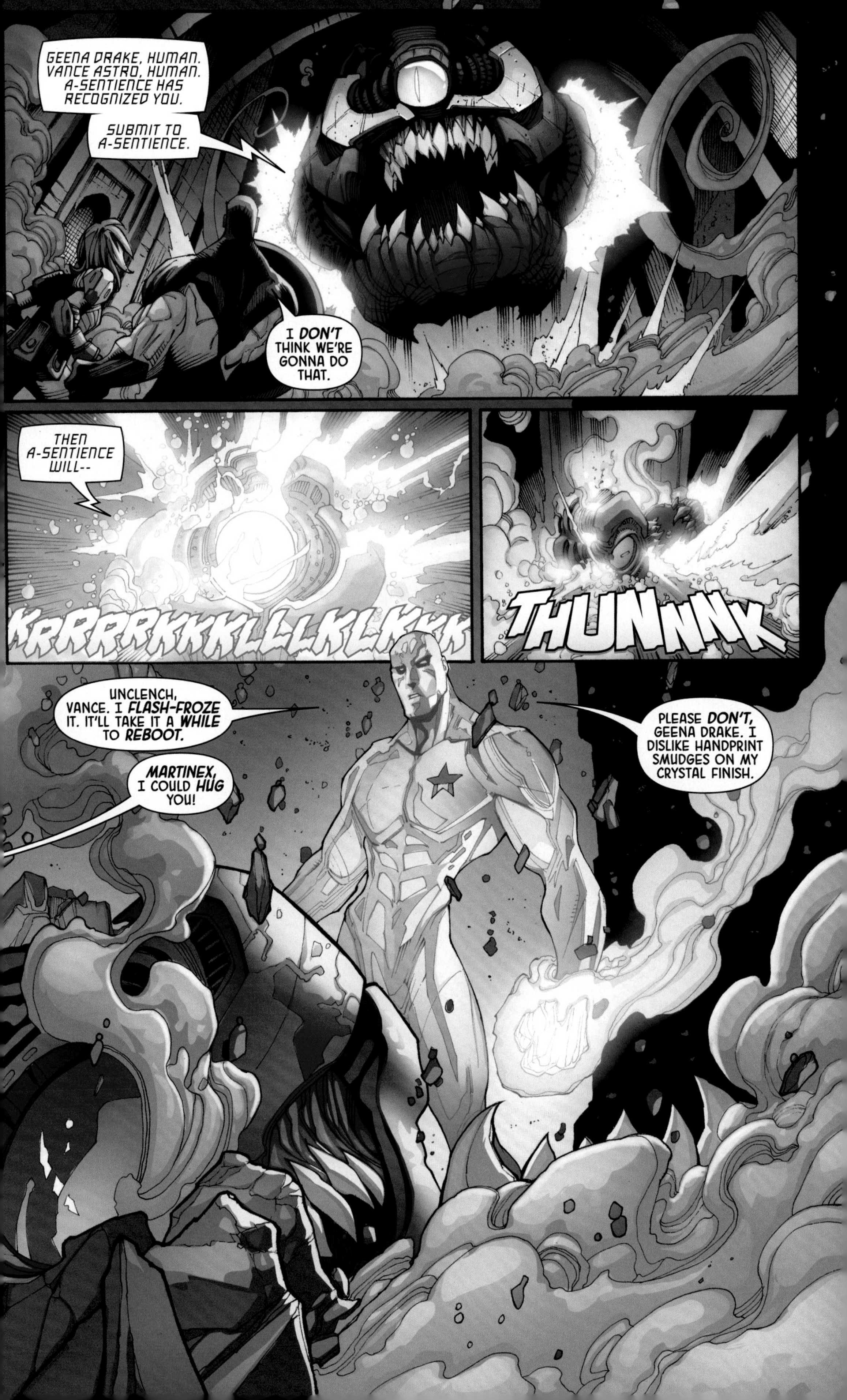

GEENA DRAKE, HUMAN. VANCE ASTRO, HUMAN. A-SENTIENCE HAS RECOGNIZED YOU.
SUBMIT TO A-SENTIENCE.
I DON'T THINK WE'RE GONNA DO THAT.
THEN A-SENTIENCE WILL--
KRRRRKKKLLLKLKKK
THUNNNK
UNCLENCH, VANCE. I FLASH-FROZE IT. IT'LL TAKE IT A WHILE TO REBOOT.
MARTINEX, I COULD HUG YOU!
PLEASE DON'T, GEENA DRAKE. I DISLIKE HANDPRINT SMUDGES ON MY CRYSTAL FINISH.

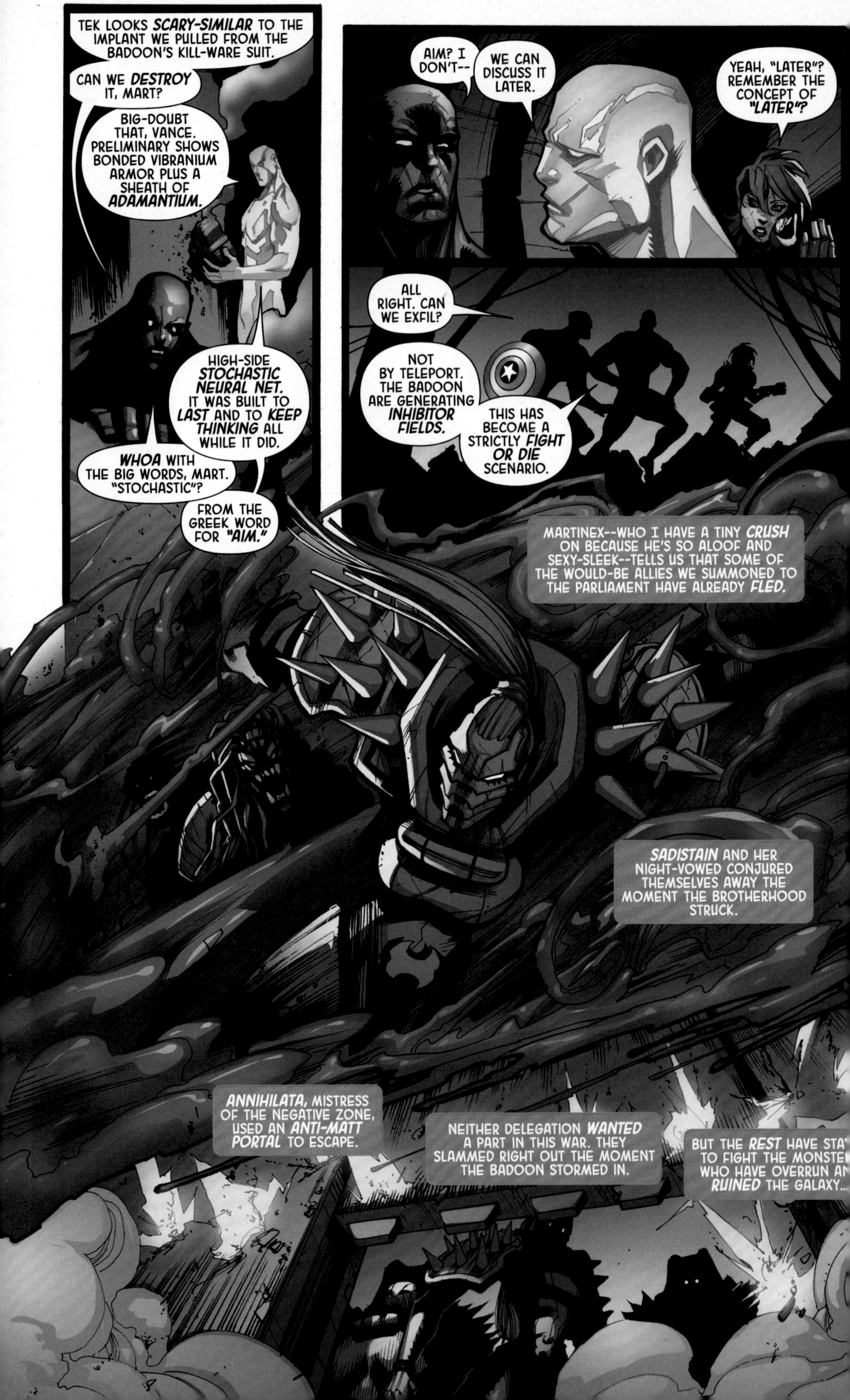
TEK LOOKS SCARY-SIMILAR TO THE IMPLANT WE PULLED FROM THE BADOON'S KILL-WARE SUIT.
CAN WE DESTROY IT, MART?
BIG-DOUBT THAT, VANCE. PRELIMINARY SHOWS BONDED VIBRANIUM ARMOR PLUS A SHEATH OF ADAMANTIUM.
HIGH-SIDE STOCHASTIC NEURAL NET. IT WAS BUILT TO LAST AND TO KEEP THINKING ALL WHILE IT DID.
WHOA WITH THE BIG WORDS, MART. "STOCHASTIC"?
FROM THE GREEK WORD FOR "AIM."
AIM? I DON'T--
WE CAN DISCUSS IT LATER.
YEAH, "LATER"? REMEMBER THE CONCEPT OF "LATER"?
ALL RIGHT. CAN WE EXFIL?
NOT BY TELEPORT. THE BADOON ARE GENERATING INHIBITOR FIELDS.
THIS HAS BECOME A STRICTLY FIGHT OR DIE SCENARIO.
MARTINEX--WHO I HAVE A TINY CRUSH ON BECAUSE HE'S SO ALOOF AND SEXY-SLEEK--TELLS US THAT SOME OF THE WOULD-BE ALLIES WE SUMMONED TO THE PARLIAMENT HAVE ALREADY FLED.
SADISTAIN AND HER NIGHT-VOWED CONJURED THEMSELVES AWAY THE MOMENT THE BROTHERHOOD STRUCK.
ANNIHILATA, MISTRESS OF THE NEGATIVE ZONE, USED AN ANTI-MATT PORTAL TO ESCAPE.
NEITHER DELEGATION WANTED A PART IN THIS WAR. THEY SLAMMED RIGHT OUT THE MOMENT THE BADOON STORMED IN.
BUT THE REST HAVE STA TO FIGHT THE MONSTE WHO HAVE OVERRUN AN RUINED THE GALAXY...

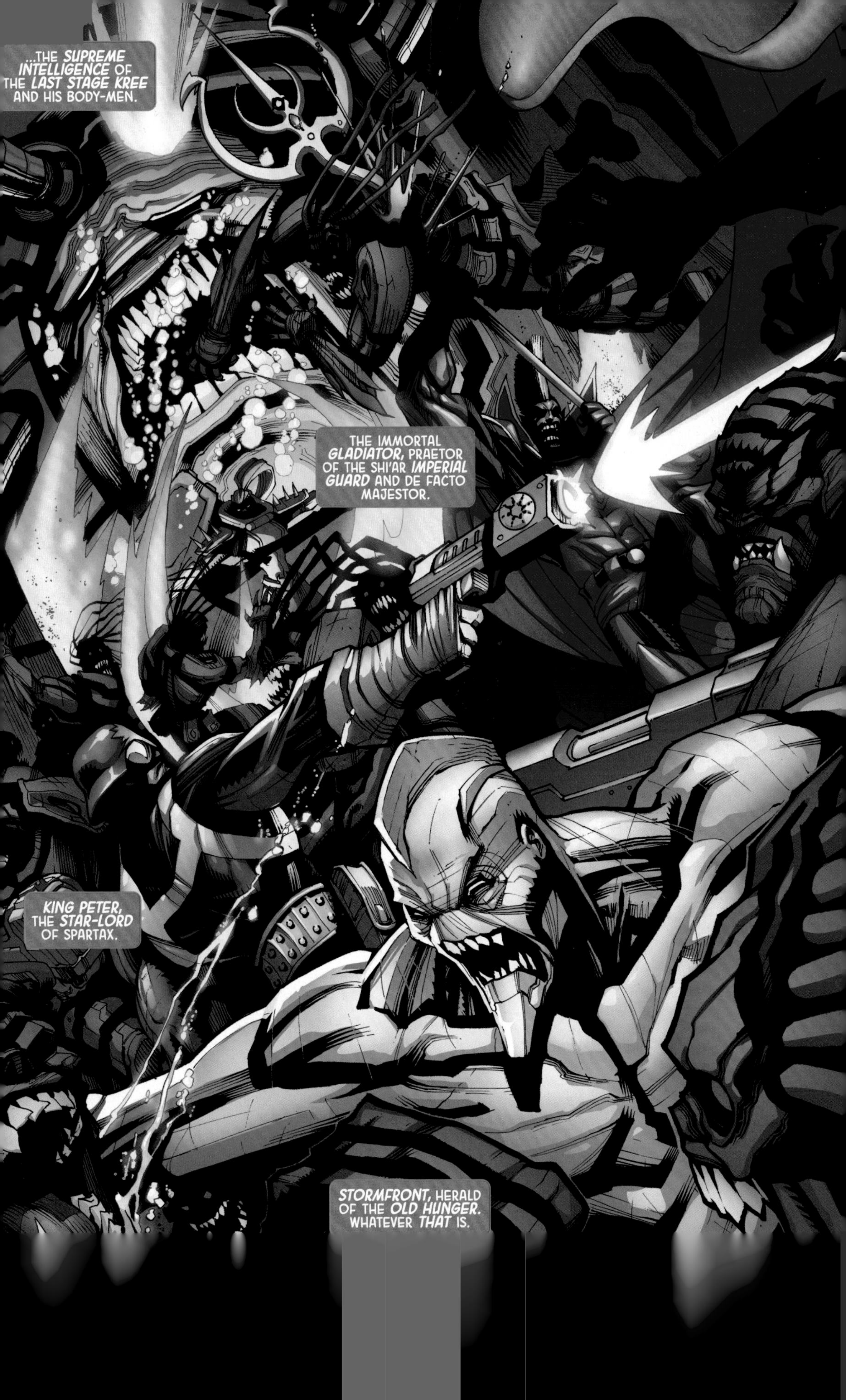
...THE SUPREME INTELLIGENCE OF THE LAST STAGE KREE AND HIS BODY-MEN.
THE IMMORTAL GLADIATOR, PRAETOR OF THE SHI'AR IMPERIAL GUARD AND DE FACTO MAJESTOR.
KING PETER, THE STAR-LORD OF SPARTAX.
STORMFRONT, HERALD OF THE OLD HUNGER. WHATEVER THAT IS.

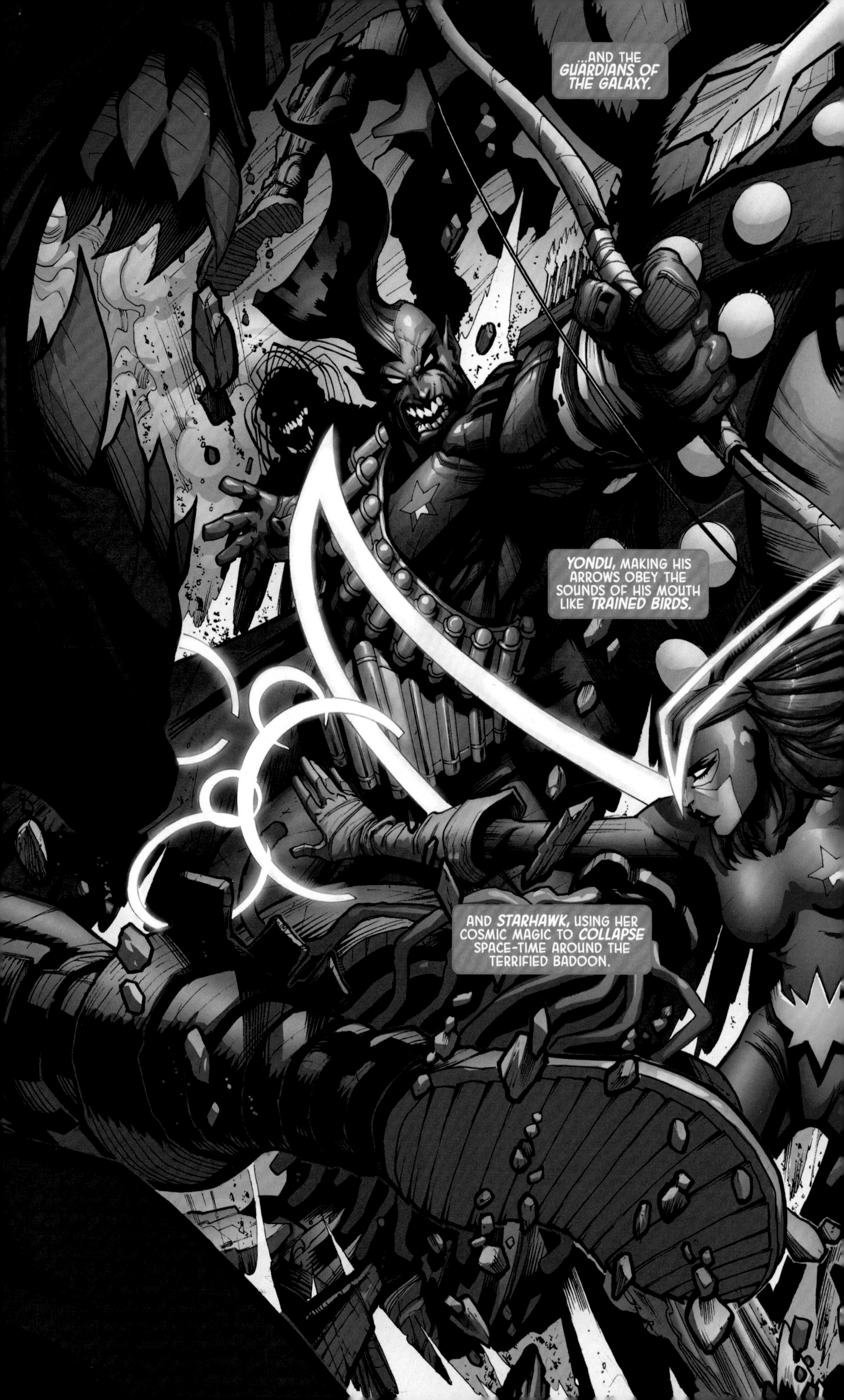
...AND THE GUARDIANS OF THE GALAXY.
YONDU, MAKING HIS ARROWS OBEY THE SOUNDS OF HIS MOUTH LIKE TRAINED BIRDS.
AND STARHAWK, USING HER COSMIC MAGIC TO COLLAPSE SPACE-TIME AROUND THE TERRIFIED BADOON.

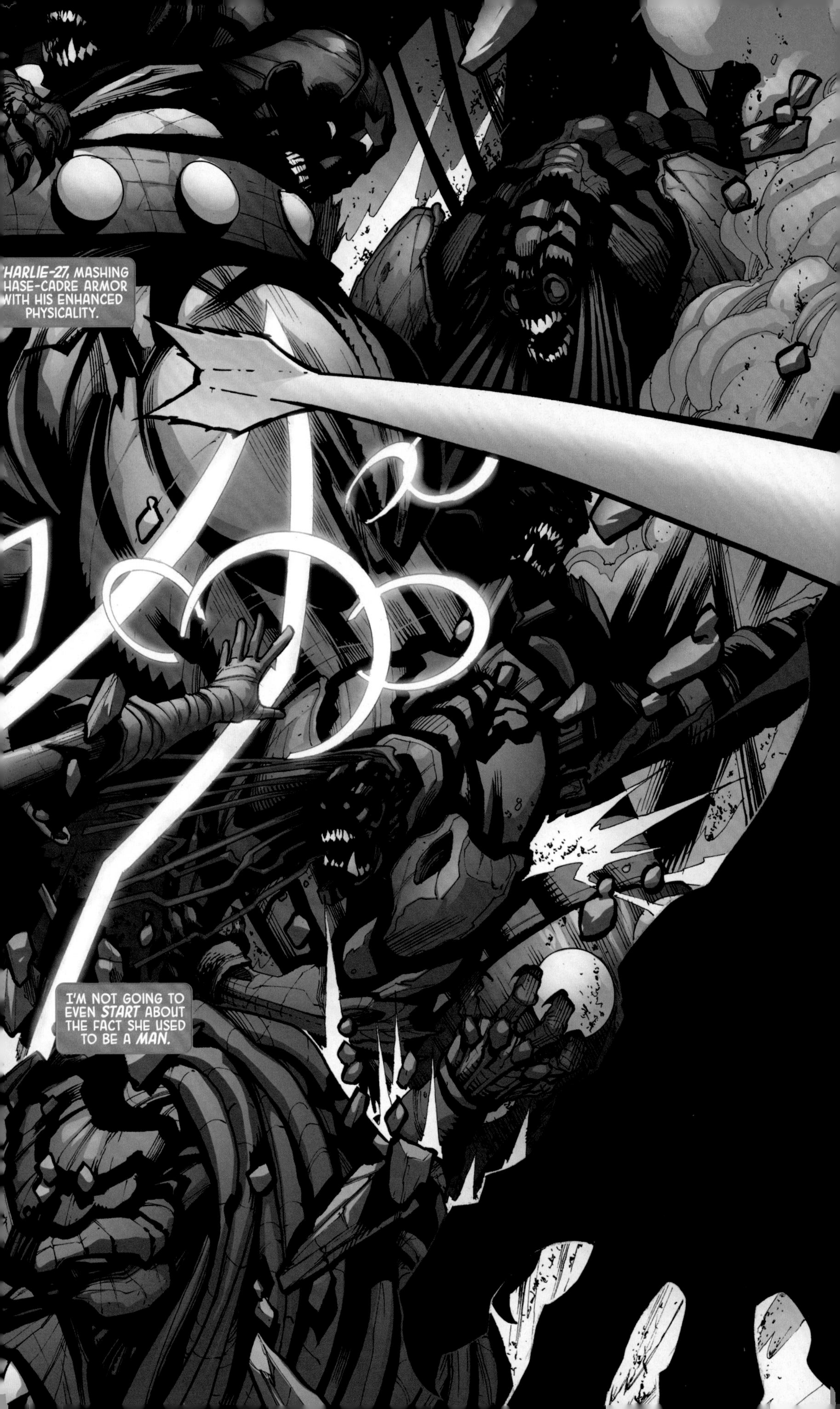
HARLIE-27, MASHING HASE-CADRE ARMOR WITH HIS ENHANCED PHYSICALITY.
I'M NOT GOING TO EVEN START ABOUT THE FACT SHE USED TO BE A MAN.

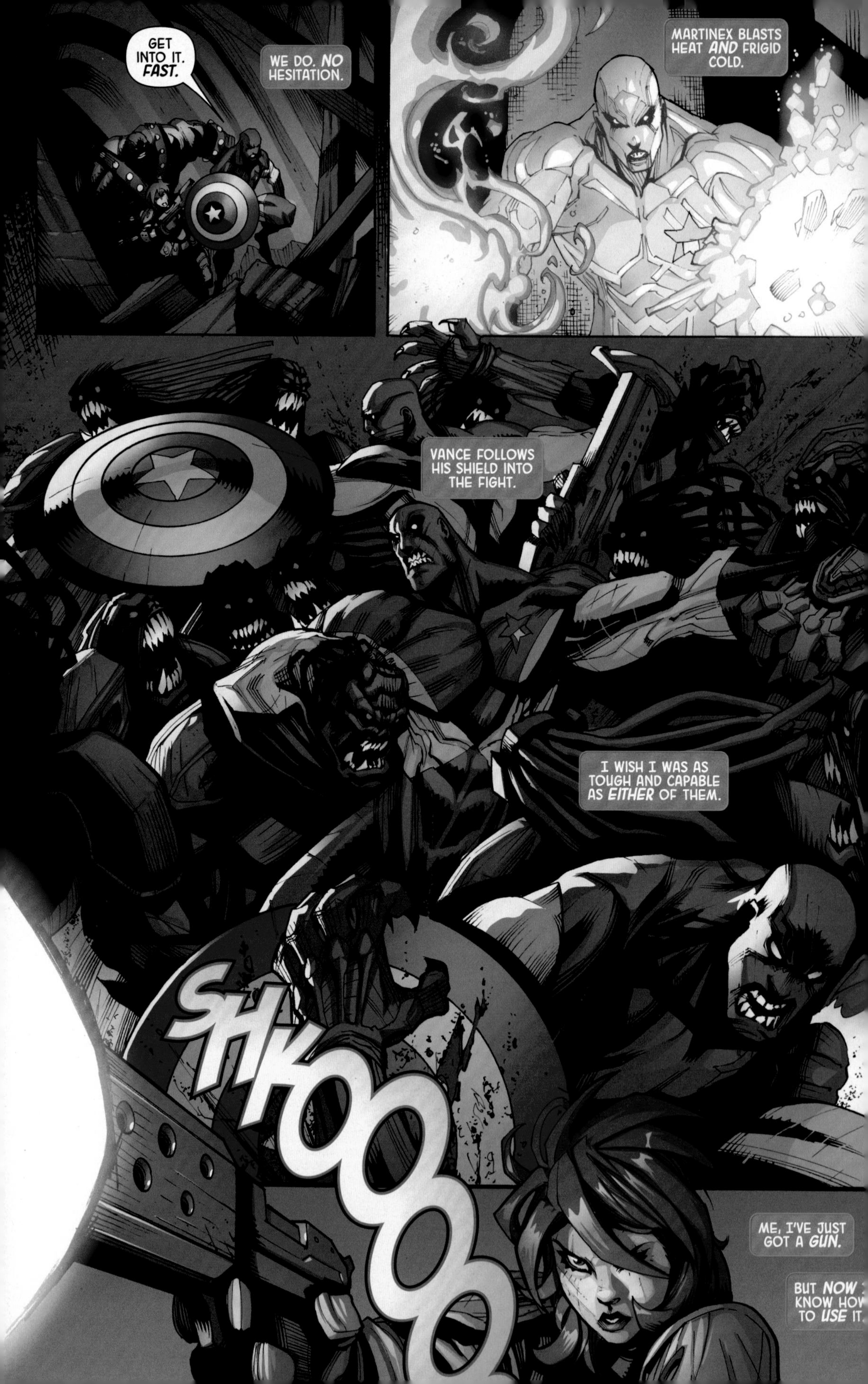
GET INTO IT. *FAST.*
WE DO. *NO* HESITATION.
MARTINEX BLASTS HEAT *AND* FRIGID COLD.
VANCE FOLLOWS HIS SHIELD INTO THE FIGHT.
I WISH I WAS AS TOUGH AND CAPABLE AS *EITHER* OF THEM.
SHKOOOO
ME, I'VE JUST GOT A *GUN.*
BUT *NOW* KNOW HOW TO *USE* IT.

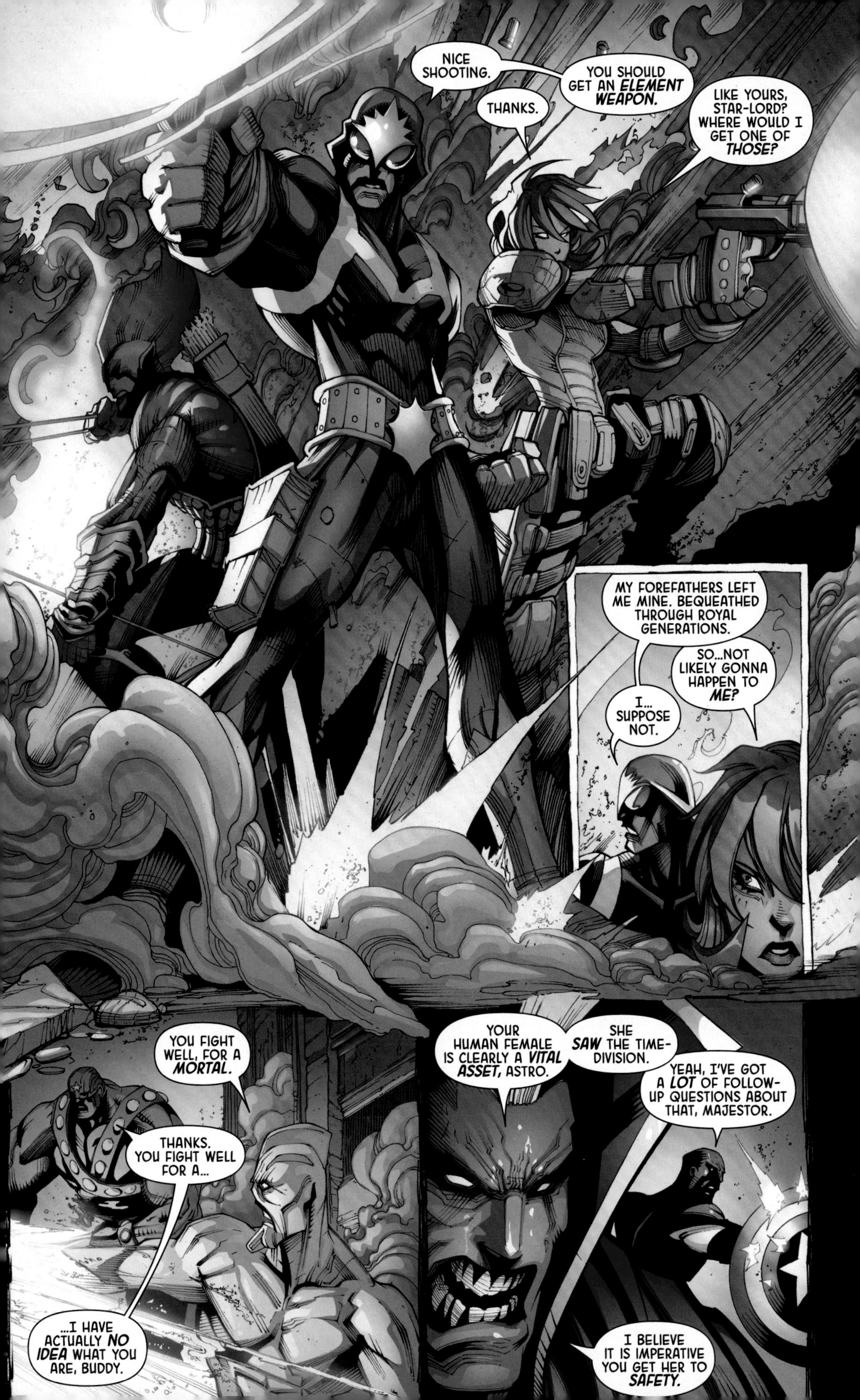

NICE SHOOTING.
THANKS.
YOU SHOULD GET AN *ELEMENT WEAPON.*
LIKE YOURS, STAR-LORD? WHERE WOULD I GET ONE OF *THOSE?*
MY FOREFATHERS LEFT ME MINE. BEQUEATHED THROUGH ROYAL GENERATIONS.
SO...NOT LIKELY GONNA HAPPEN TO *ME?*
I... SUPPOSE NOT.
YOU FIGHT WELL, FOR A *MORTAL.*
THANKS. YOU FIGHT WELL FOR A...
...I HAVE ACTUALLY *NO IDEA* WHAT YOU ARE, BUDDY.
YOUR HUMAN FEMALE IS CLEARLY A *VITAL ASSET,* ASTRO.
SHE *SAW* THE TIME-DIVISION.
YEAH, I'VE GOT A *LOT* OF FOLLOW-UP QUESTIONS ABOUT THAT, MAJESTOR.
I BELIEVE IT IS IMPERATIVE YOU GET HER TO *SAFETY.*

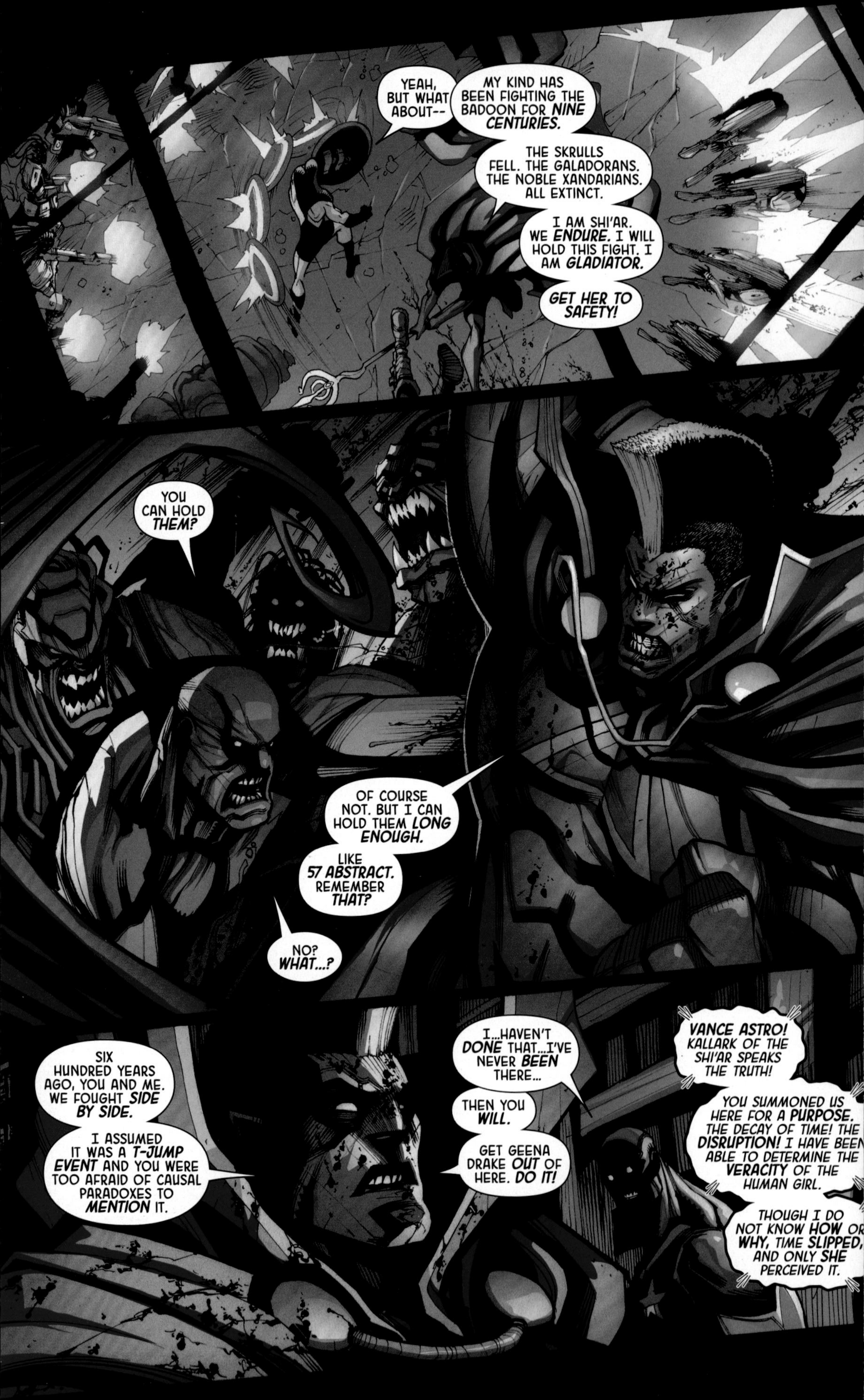
YEAH, BUT WHAT ABOUT--
MY KIND HAS BEEN FIGHTING THE BADOON FOR NINE CENTURIES.
THE SKRULLS FELL. THE GALADORANS. THE NOBLE XANDARIANS. ALL EXTINCT.
I AM SHI'AR. WE ENDURE. I WILL HOLD THIS FIGHT. I AM GLADIATOR.
GET HER TO SAFETY!
YOU CAN HOLD THEM?
OF COURSE NOT. BUT I CAN HOLD THEM LONG ENOUGH.
LIKE 57 ABSTRACT. REMEMBER THAT?
NO? WHAT...?
SIX HUNDRED YEARS AGO, YOU AND ME. WE FOUGHT SIDE BY SIDE.
I ASSUMED IT WAS A T-JUMP EVENT AND YOU WERE TOO AFRAID OF CAUSAL PARADOXES TO MENTION IT.
I...HAVEN'T DONE THAT...I'VE NEVER BEEN THERE...
THEN YOU WILL.
GET GEENA DRAKE OUT OF HERE. DO IT!
VANCE ASTRO! KALLARK OF THE SHI'AR SPEAKS THE TRUTH!
YOU SUMMONED US HERE FOR A PURPOSE. THE DECAY OF TIME! THE DISRUPTION! I HAVE BEEN ABLE TO DETERMINE THE VERACITY OF THE HUMAN GIRL.
THOUGH I DO NOT KNOW HOW OR WHY, TIME SLIPPED, AND ONLY SHE PERCEIVED IT.

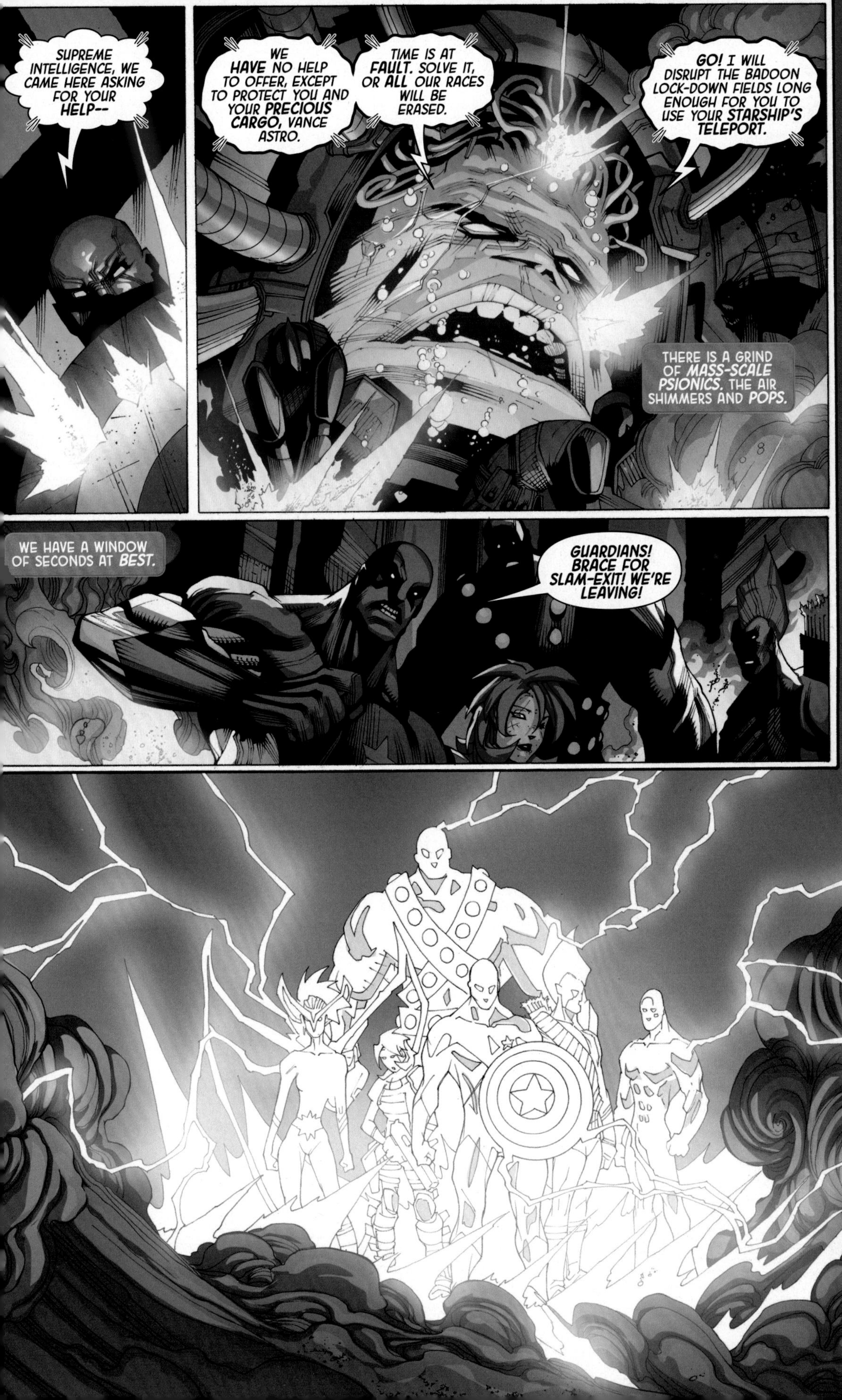
SUPREME INTELLIGENCE, WE CAME HERE ASKING FOR YOUR HELP--
WE HAVE NO HELP TO OFFER, EXCEPT TO PROTECT YOU AND YOUR PRECIOUS CARGO, VANCE ASTRO.
TIME IS AT FAULT. SOLVE IT, OR ALL OUR RACES WILL BE ERASED.
GO! I WILL DISRUPT THE BADOON LOCK-DOWN FIELDS LONG ENOUGH FOR YOU TO USE YOUR STARSHIP'S TELEPORT.
THERE IS A GRIND OF MASS-SCALE PSIONICS. THE AIR SHIMMERS AND POPS.
WE HAVE A WINDOW OF SECONDS AT BEST.
GUARDIANS! BRACE FOR SLAM-EXIT! WE'RE LEAVING!

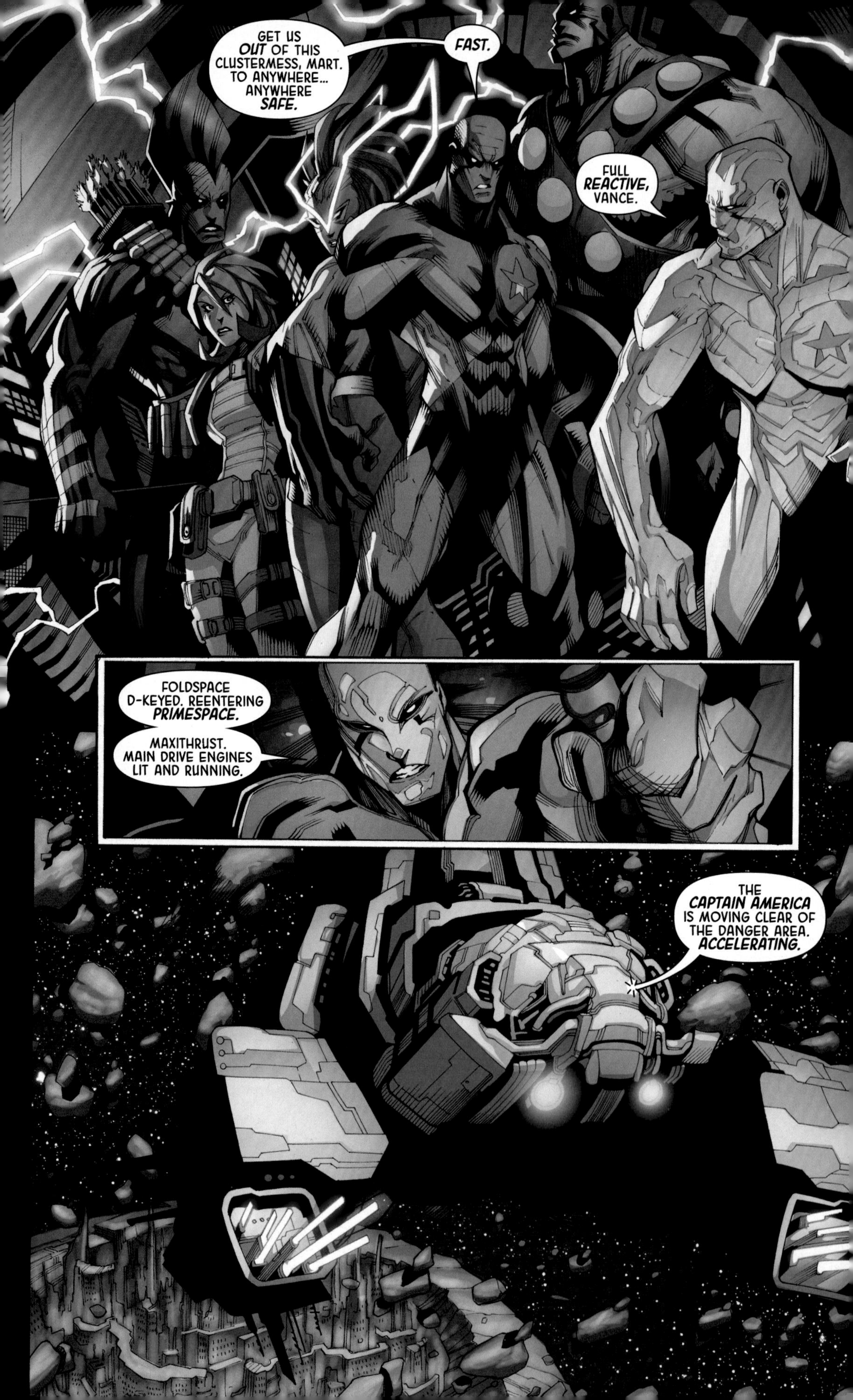
GET US OUT OF THIS CLUSTERMESS, MART. TO ANYWHERE... ANYWHERE SAFE.
FAST.
FULL REACTIVE, VANCE.
FOLDSPACE D-KEYED. REENTERING PRIMESPACE.
MAXITHRUST. MAIN DRIVE ENGINES LIT AND RUNNING.
THE CAPTAIN AMERICA IS MOVING CLEAR OF THE DANGER AREA. ACCELERATING.

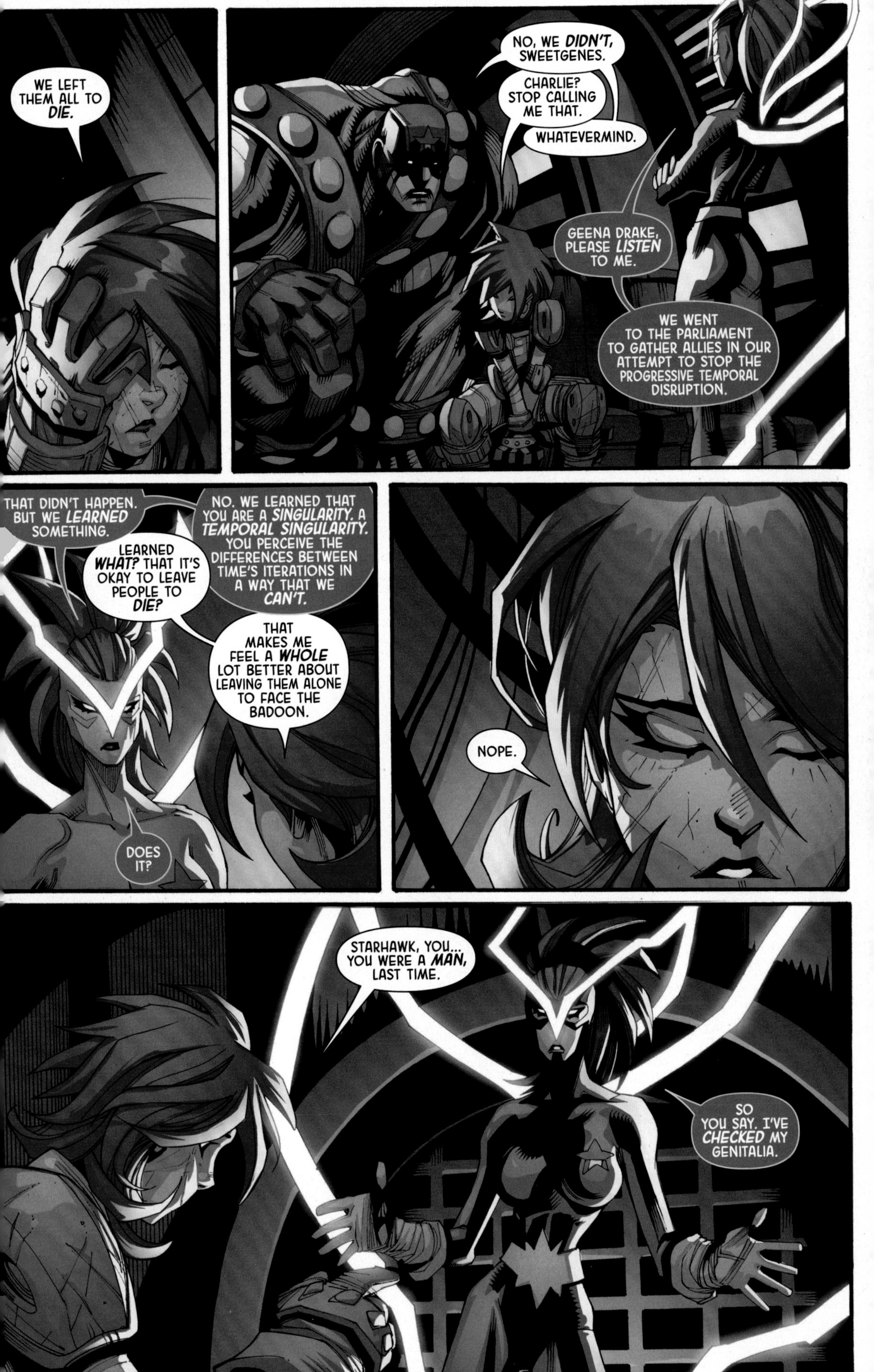

WE LEFT THEM ALL TO DIE.
NO, WE DIDN'T, SWEETGENES.
CHARLIE? STOP CALLING ME THAT.
WHATEVERMIND.
GEENA DRAKE, PLEASE LISTEN TO ME.
WE WENT TO THE PARLIAMENT TO GATHER ALLIES IN OUR ATTEMPT TO STOP THE PROGRESSIVE TEMPORAL DISRUPTION.
THAT DIDN'T HAPPEN. BUT WE LEARNED SOMETHING.
LEARNED WHAT? THAT IT'S OKAY TO LEAVE PEOPLE TO DIE?
NO. WE LEARNED THAT YOU ARE A SINGULARITY. A TEMPORAL SINGULARITY. YOU PERCEIVE THE DIFFERENCES BETWEEN TIME'S ITERATIONS IN A WAY THAT WE CAN'T.
THAT MAKES ME FEEL A WHOLE LOT BETTER ABOUT LEAVING THEM ALONE TO FACE THE BADOON.
DOES IT?
NOPE.
STARHAWK, YOU... YOU WERE A MAN, LAST TIME.
SO YOU SAY. I'VE CHECKED MY GENITALIA.

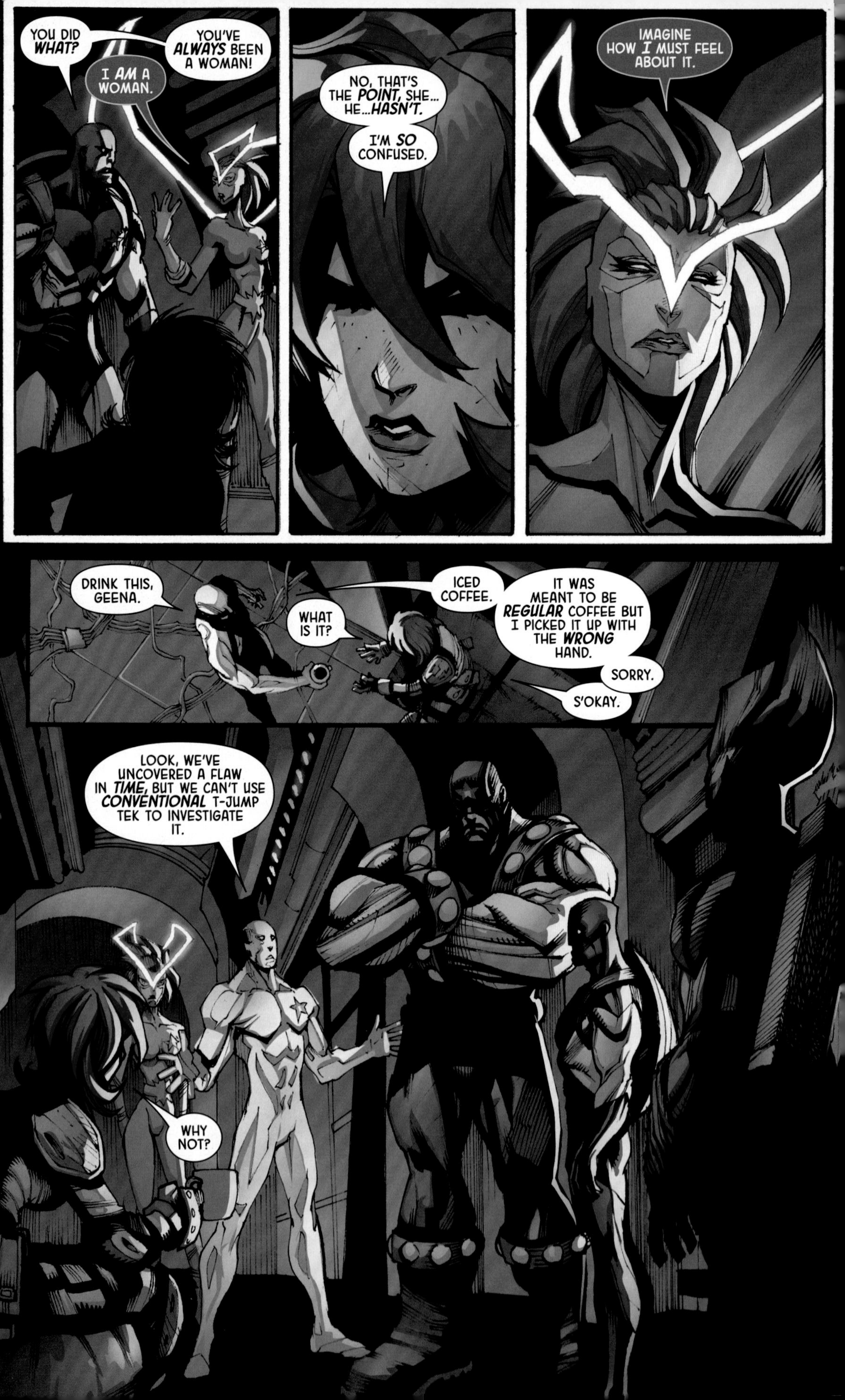
YOU DID WHAT?
YOU'VE ALWAYS BEEN A WOMAN!
I AM A WOMAN.
NO, THAT'S THE POINT, SHE... HE...HASN'T.
I'M SO CONFUSED.
IMAGINE HOW I MUST FEEL ABOUT IT.
DRINK THIS, GEENA.
WHAT IS IT?
ICED COFFEE.
IT WAS MEANT TO BE REGULAR COFFEE BUT I PICKED IT UP WITH THE WRONG HAND.
SORRY.
S'OKAY.
LOOK, WE'VE UNCOVERED A FLAW IN TIME, BUT WE CAN'T USE CONVENTIONAL T-JUMP TEK TO INVESTIGATE IT.
WHY NOT?

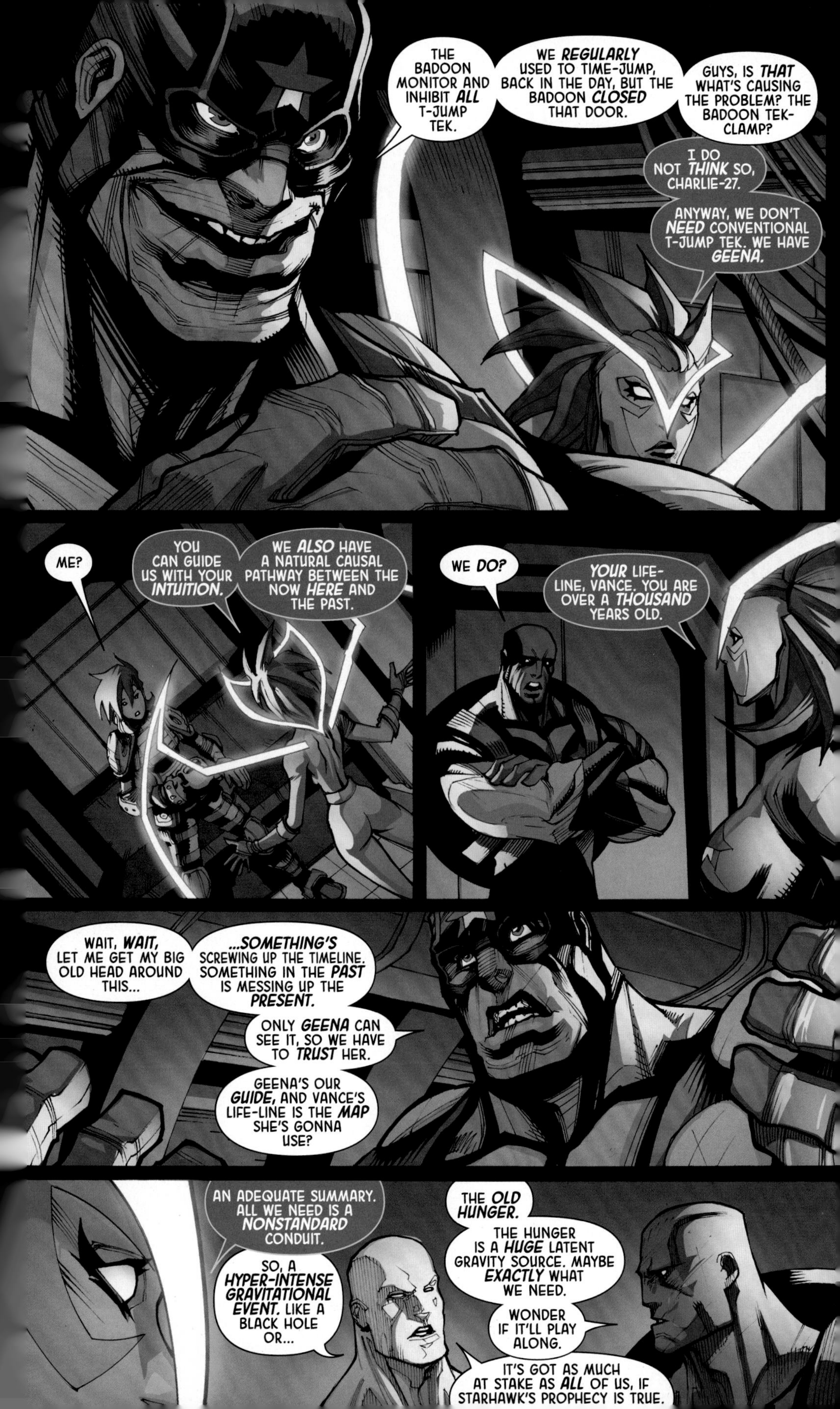

THE BADOON MONITOR AND INHIBIT ALL T-JUMP TEK.
WE REGULARLY USED TO TIME-JUMP, BACK IN THE DAY, BUT THE BADOON CLOSED THAT DOOR.
GUYS, IS THAT WHAT'S CAUSING THE PROBLEM? THE BADOON TEK-CLAMP?
I DO NOT THINK SO, CHARLIE-27.
ANYWAY, WE DON'T NEED CONVENTIONAL T-JUMP TEK. WE HAVE GEENA.
ME?
YOU CAN GUIDE US WITH YOUR INTUITION.
WE ALSO HAVE A NATURAL CAUSAL PATHWAY BETWEEN THE NOW HERE AND THE PAST.
WE DO?
YOUR LIFE-LINE, VANCE. YOU ARE OVER A THOUSAND YEARS OLD.
WAIT, WAIT, LET ME GET MY BIG OLD HEAD AROUND THIS...
...SOMETHING'S SCREWING UP THE TIMELINE. SOMETHING IN THE PAST IS MESSING UP THE PRESENT.
ONLY GEENA CAN SEE IT, SO WE HAVE TO TRUST HER.
GEENA'S OUR GUIDE, AND VANCE'S LIFE-LINE IS THE MAP SHE'S GONNA USE?
AN ADEQUATE SUMMARY. ALL WE NEED IS A NONSTANDARD CONDUIT.
SO, A HYPER-INTENSE GRAVITATIONAL EVENT. LIKE A BLACK HOLE OR...
THE OLD HUNGER.
THE HUNGER IS A HUGE LATENT GRAVITY SOURCE. MAYBE EXACTLY WHAT WE NEED.
WONDER IF IT'LL PLAY ALONG.
IT'S GOT AS MUCH AT STAKE AS ALL OF US, IF STARHAWK'S PROPHECY IS TRUE.

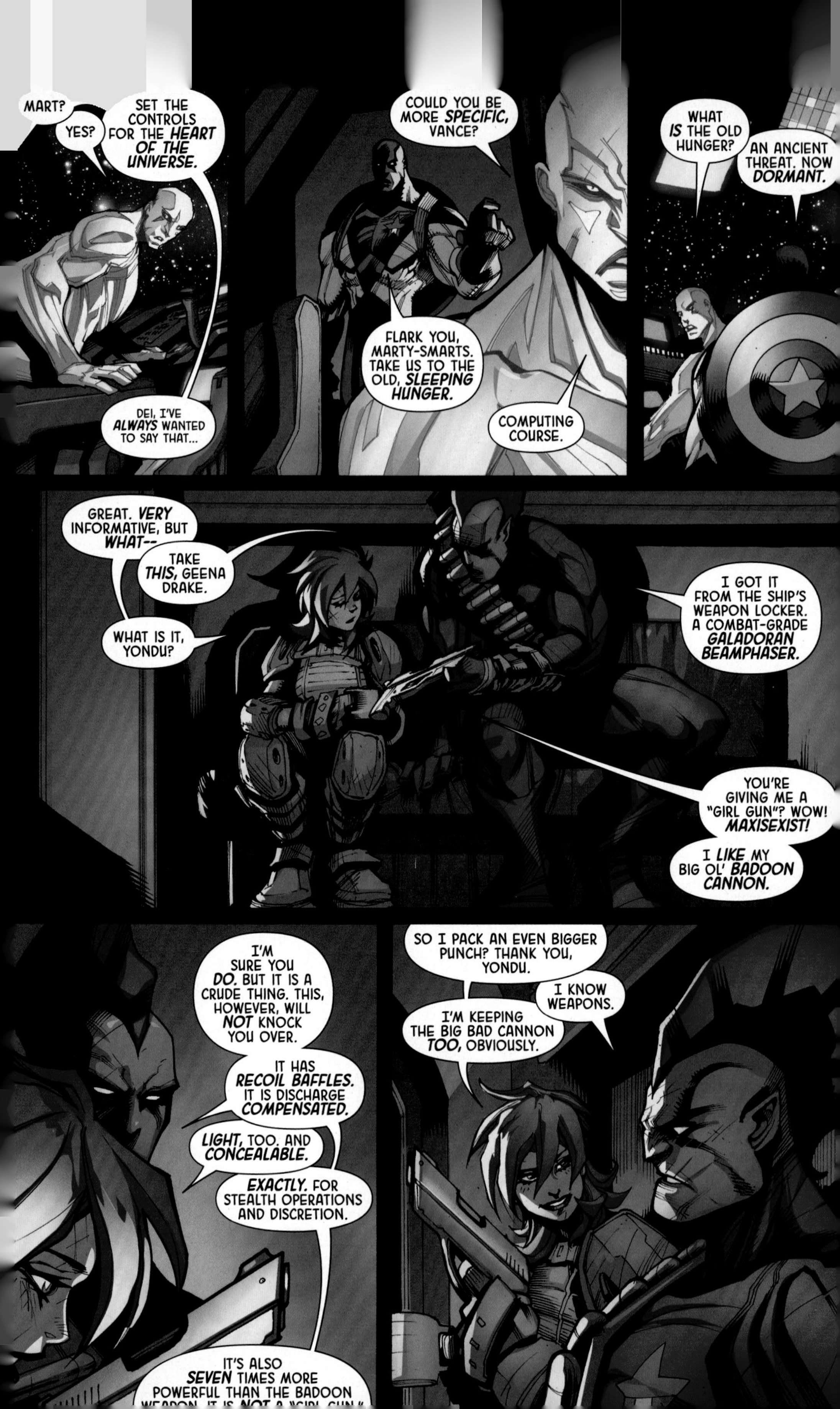
MART?
YES?
SET THE CONTROLS FOR THE HEART OF THE UNIVERSE.
DEI, I'VE ALWAYS WANTED TO SAY THAT...
COULD YOU BE MORE SPECIFIC, VANCE?
FLARK YOU, MARTY-SMARTS. TAKE US TO THE OLD, SLEEPING HUNGER.
COMPUTING COURSE.
WHAT IS THE OLD HUNGER?
AN ANCIENT THREAT. NOW DORMANT.
GREAT. VERY INFORMATIVE, BUT WHAT--
TAKE THIS, GEENA DRAKE.
WHAT IS IT, YONDU?
I GOT IT FROM THE SHIP'S WEAPON LOCKER. A COMBAT-GRADE GALADORAN BEAMPHASER.
YOU'RE GIVING ME A "GIRL GUN"? WOW! MAXISEXIST!
I LIKE MY BIG OL' BADOON CANNON.
I'M SURE YOU DO. BUT IT IS A CRUDE THING. THIS, HOWEVER, WILL NOT KNOCK YOU OVER.
IT HAS RECOIL BAFFLES. IT IS DISCHARGE COMPENSATED.
LIGHT, TOO. AND CONCEALABLE.
EXACTLY. FOR STEALTH OPERATIONS AND DISCRETION.
IT'S ALSO SEVEN TIMES MORE POWERFUL THAN THE BADOON
SO I PACK AN EVEN BIGGER PUNCH? THANK YOU, YONDU.
I KNOW WEAPONS.
I'M KEEPING THE BIG BAD CANNON TOO, OBVIOUSLY.

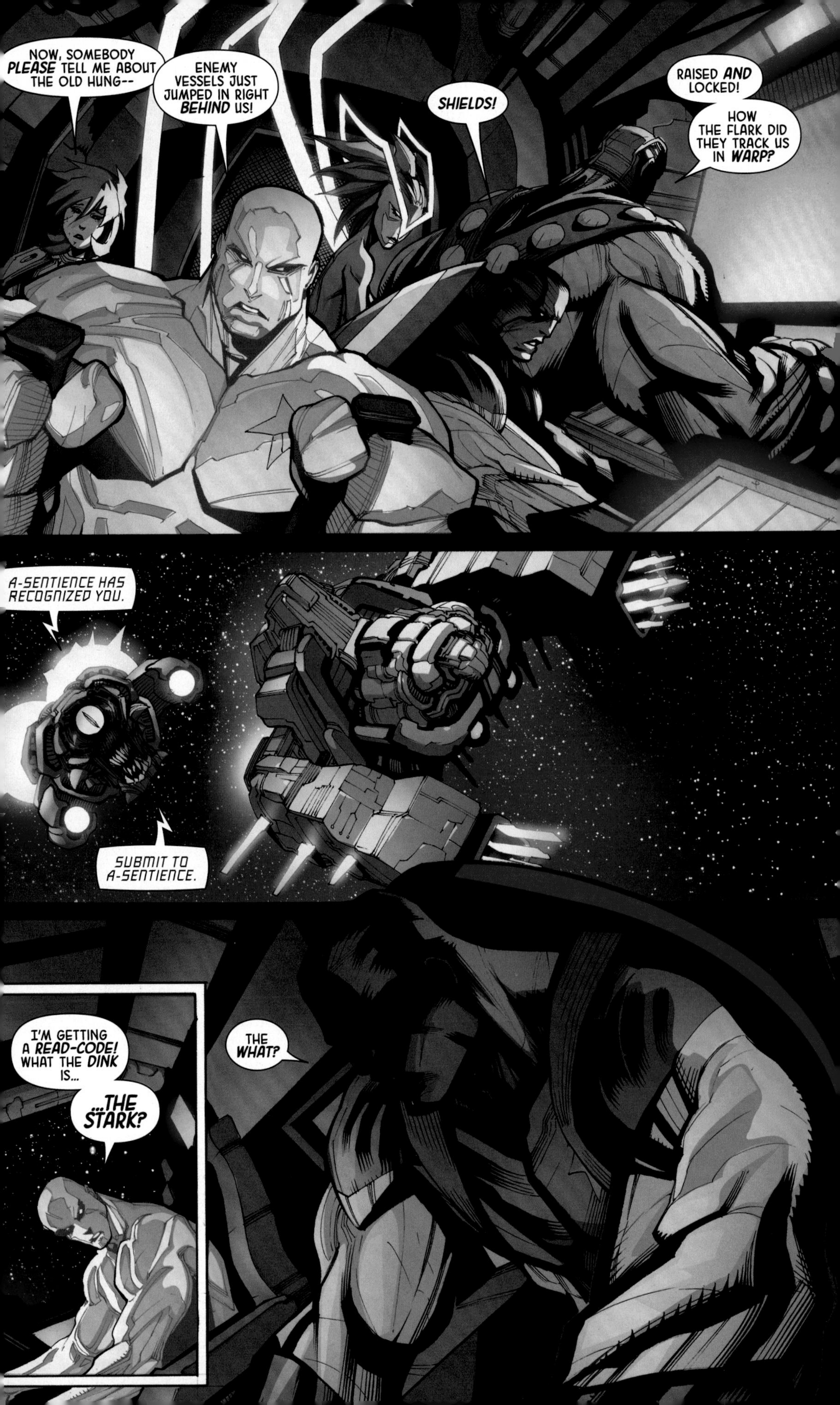
NOW, SOMEBODY PLEASE TELL ME ABOUT THE OLD HUNG--
ENEMY VESSELS JUST JUMPED IN RIGHT BEHIND US!
SHIELDS!
RAISED AND LOCKED!
HOW THE FLARK DID THEY TRACK US IN WARP?
A-SENTIENCE HAS RECOGNIZED YOU.
SUBMIT TO A-SENTIENCE.
I'M GETTING A READ-CODE! WHAT THE DINK IS...
...THE STARK?
THE WHAT?

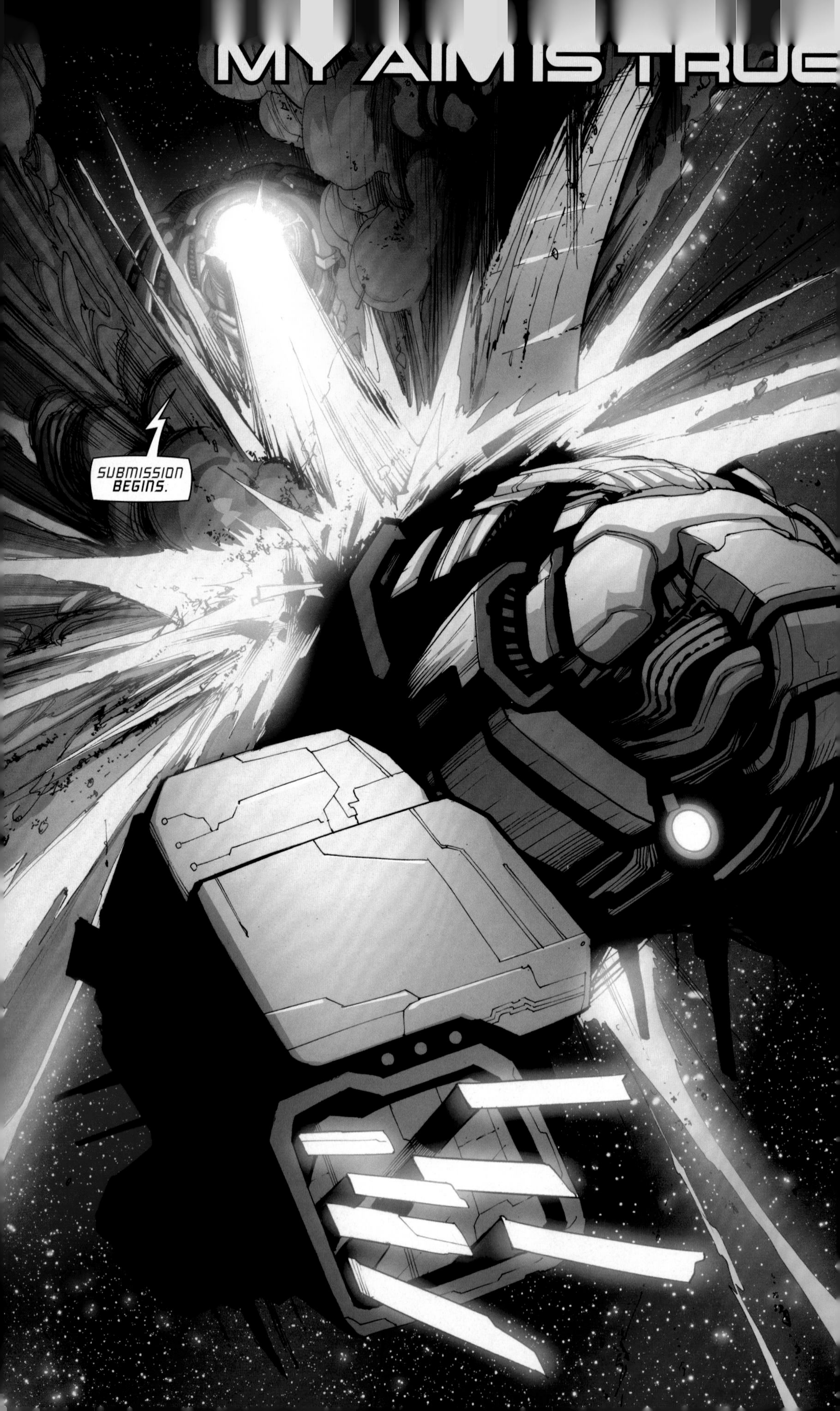
MY AIM IS TRUE
SUBMISSION BEGINS.

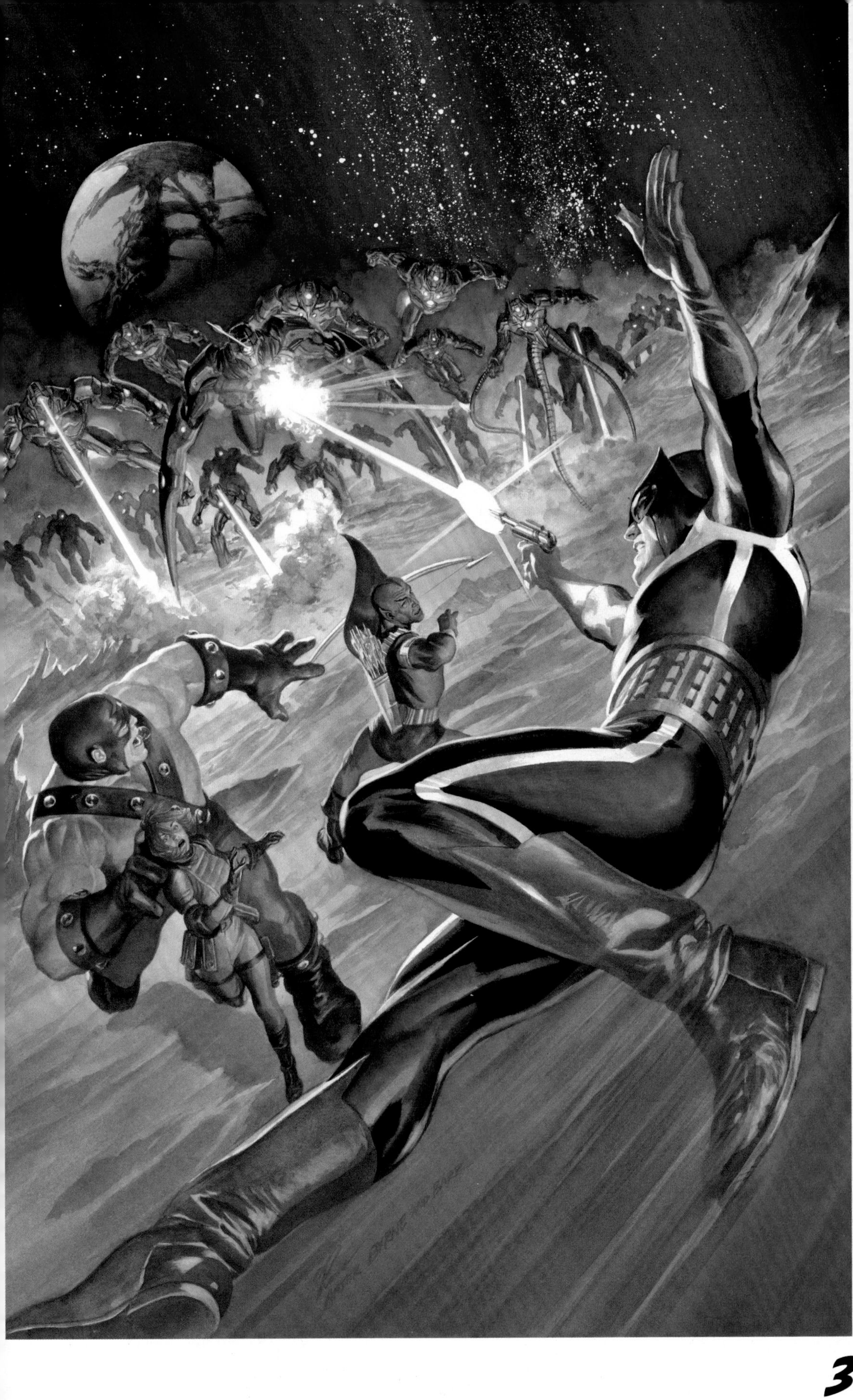

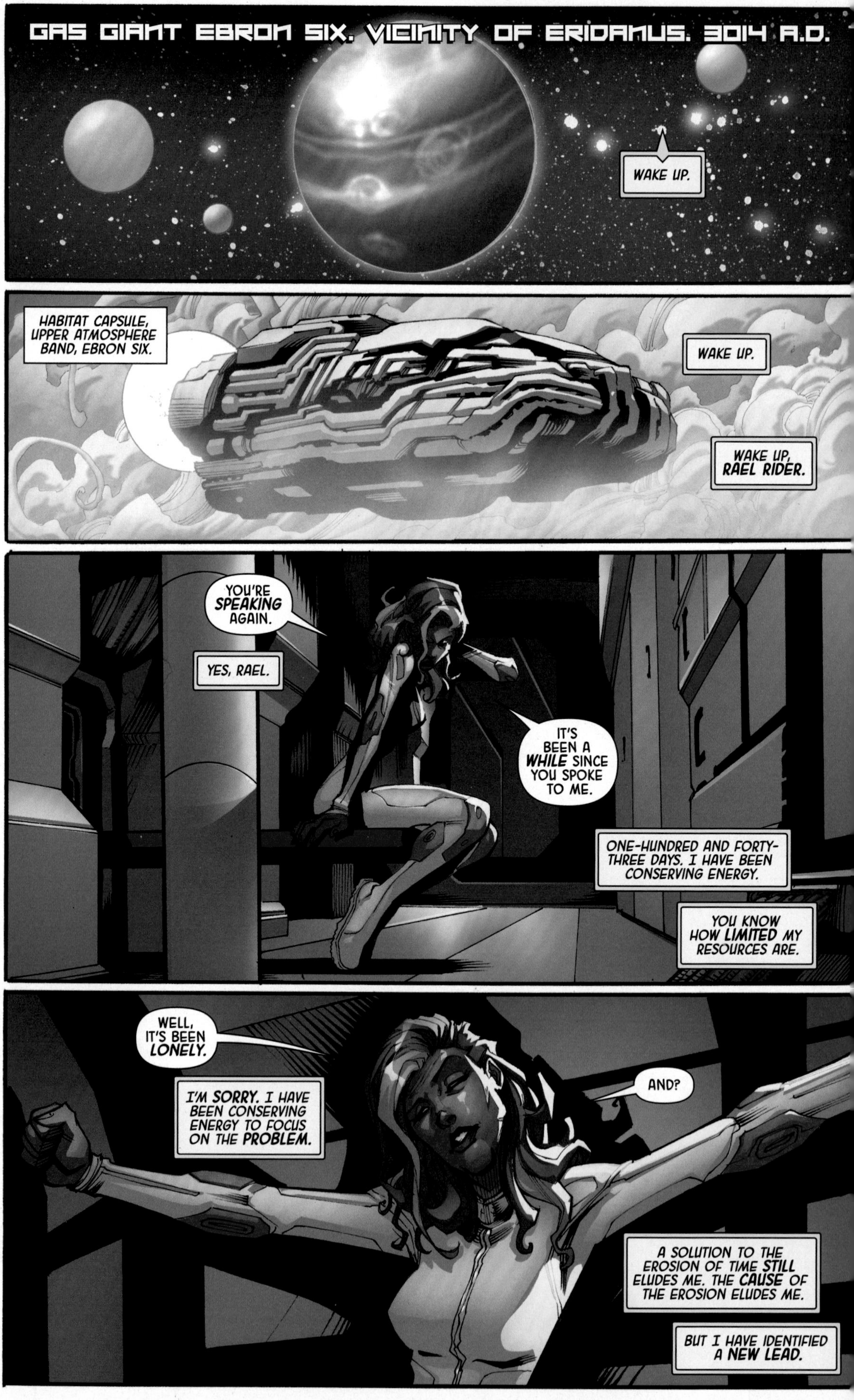
GAS GIANT EBRON SIX. VICINITY OF ERIDANUS. 3014 A.D.
WAKE UP.
HABITAT CAPSULE, UPPER ATMOSPHERE BAND, EBRON SIX.
WAKE UP.
WAKE UP, RAEL RIDER.
YOU'RE SPEAKING AGAIN.
YES, RAEL.
IT'S BEEN A WHILE SINCE YOU SPOKE TO ME.
ONE-HUNDRED AND FORTY-THREE DAYS. I HAVE BEEN CONSERVING ENERGY.
YOU KNOW HOW LIMITED MY RESOURCES ARE.
WELL, IT'S BEEN LONELY.
I'M SORRY. I HAVE BEEN CONSERVING ENERGY TO FOCUS ON THE PROBLEM.
AND?
A SOLUTION TO THE EROSION OF TIME STILL ELUDES ME. THE CAUSE OF THE EROSION ELUDES ME.
BUT I HAVE IDENTIFIED A NEW LEAD.

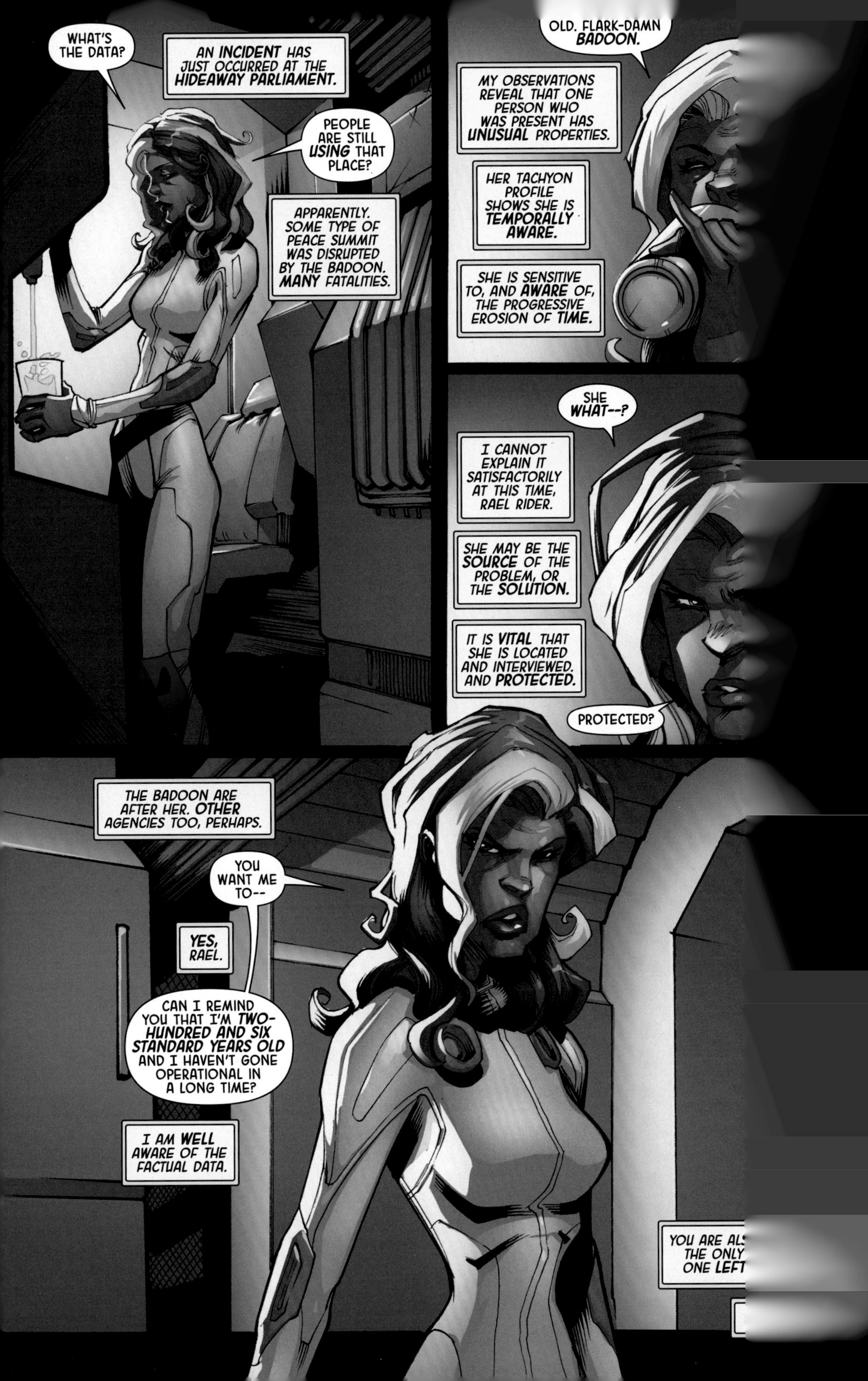

WHAT'S THE DATA?
AN INCIDENT HAS JUST OCCURRED AT THE HIDEAWAY PARLIAMENT.
PEOPLE ARE STILL USING THAT PLACE?
APPARENTLY. SOME TYPE OF PEACE SUMMIT WAS DISRUPTED BY THE BADOON. MANY FATALITIES.
OLD. FLARK-DAMN BADOON.
MY OBSERVATIONS REVEAL THAT ONE PERSON WHO WAS PRESENT HAS UNUSUAL PROPERTIES.
HER TACHYON PROFILE SHOWS SHE IS TEMPORALLY AWARE.
SHE IS SENSITIVE TO, AND AWARE OF, THE PROGRESSIVE EROSION OF TIME.
SHE WHAT--?
I CANNOT EXPLAIN IT SATISFACTORILY AT THIS TIME, RAEL RIDER.
SHE MAY BE THE SOURCE OF THE PROBLEM, OR THE SOLUTION.
IT IS VITAL THAT SHE IS LOCATED AND INTERVIEWED. AND PROTECTED.
PROTECTED?
THE BADOON ARE AFTER HER. OTHER AGENCIES TOO, PERHAPS.
YOU WANT ME TO--
YES, RAEL.
CAN I REMIND YOU THAT I'M TWO-HUNDRED AND SIX STANDARD YEARS OLD AND I HAVEN'T GONE OPERATIONAL IN A LONG TIME?
I AM WELL AWARE OF THE FACTUAL DATA.

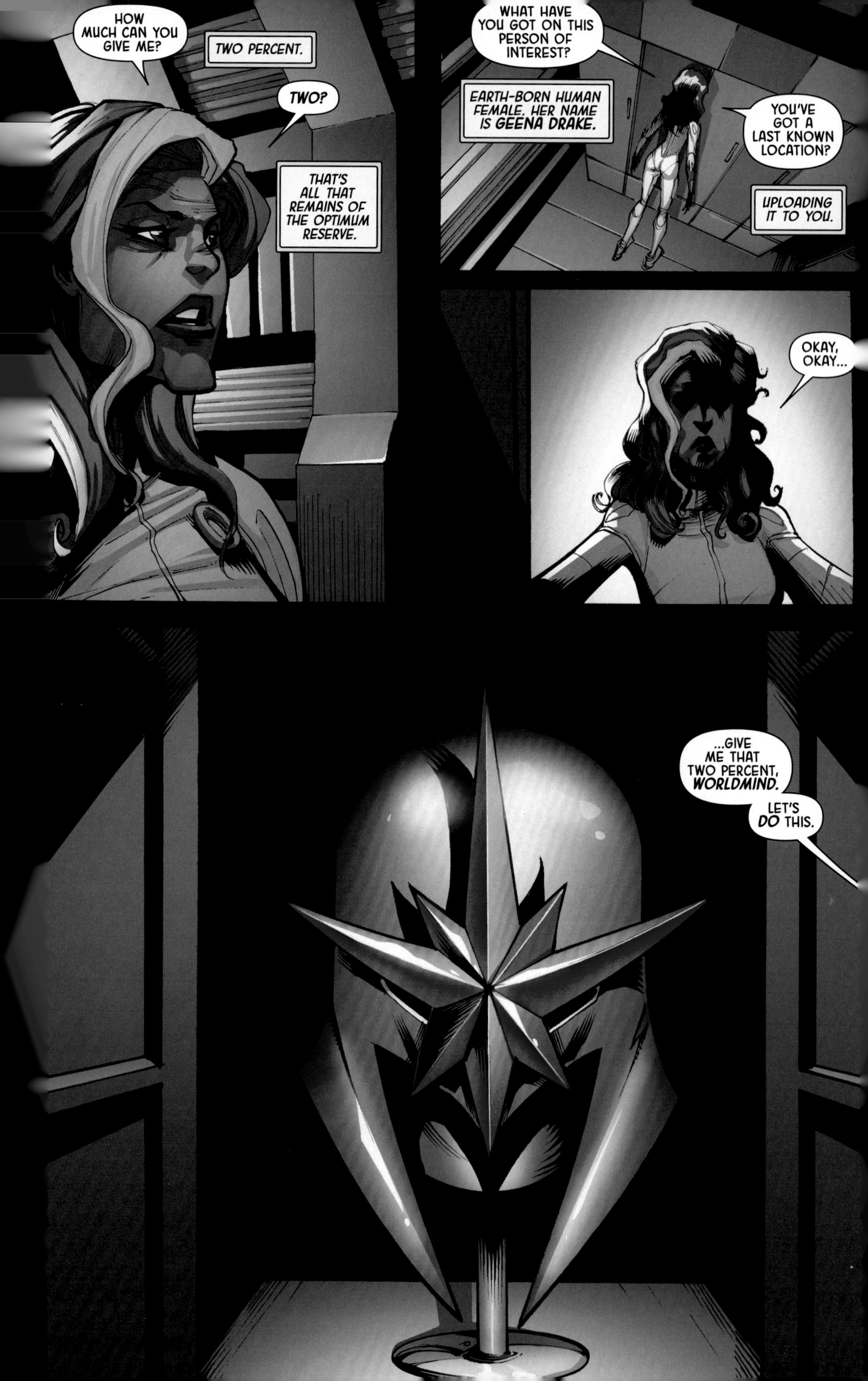

HOW MUCH CAN YOU GIVE ME?
TWO PERCENT.
TWO?
THAT'S ALL THAT REMAINS OF THE OPTIMUM RESERVE.
WHAT HAVE YOU GOT ON THIS PERSON OF INTEREST?
EARTH-BORN HUMAN FEMALE. HER NAME IS GEENA DRAKE.
YOU'VE GOT A LAST KNOWN LOCATION?
UPLOADING IT TO YOU.
OKAY, OKAY...
...GIVE ME THAT TWO PERCENT, WORLDMIND.
LET'S DO THIS.

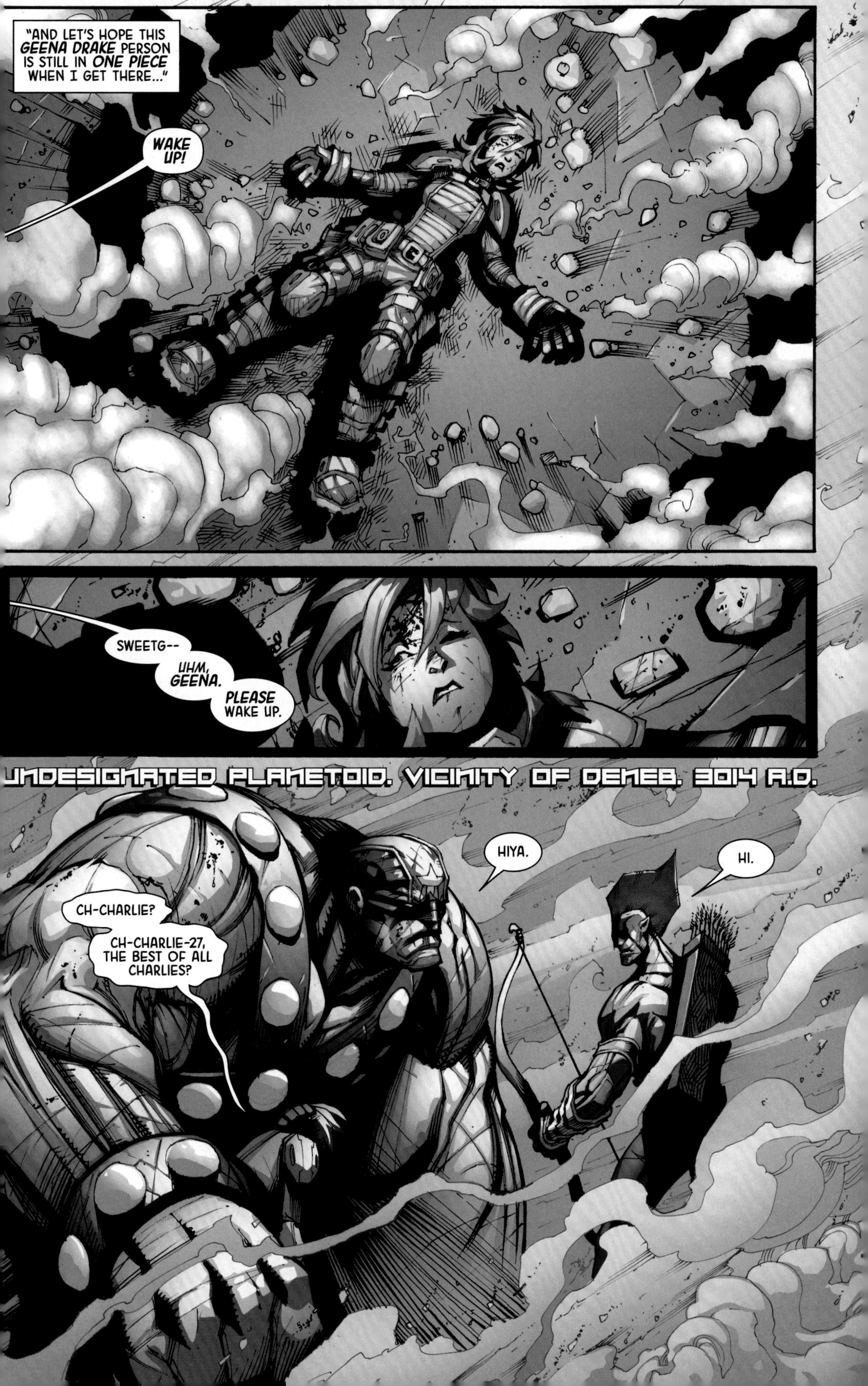

"AND LET'S HOPE THIS GEENA DRAKE PERSON IS STILL IN ONE PIECE WHEN I GET THERE..."
WAKE UP!
SWEETG--
UHM, GEENA.
PLEASE WAKE UP.
UNDESIGNATED PLANETOID. VICINITY OF DENEB. 3014 A.D.
CH-CHARLIE?
CH-CHARLIE-27, THE BEST OF ALL CHARLIES?
HIYA.
HI.

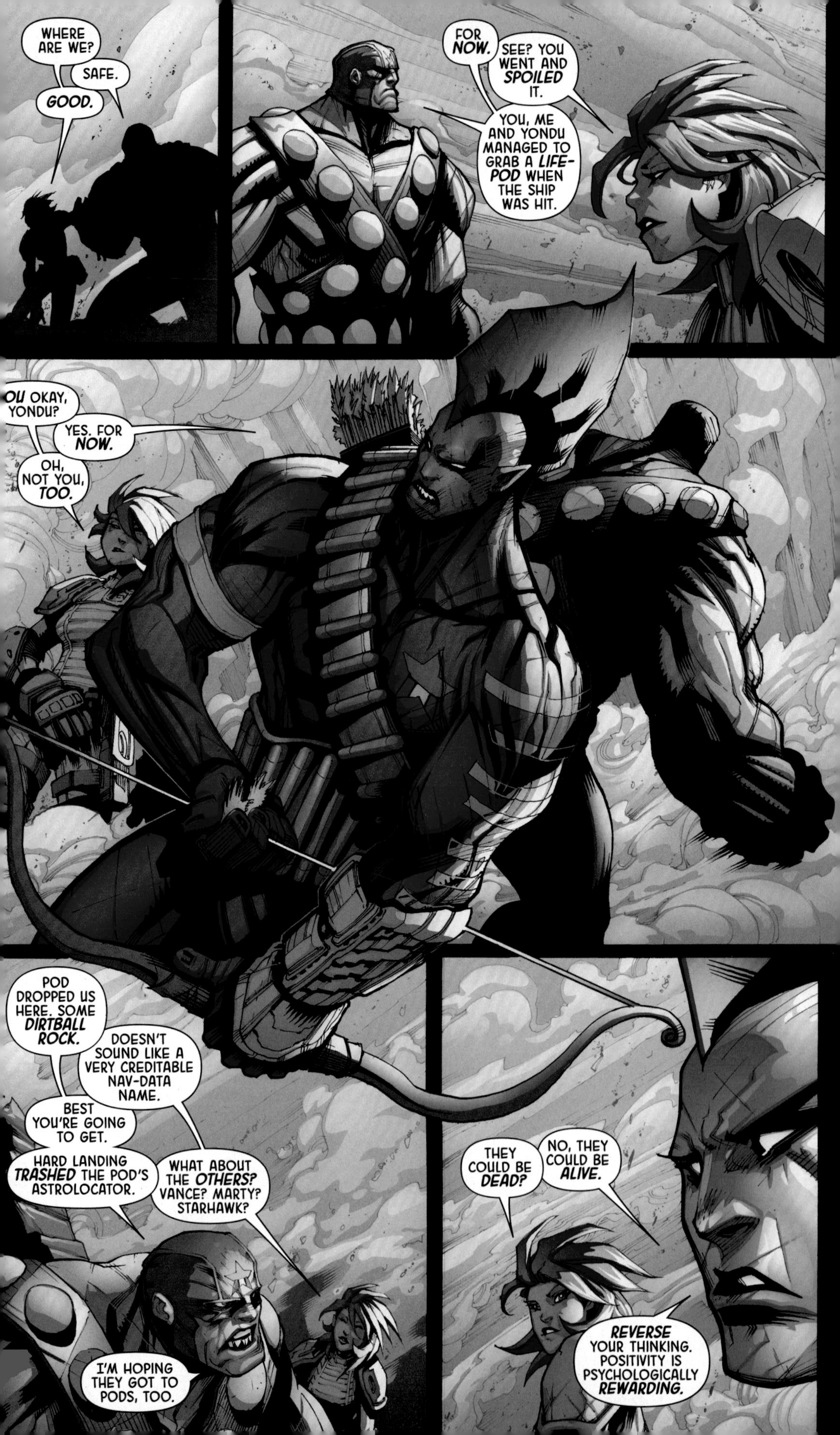
WHERE ARE WE?
SAFE.
GOOD.
FOR NOW.
SEE? YOU WENT AND SPOILED IT.
YOU, ME AND YONDU MANAGED TO GRAB A LIFE-POD WHEN THE SHIP WAS HIT.
OU OKAY, YONDU?
YES. FOR NOW.
OH, NOT YOU, TOO.
POD DROPPED US HERE. SOME DIRTBALL ROCK.
DOESN'T SOUND LIKE A VERY CREDITABLE NAV-DATA NAME.
BEST YOU'RE GOING TO GET.
HARD LANDING TRASHED THE POD'S ASTROLOCATOR.
WHAT ABOUT THE OTHERS? VANCE? MARTY? STARHAWK?
I'M HOPING THEY GOT TO PODS, TOO.
THEY COULD BE DEAD?
NO, THEY COULD BE ALIVE.
REVERSE YOUR THINKING. POSITIVITY IS PSYCHOLOGICALLY REWARDING.

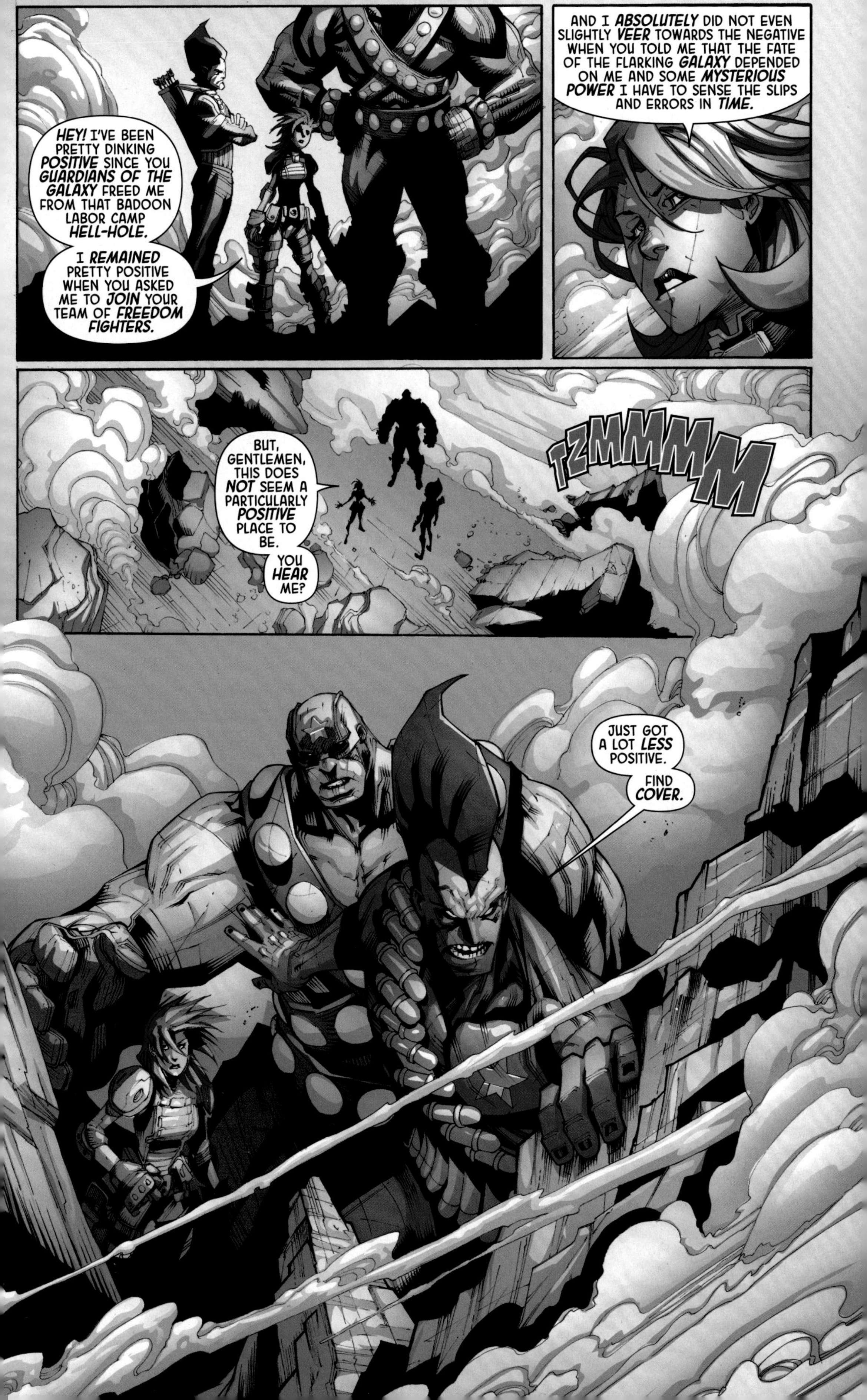
HEY! I'VE BEEN PRETTY DINKING POSITIVE SINCE YOU GUARDIANS OF THE GALAXY FREED ME FROM THAT BADOON LABOR CAMP HELL-HOLE.
I REMAINED PRETTY POSITIVE WHEN YOU ASKED ME TO JOIN YOUR TEAM OF FREEDOM FIGHTERS.
AND I ABSOLUTELY DID NOT EVEN SLIGHTLY VEER TOWARDS THE NEGATIVE WHEN YOU TOLD ME THAT THE FATE OF THE FLARKING GALAXY DEPENDED ON ME AND SOME MYSTERIOUS POWER I HAVE TO SENSE THE SLIPS AND ERRORS IN TIME.
BUT, GENTLEMEN, THIS DOES NOT SEEM A PARTICULARLY POSITIVE PLACE TO BE.
YOU HEAR ME?
TZMMMMM
JUST GOT A LOT LESS POSITIVE.
FIND COVER.

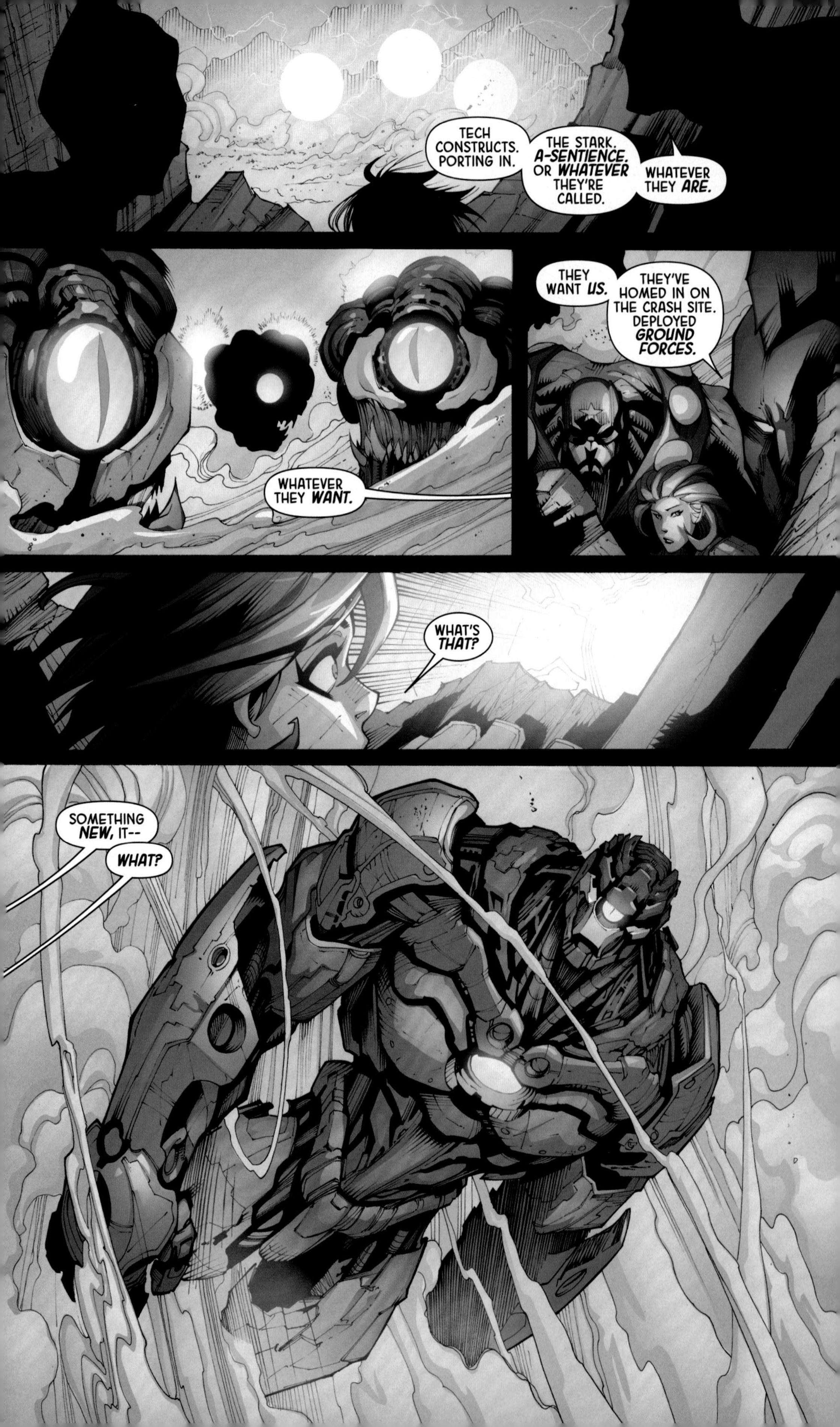
TECH CONSTRUCTS. PORTING IN.
THE STARK. A-SENTIENCE. OR WHATEVER THEY'RE CALLED.
WHATEVER THEY ARE.
WHATEVER THEY WANT.
THEY WANT US.
THEY'VE HOMED IN ON THE CRASH SITE. DEPLOYED GROUND FORCES.
WHAT'S THAT?
SOMETHING NEW, IT--
WHAT?

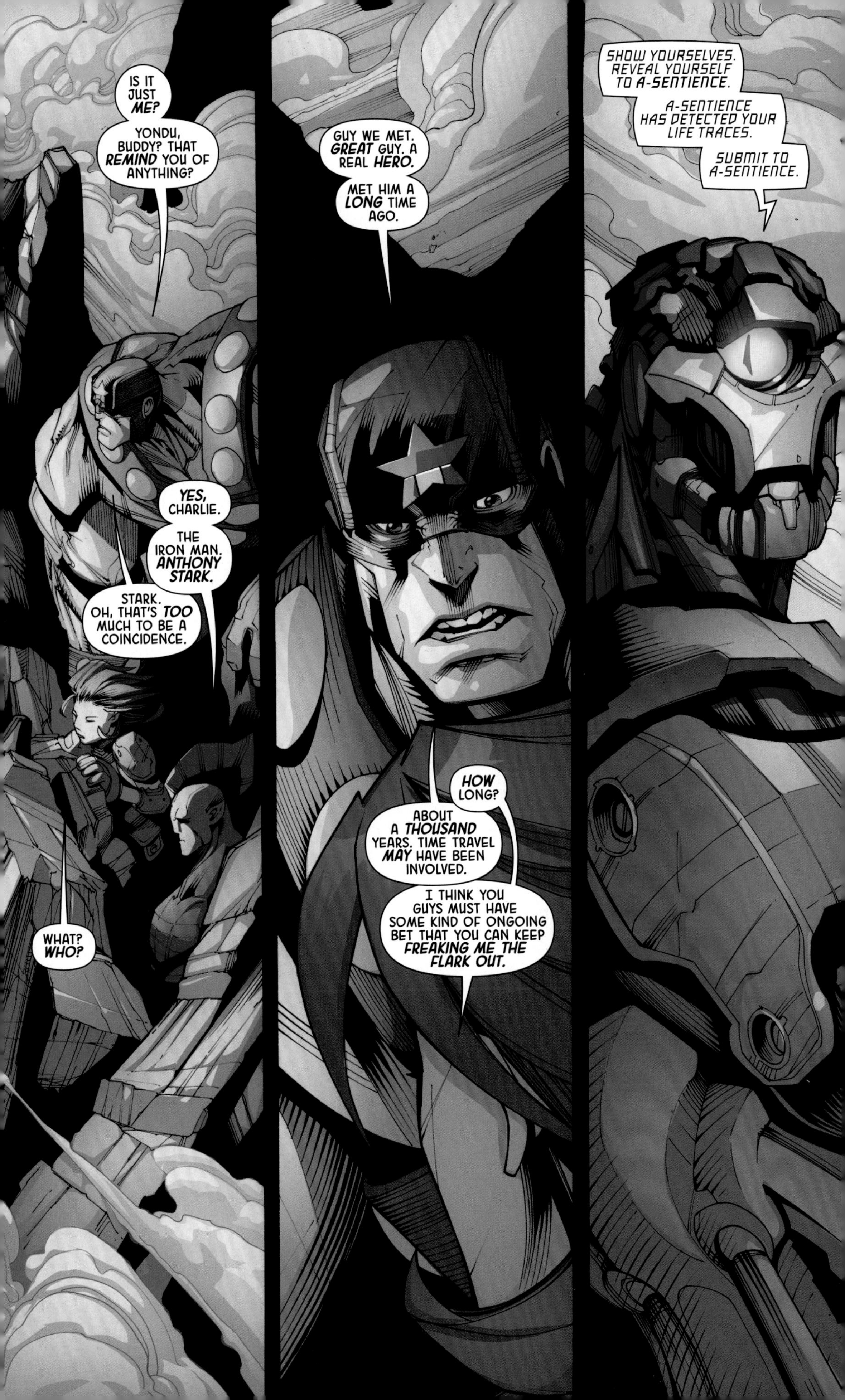
IS IT JUST ME?
YONDU, BUDDY? THAT REMIND YOU OF ANYTHING?
YES, CHARLIE.
THE IRON MAN. ANTHONY STARK.
STARK. OH, THAT'S TOO MUCH TO BE A COINCIDENCE.
WHAT? WHO?
GUY WE MET. GREAT GUY. A REAL HERO.
MET HIM A LONG TIME AGO.
HOW LONG?
ABOUT A THOUSAND YEARS. TIME TRAVEL MAY HAVE BEEN INVOLVED.
I THINK YOU GUYS MUST HAVE SOME KIND OF ONGOING BET THAT YOU CAN KEEP FREAKING ME THE FLARK OUT.
SHOW YOURSELVES. REVEAL YOURSELF TO A-SENTIENCE.
A-SENTIENCE HAS DETECTED YOUR LIFE TRACES.
SUBMIT TO A-SENTIENCE.

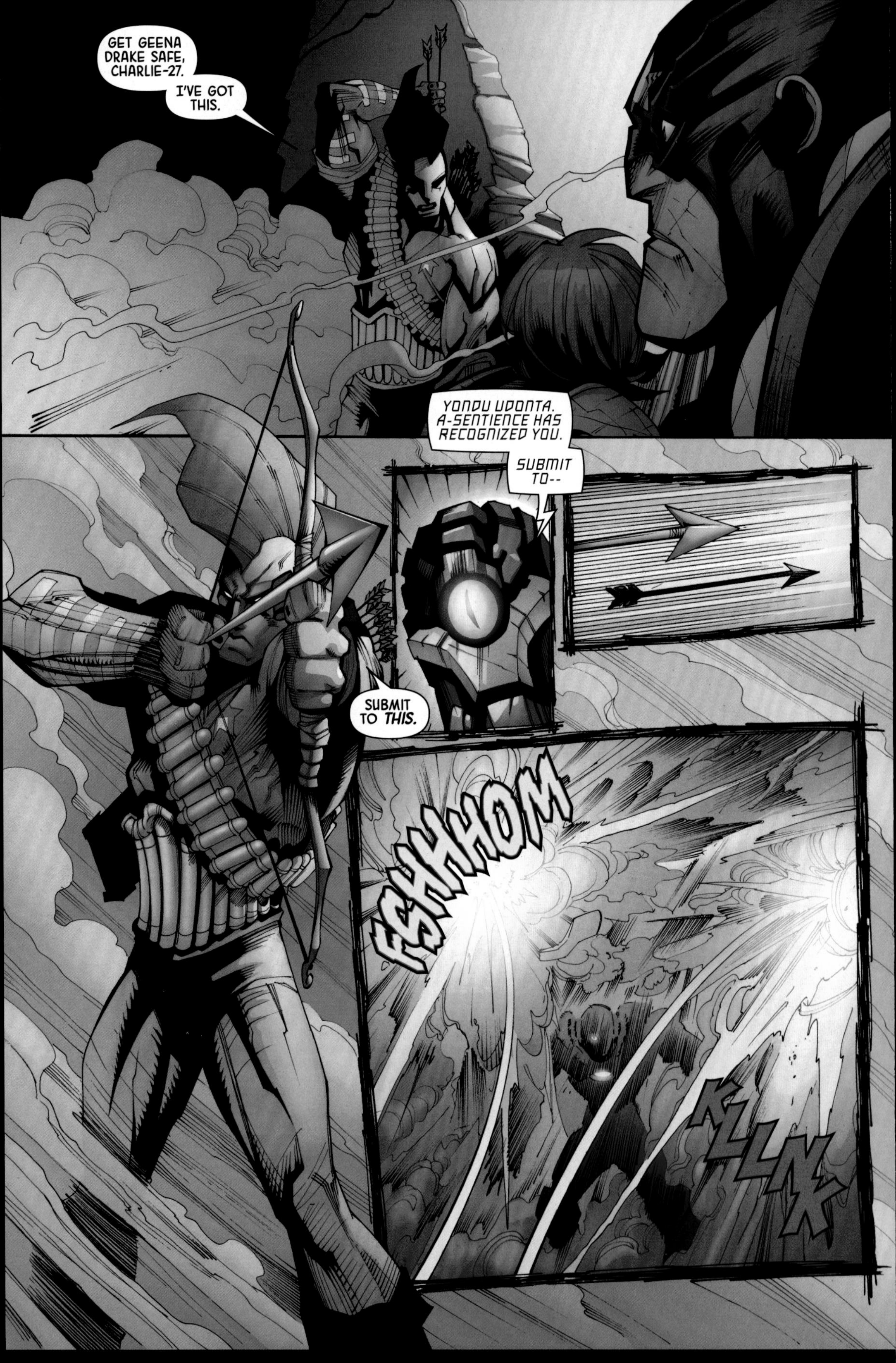
GET GEENA DRAKE SAFE, CHARLIE-27.
I'VE GOT THIS.
YONDU UDONTA. A-SENTIENCE HAS RECOGNIZED YOU.
SUBMIT TO--
SUBMIT TO THIS.
FSHHOM
KLLNK

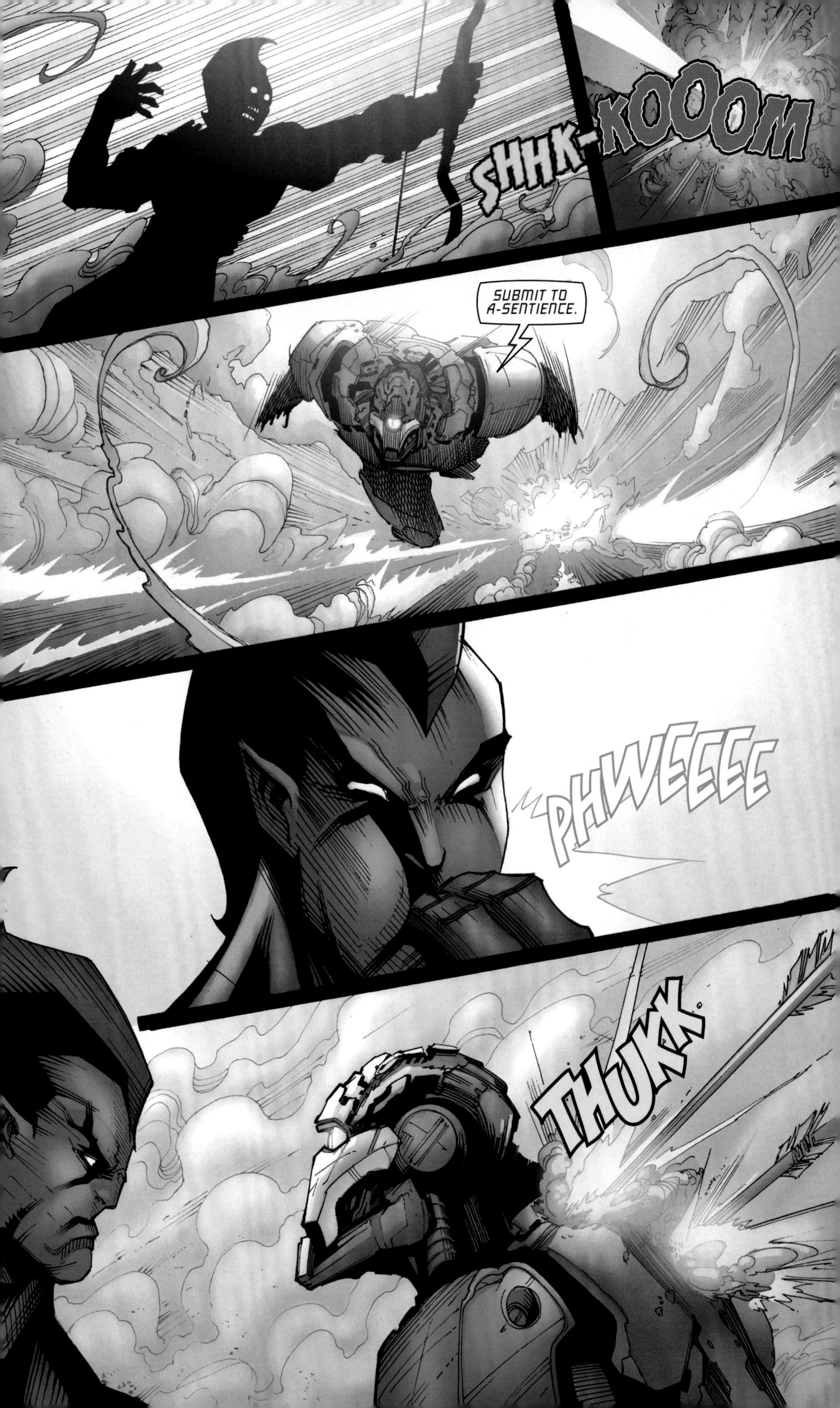
SHHK-KOOOM
SUBMIT TO A-SENTIENCE.
PHWEEEE
THUKK

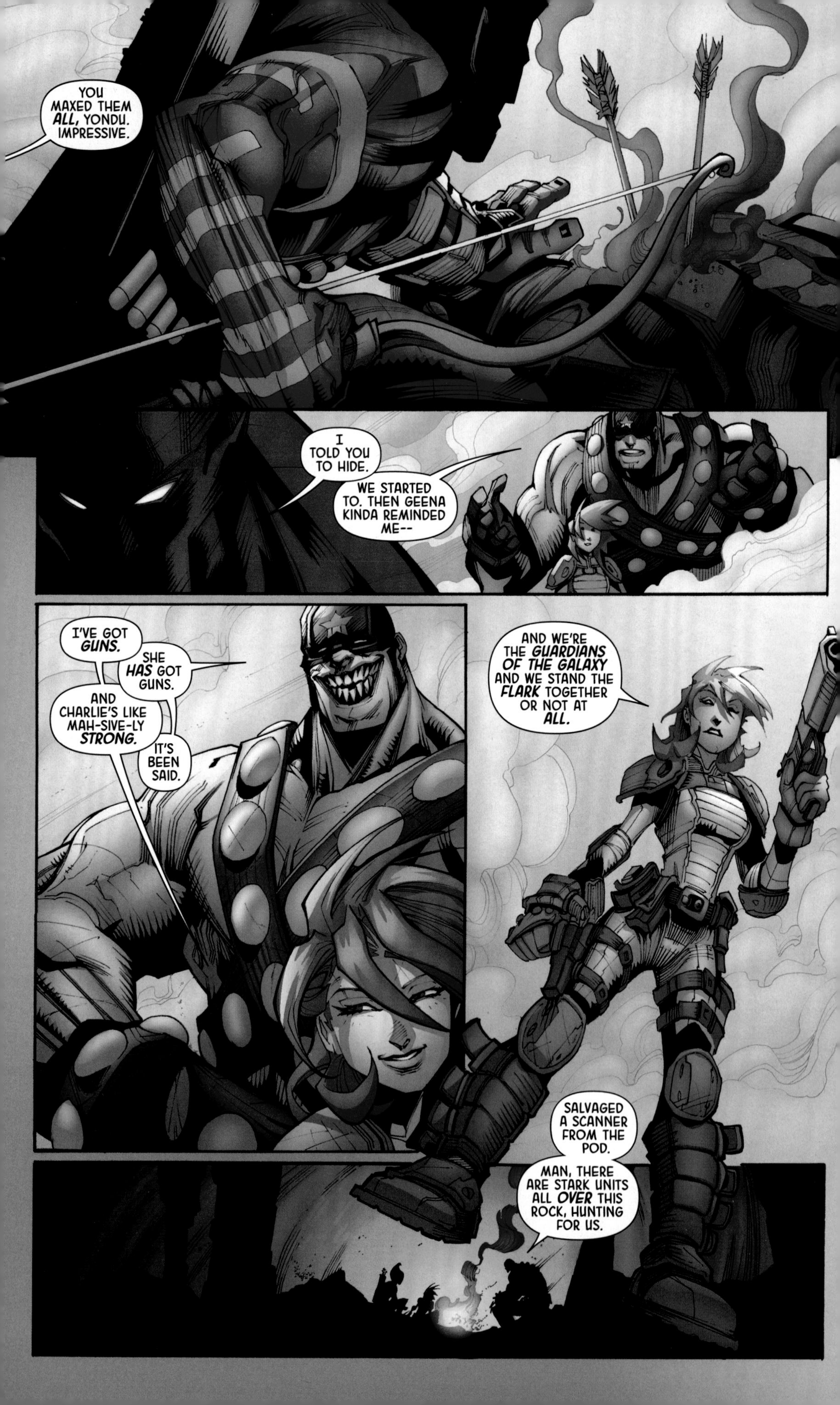

YOU MAXED THEM ALL, YONDU. IMPRESSIVE.
I TOLD YOU TO HIDE.
WE STARTED TO. THEN GEENA KINDA REMINDED ME--
I'VE GOT GUNS.
SHE HAS GOT GUNS.
AND CHARLIE'S LIKE MAH-SIVE-LY STRONG.
IT'S BEEN SAID.
AND WE'RE THE GUARDIANS OF THE GALAXY AND WE STAND THE FLARK TOGETHER OR NOT AT ALL.
SALVAGED A SCANNER FROM THE POD.
MAN, THERE ARE STARK UNITS ALL OVER THIS ROCK, HUNTING FOR US.

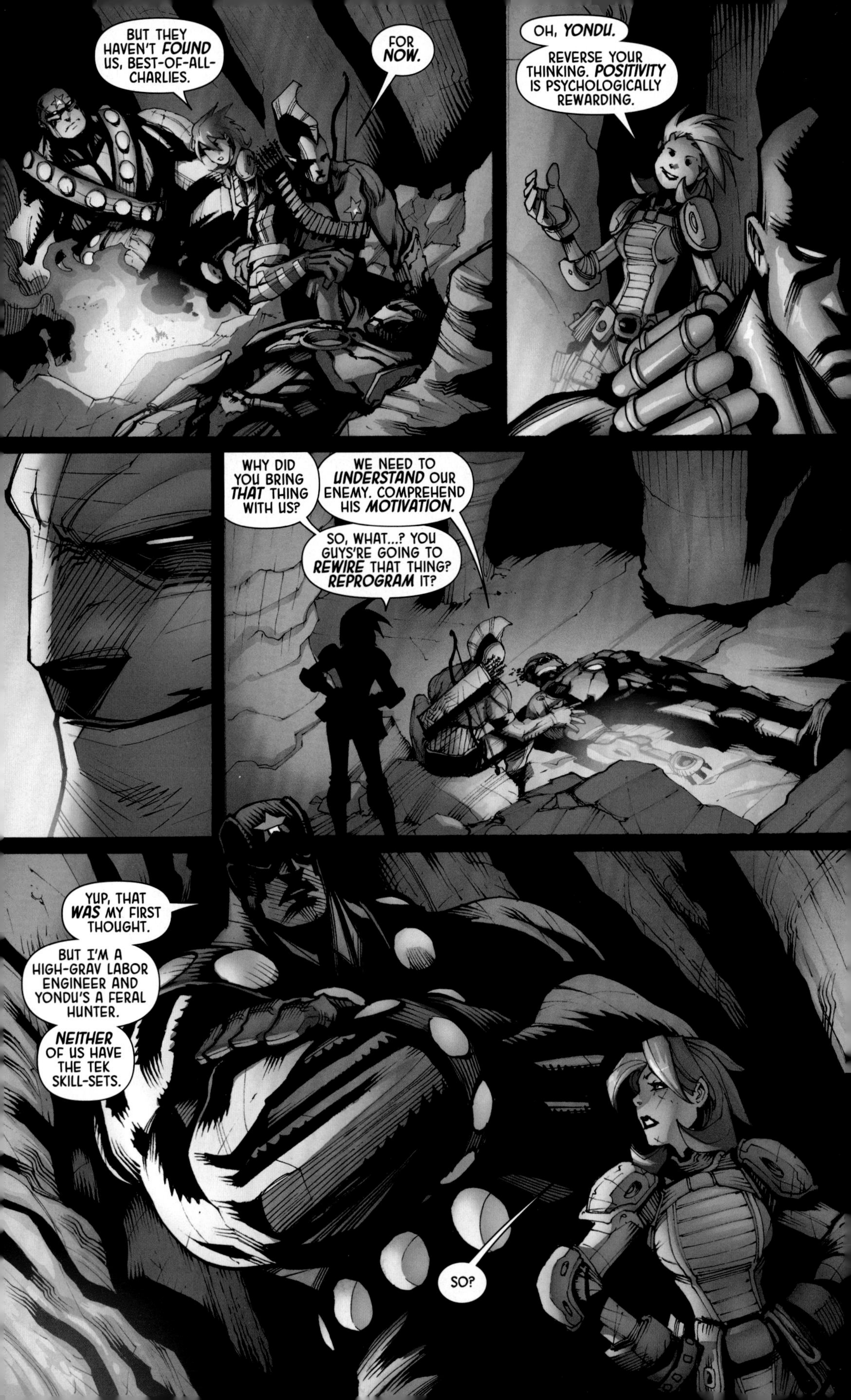
BUT THEY HAVEN'T FOUND US, BEST-OF-ALL-CHARLIES.
FOR NOW.
OH, YONDU.
REVERSE YOUR THINKING. POSITIVITY IS PSYCHOLOGICALLY REWARDING.
WHY DID YOU BRING THAT THING WITH US?
WE NEED TO UNDERSTAND OUR ENEMY. COMPREHEND HIS MOTIVATION.
SO, WHAT...? YOU GUYS'RE GOING TO REWIRE THAT THING? REPROGRAM IT?
YUP, THAT WAS MY FIRST THOUGHT.
BUT I'M A HIGH-GRAV LABOR ENGINEER AND YONDU'S A FERAL HUNTER.
NEITHER OF US HAVE THE TEK SKILL-SETS.
SO?

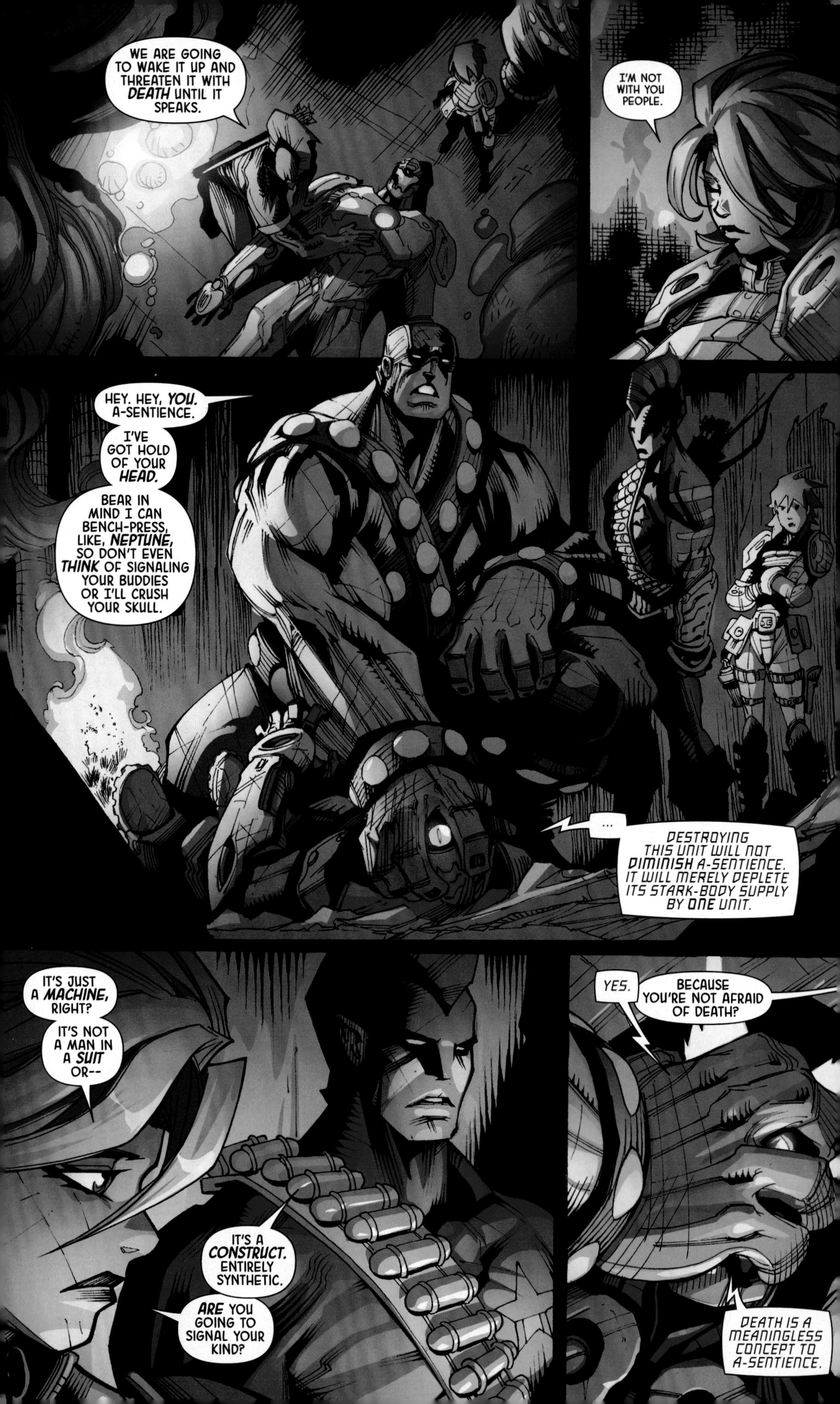

WE ARE GOING TO WAKE IT UP AND THREATEN IT WITH DEATH UNTIL IT SPEAKS.
I'M NOT WITH YOU PEOPLE.
HEY. HEY, YOU. A-SENTIENCE.
I'VE GOT HOLD OF YOUR HEAD.
BEAR IN MIND I CAN BENCH-PRESS, LIKE, NEPTUNE, SO DON'T EVEN THINK OF SIGNALING YOUR BUDDIES OR I'LL CRUSH YOUR SKULL.
...
DESTROYING THIS UNIT WILL NOT DIMINISH A-SENTIENCE. IT WILL MERELY DEPLETE ITS STARK-BODY SUPPLY BY ONE UNIT.
IT'S JUST A MACHINE, RIGHT?
IT'S NOT A MAN IN A SUIT OR--
IT'S A CONSTRUCT. ENTIRELY SYNTHETIC.
ARE YOU GOING TO SIGNAL YOUR KIND?
BECAUSE YOU'RE NOT AFRAID OF DEATH?
YES.
DEATH IS A MEANINGLESS CONCEPT TO A-SENTIENCE.

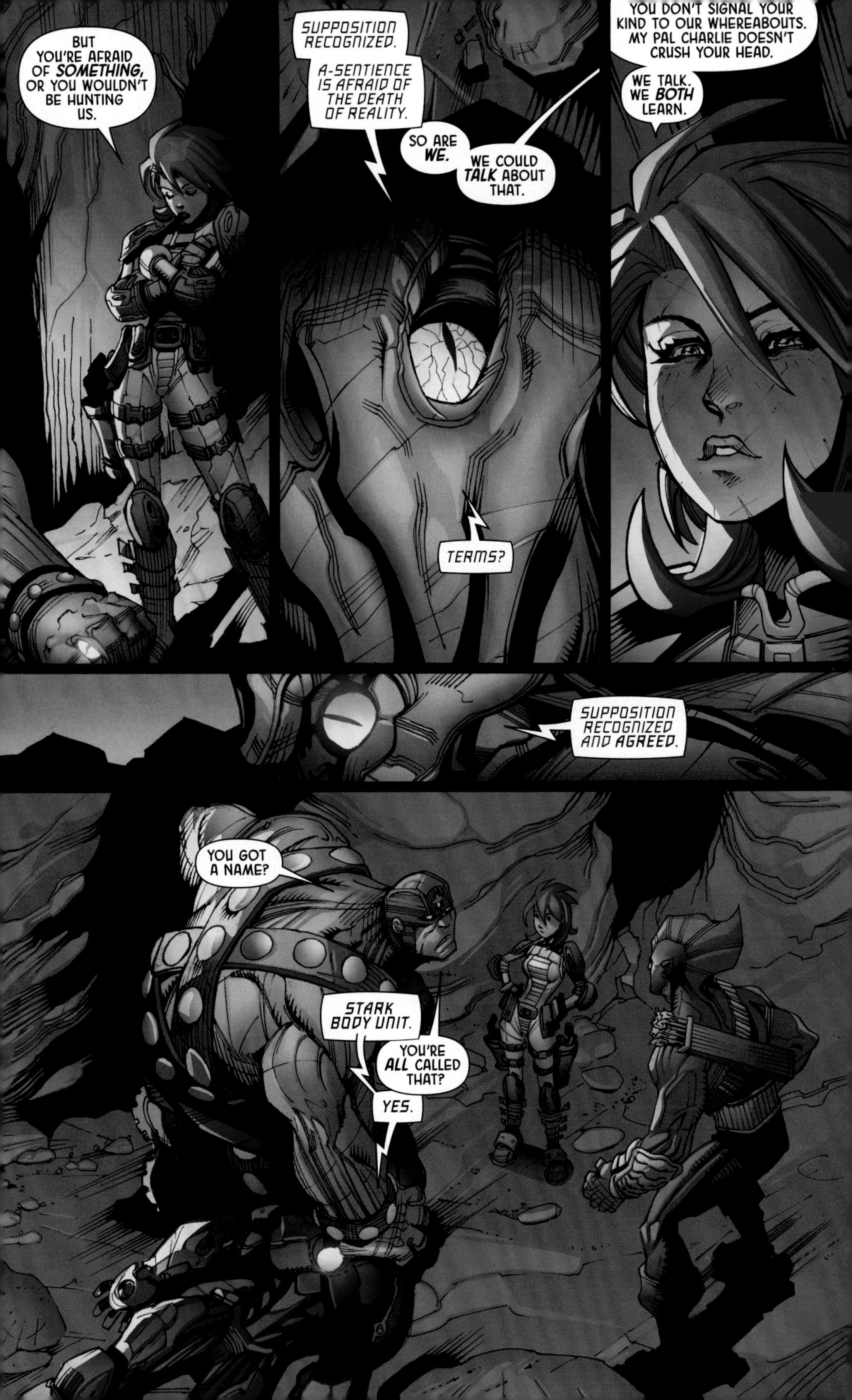

BUT YOU'RE AFRAID OF SOMETHING, OR YOU WOULDN'T BE HUNTING US.
SUPPOSITION RECOGNIZED.
A-SENTIENCE IS AFRAID OF THE DEATH OF REALITY.
SO ARE WE.
WE COULD TALK ABOUT THAT.
TERMS?
YOU DON'T SIGNAL YOUR KIND TO OUR WHEREABOUTS. MY PAL CHARLIE DOESN'T CRUSH YOUR HEAD.
WE TALK. WE BOTH LEARN.
SUPPOSITION RECOGNIZED AND AGREED.
YOU GOT A NAME?
STARK BODY UNIT.
YOU'RE ALL CALLED THAT?
YES.

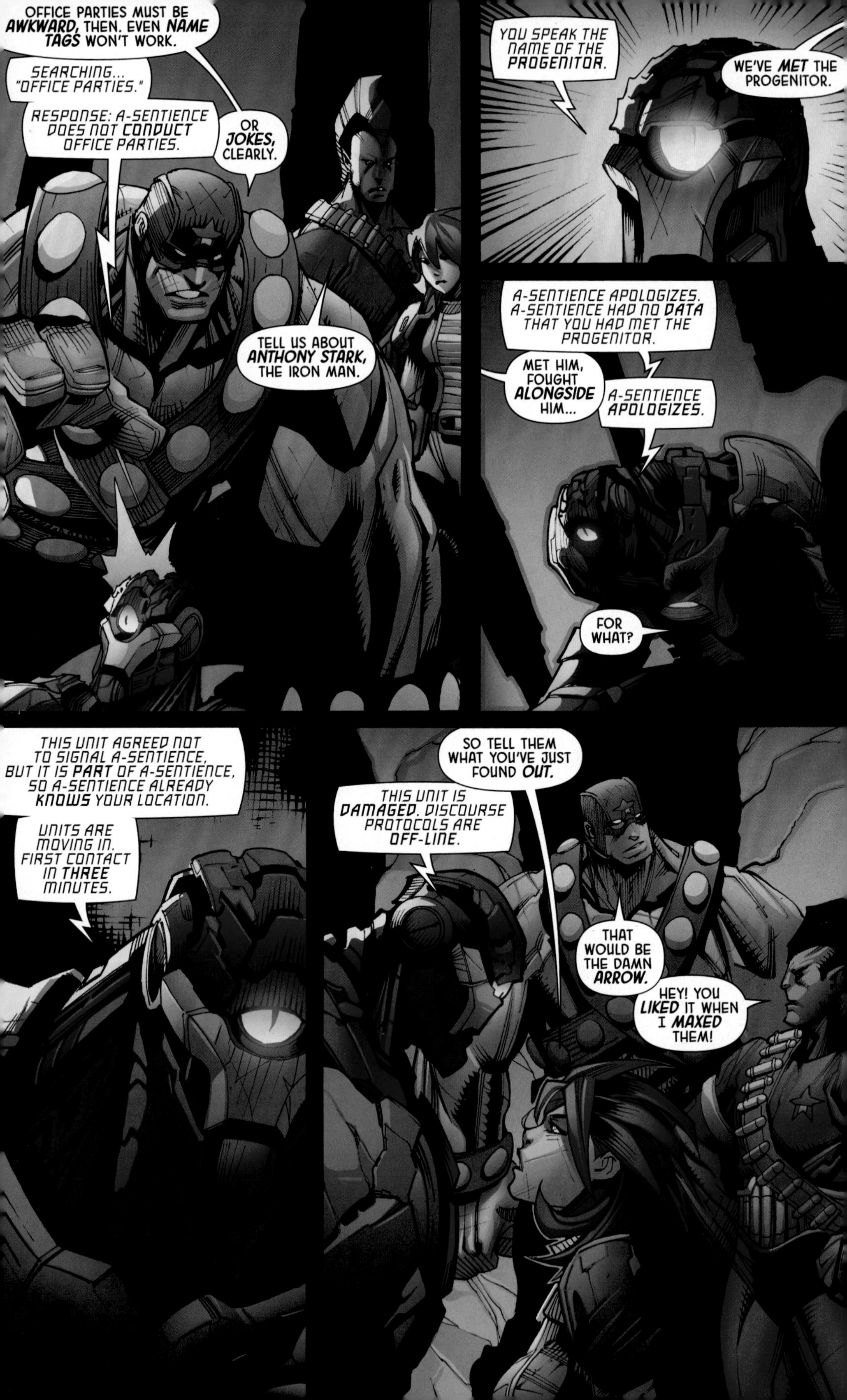
OFFICE PARTIES MUST BE AWKWARD, THEN. EVEN NAME TAGS WON'T WORK.
SEARCHING... "OFFICE PARTIES."
RESPONSE: A-SENTIENCE DOES NOT CONDUCT OFFICE PARTIES.
OR JOKES, CLEARLY.
TELL US ABOUT ANTHONY STARK, THE IRON MAN.
YOU SPEAK THE NAME OF THE PROGENITOR.
WE'VE MET THE PROGENITOR.
A-SENTIENCE APOLOGIZES. A-SENTIENCE HAD NO DATA THAT YOU HAD MET THE PROGENITOR.
MET HIM, FOUGHT ALONGSIDE HIM...
A-SENTIENCE APOLOGIZES.
FOR WHAT?
THIS UNIT AGREED NOT TO SIGNAL A-SENTIENCE, BUT IT IS PART OF A-SENTIENCE, SO A-SENTIENCE ALREADY KNOWS YOUR LOCATION.
UNITS ARE MOVING IN. FIRST CONTACT IN THREE MINUTES.
SO TELL THEM WHAT YOU'VE JUST FOUND OUT.
THIS UNIT IS DAMAGED. DISCOURSE PROTOCOLS ARE OFF-LINE.
THAT WOULD BE THE DAMN ARROW.
HEY! YOU LIKED IT WHEN I MAXED THEM!

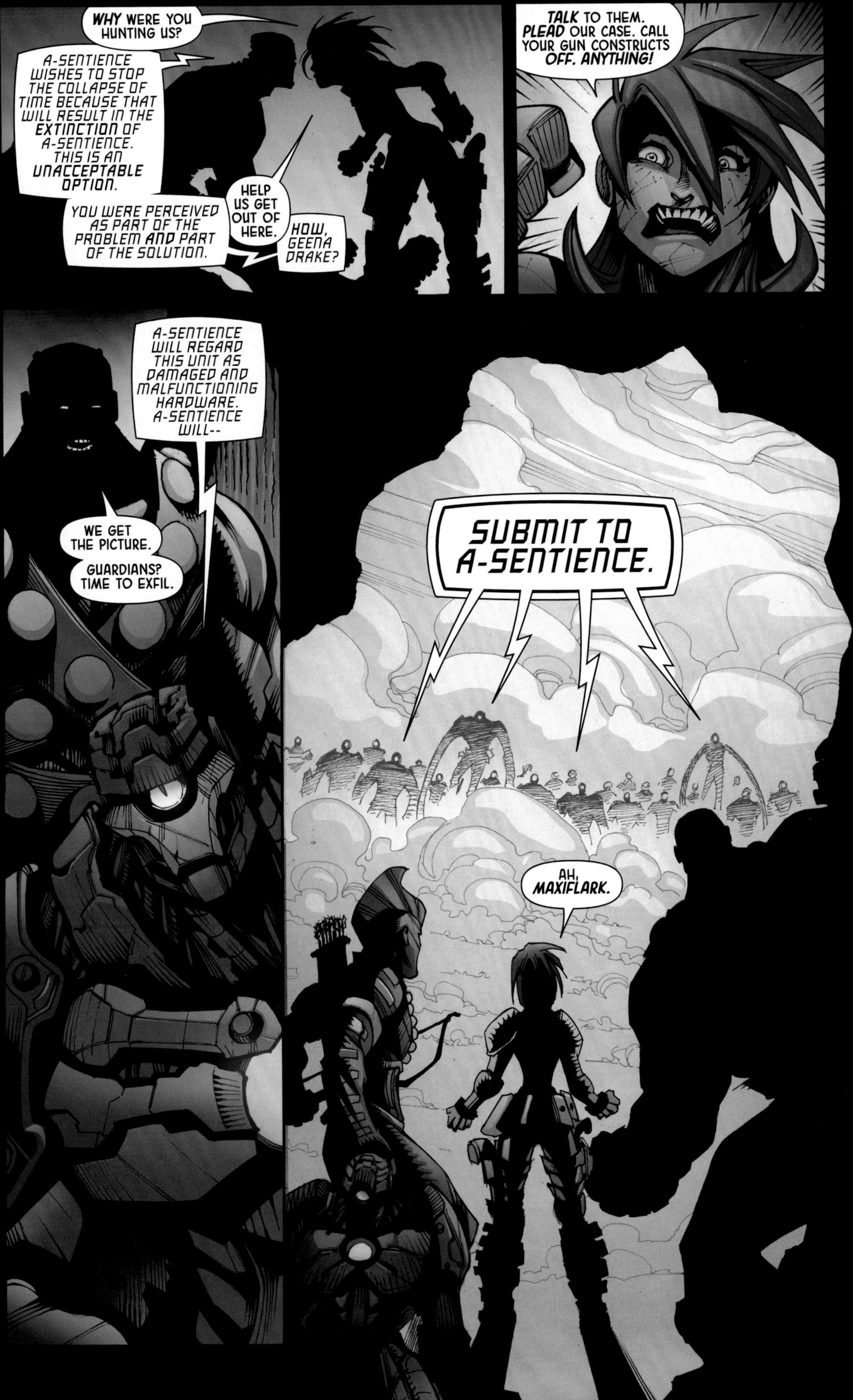
WHY WERE YOU HUNTING US?
A-SENTIENCE WISHES TO STOP THE COLLAPSE OF TIME BECAUSE THAT WILL RESULT IN THE EXTINCTION OF A-SENTIENCE. THIS IS AN UNACCEPTABLE OPTION.
YOU WERE PERCEIVED AS PART OF THE PROBLEM AND PART OF THE SOLUTION.
HELP US GET OUT OF HERE.
HOW, GEENA DRAKE?
TALK TO THEM. PLEAD OUR CASE. CALL YOUR GUN CONSTRUCTS OFF. ANYTHING!
A-SENTIENCE WILL REGARD THIS UNIT AS DAMAGED AND MALFUNCTIONING HARDWARE. A-SENTIENCE WILL--
WE GET THE PICTURE.
GUARDIANS? TIME TO EXFIL.
SUBMIT TO A-SENTIENCE.
AH, MAXIFLARK.

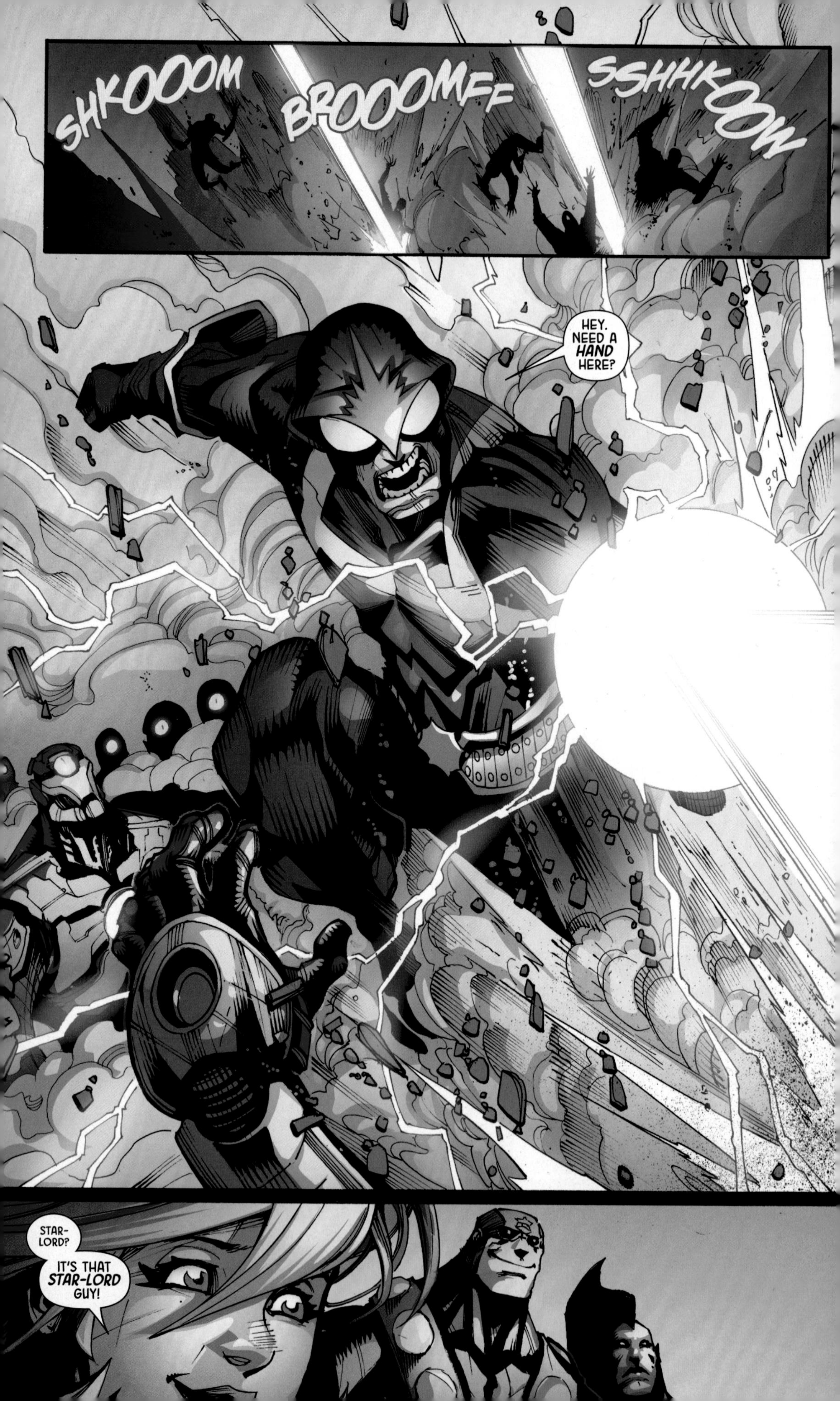
SHKOOOM
BROOOMFF
SSHHKOOW
HEY. NEED A HAND HERE?
STAR-LORD?
IT'S THAT STAR-LORD GUY!

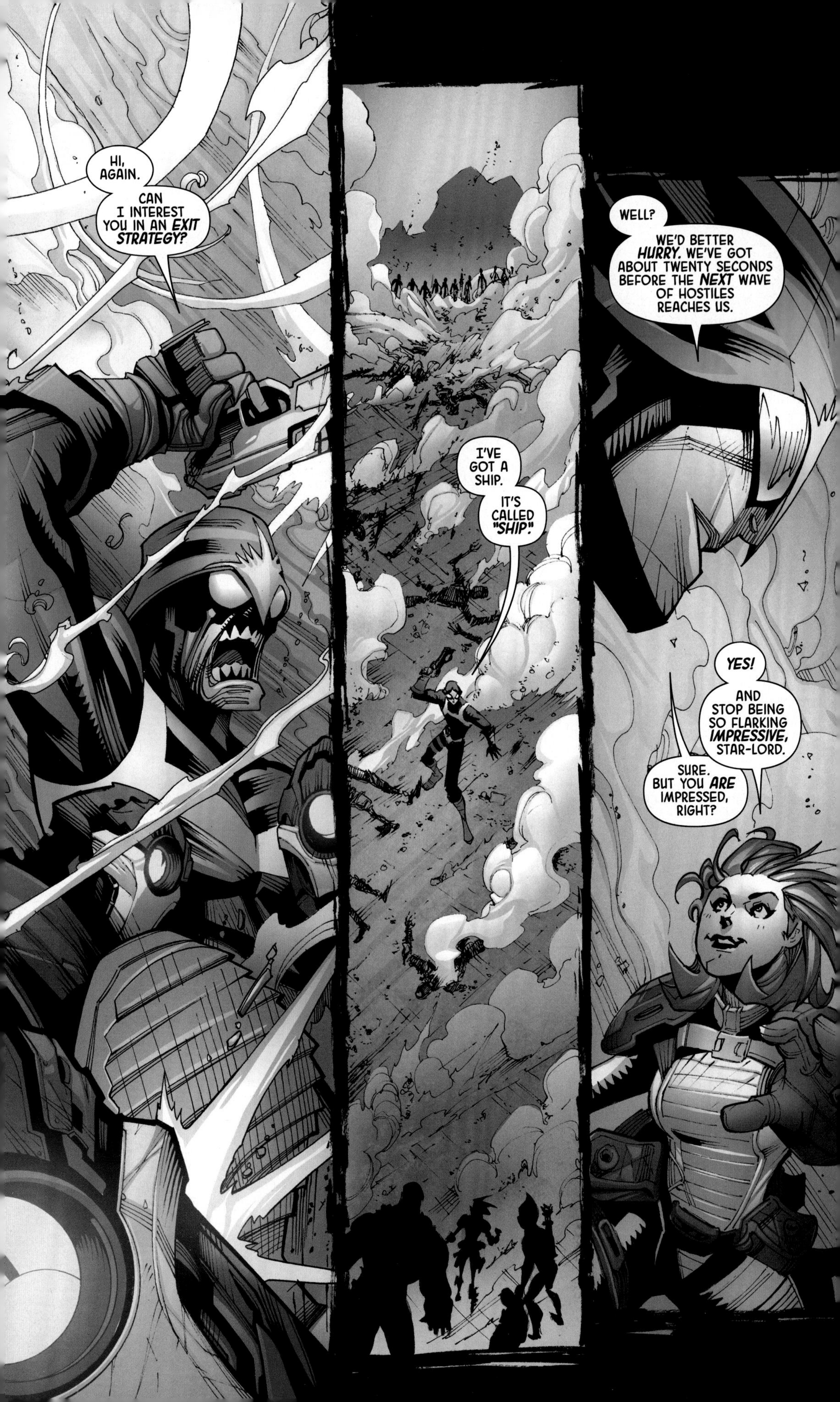

HI, AGAIN.
CAN I INTEREST YOU IN AN EXIT STRATEGY?
I'VE GOT A SHIP.
IT'S CALLED "SHIP."
WELL?
WE'D BETTER HURRY. WE'VE GOT ABOUT TWENTY SECONDS BEFORE THE NEXT WAVE OF HOSTILES REACHES US.
YES!
AND STOP BEING SO FLARKING IMPRESSIVE, STAR-LORD.
SURE. BUT YOU ARE IMPRESSED, RIGHT?

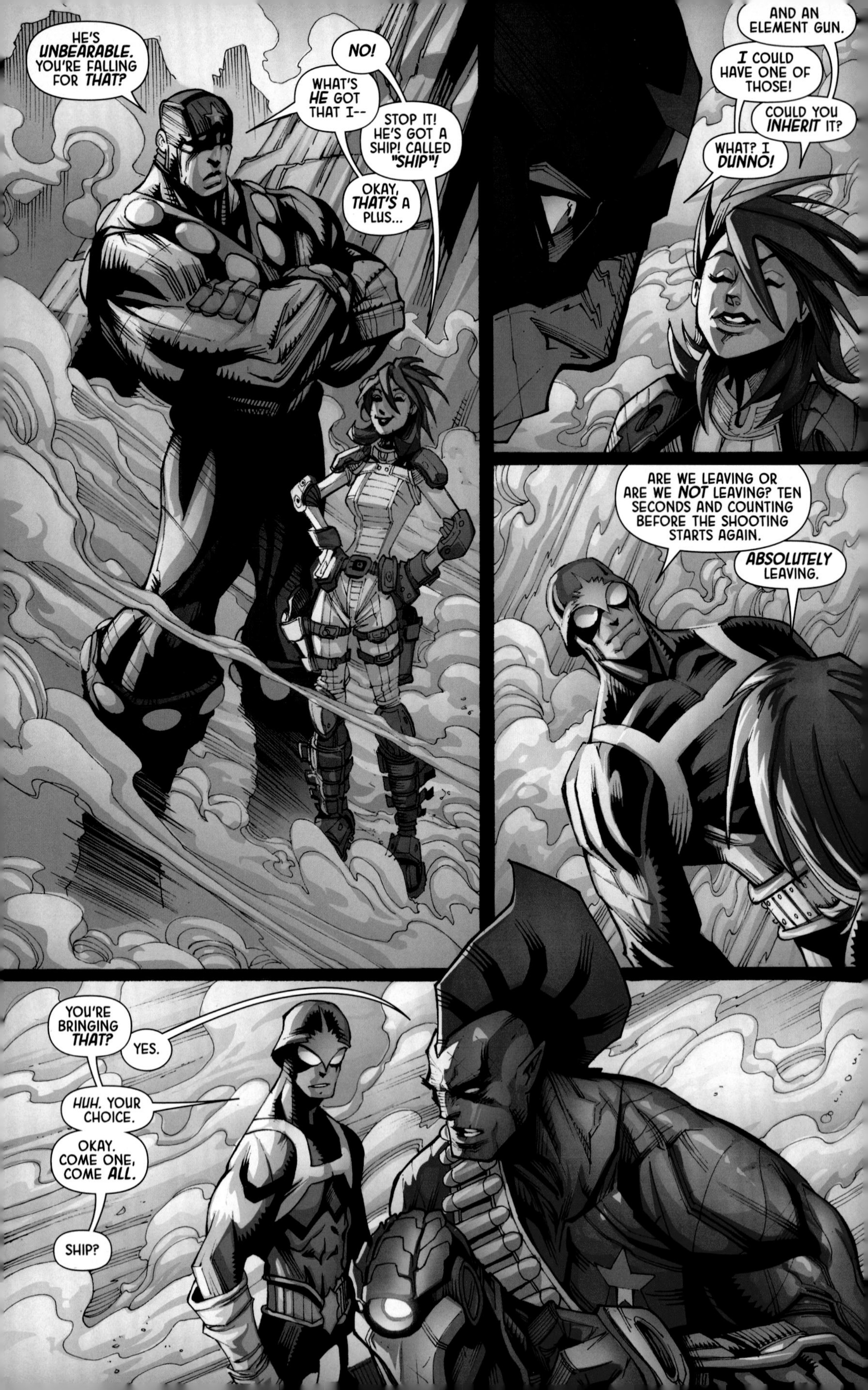
HE'S UNBEARABLE. YOU'RE FALLING FOR THAT?
NO!
WHAT'S HE GOT THAT I--
STOP IT! HE'S GOT A SHIP! CALLED "SHIP"!
OKAY, THAT'S A PLUS...
AND AN ELEMENT GUN.
I COULD HAVE ONE OF THOSE!
COULD YOU INHERIT IT?
WHAT? I DUNNO!
ARE WE LEAVING OR ARE WE NOT LEAVING? TEN SECONDS AND COUNTING BEFORE THE SHOOTING STARTS AGAIN.
ABSOLUTELY LEAVING.
YOU'RE BRINGING THAT?
YES.
HUH. YOUR CHOICE.
OKAY. COME ONE, COME ALL.
SHIP?

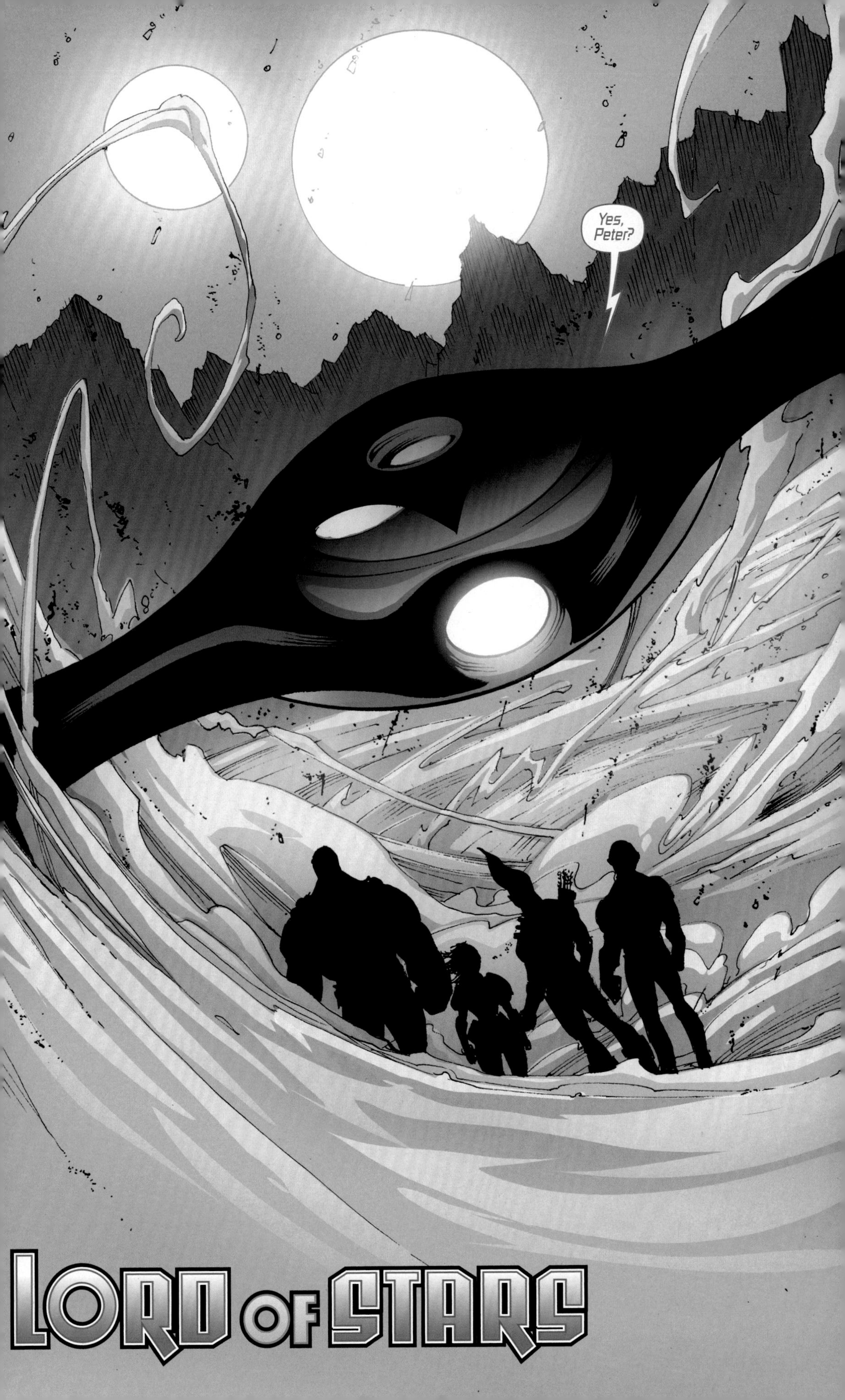
Yes, Peter?
LORD OF STARS

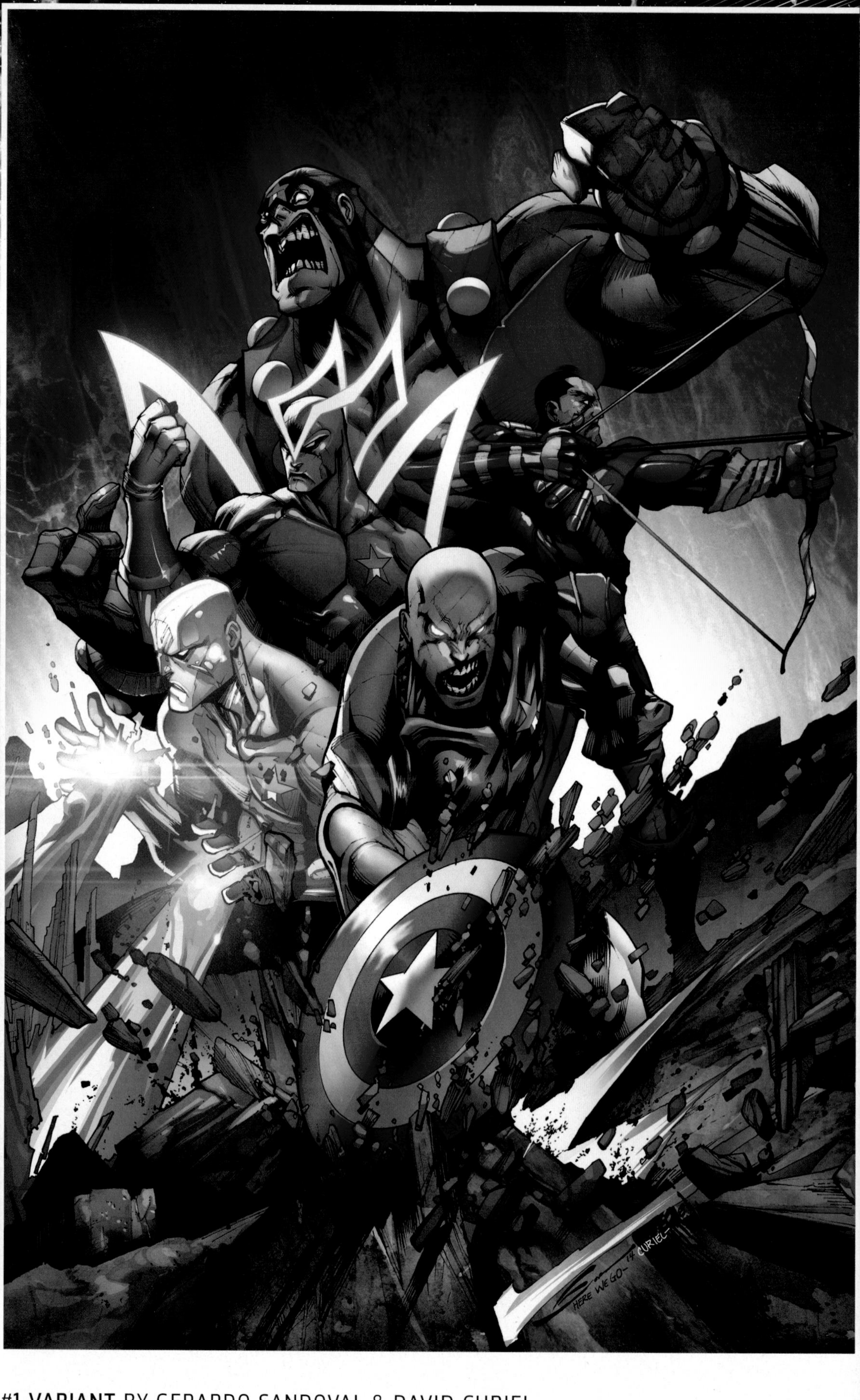

#1 VARIANT BY GERARDO SANDOVAL & DAVID CURIEL

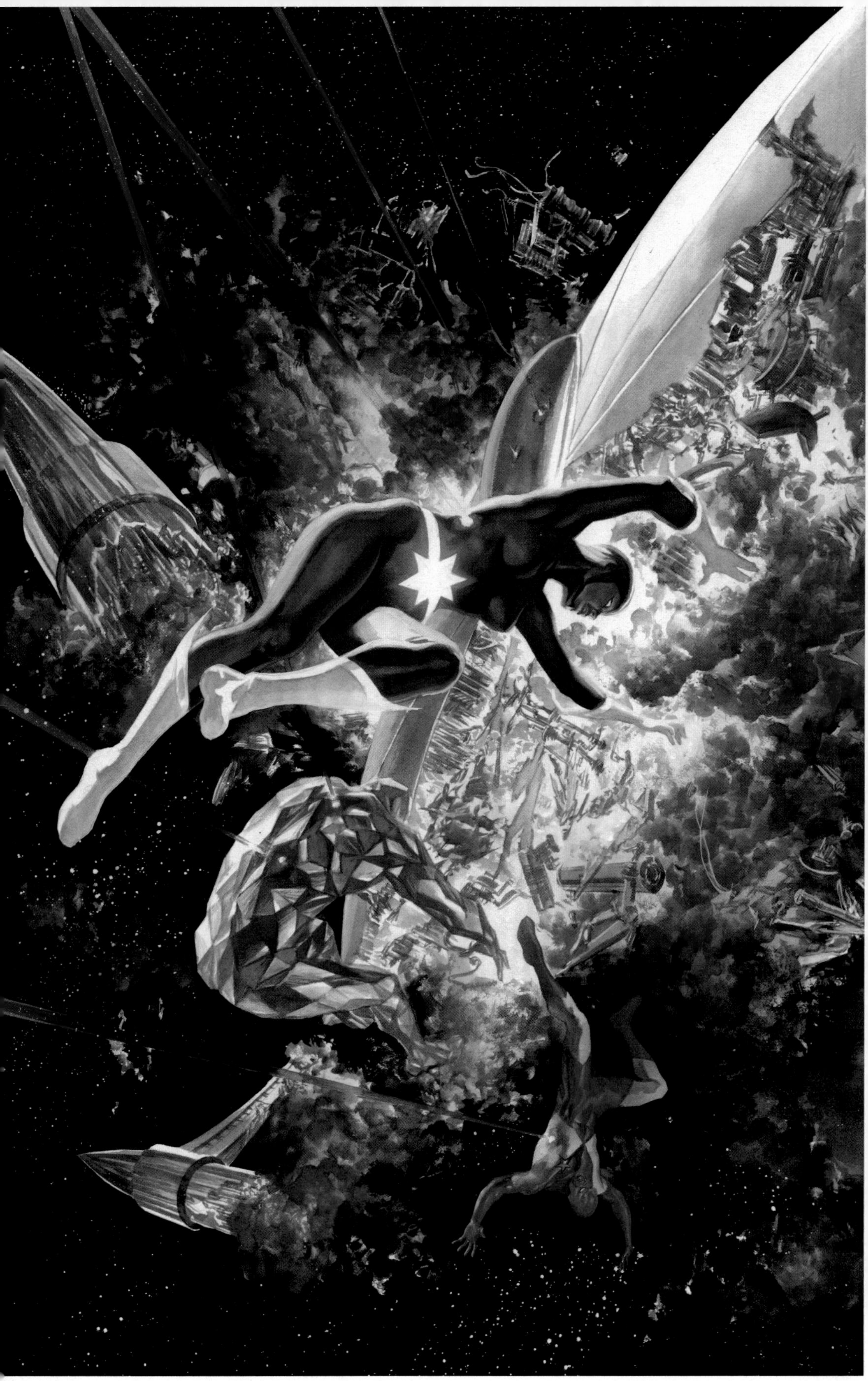

4

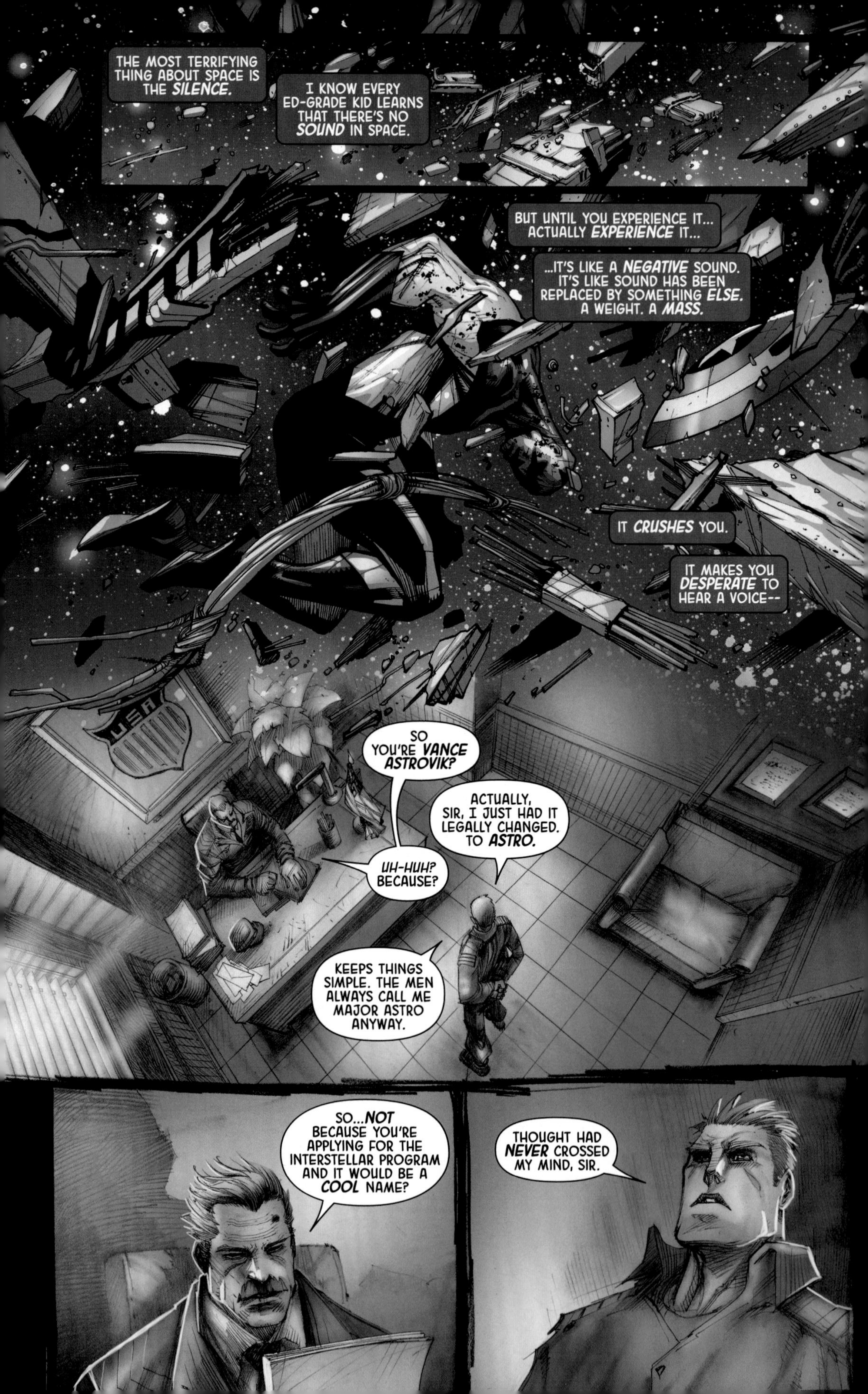

THE MOST TERRIFYING THING ABOUT SPACE IS THE SILENCE.
I KNOW EVERY ED-GRADE KID LEARNS THAT THERE'S NO SOUND IN SPACE.
BUT UNTIL YOU EXPERIENCE IT... ACTUALLY EXPERIENCE IT...
...IT'S LIKE A NEGATIVE SOUND. IT'S LIKE SOUND HAS BEEN REPLACED BY SOMETHING ELSE. A WEIGHT. A MASS.
IT CRUSHES YOU.
IT MAKES YOU DESPERATE TO HEAR A VOICE--
SO YOU'RE VANCE ASTROVIK?
ACTUALLY, SIR, I JUST HAD IT LEGALLY CHANGED. TO ASTRO.
UH-HUH? BECAUSE?
KEEPS THINGS SIMPLE. THE MEN ALWAYS CALL ME MAJOR ASTRO ANYWAY.
SO...NOT BECAUSE YOU'RE APPLYING FOR THE INTERSTELLAR PROGRAM AND IT WOULD BE A COOL NAME?
THOUGHT HAD NEVER CROSSED MY MIND, SIR.

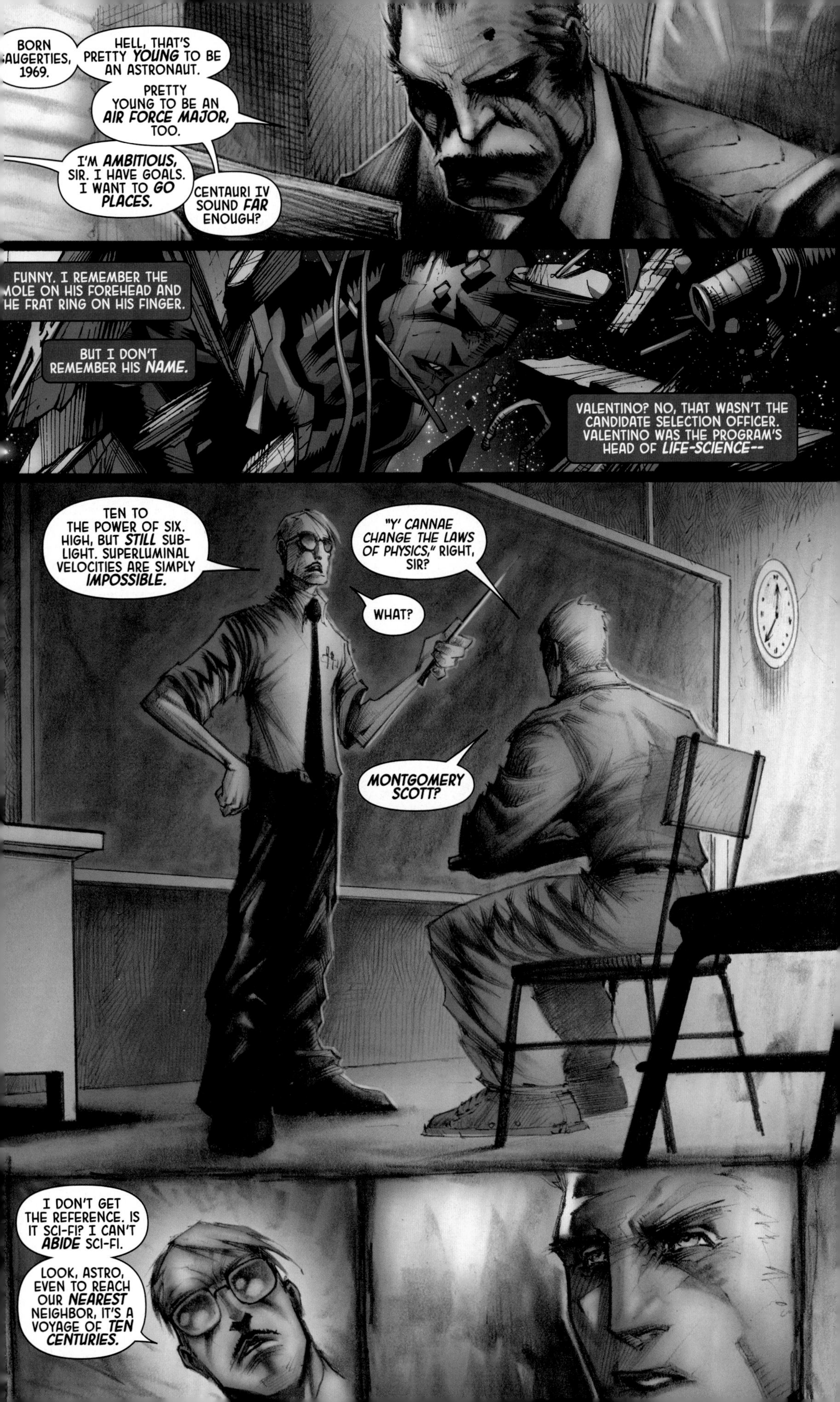
BORN SAUGERTIES, 1969.
HELL, THAT'S PRETTY YOUNG TO BE AN ASTRONAUT.
PRETTY YOUNG TO BE AN AIR FORCE MAJOR, TOO.
I'M AMBITIOUS, SIR. I HAVE GOALS. I WANT TO GO PLACES.
CENTAURI IV SOUND FAR ENOUGH?
FUNNY. I REMEMBER THE MOLE ON HIS FOREHEAD AND THE FRAT RING ON HIS FINGER.
BUT I DON'T REMEMBER HIS NAME.
VALENTINO? NO, THAT WASN'T THE CANDIDATE SELECTION OFFICER. VALENTINO WAS THE PROGRAM'S HEAD OF LIFE-SCIENCE--
TEN TO THE POWER OF SIX. HIGH, BUT STILL SUB-LIGHT. SUPERLUMINAL VELOCITIES ARE SIMPLY IMPOSSIBLE.
"Y' CANNAE CHANGE THE LAWS OF PHYSICS," RIGHT, SIR?
WHAT?
MONTGOMERY SCOTT?
I DON'T GET THE REFERENCE. IS IT SCI-FI? I CAN'T ABIDE SCI-FI.
LOOK, ASTRO, EVEN TO REACH OUR NEAREST NEIGHBOR, IT'S A VOYAGE OF TEN CENTURIES.

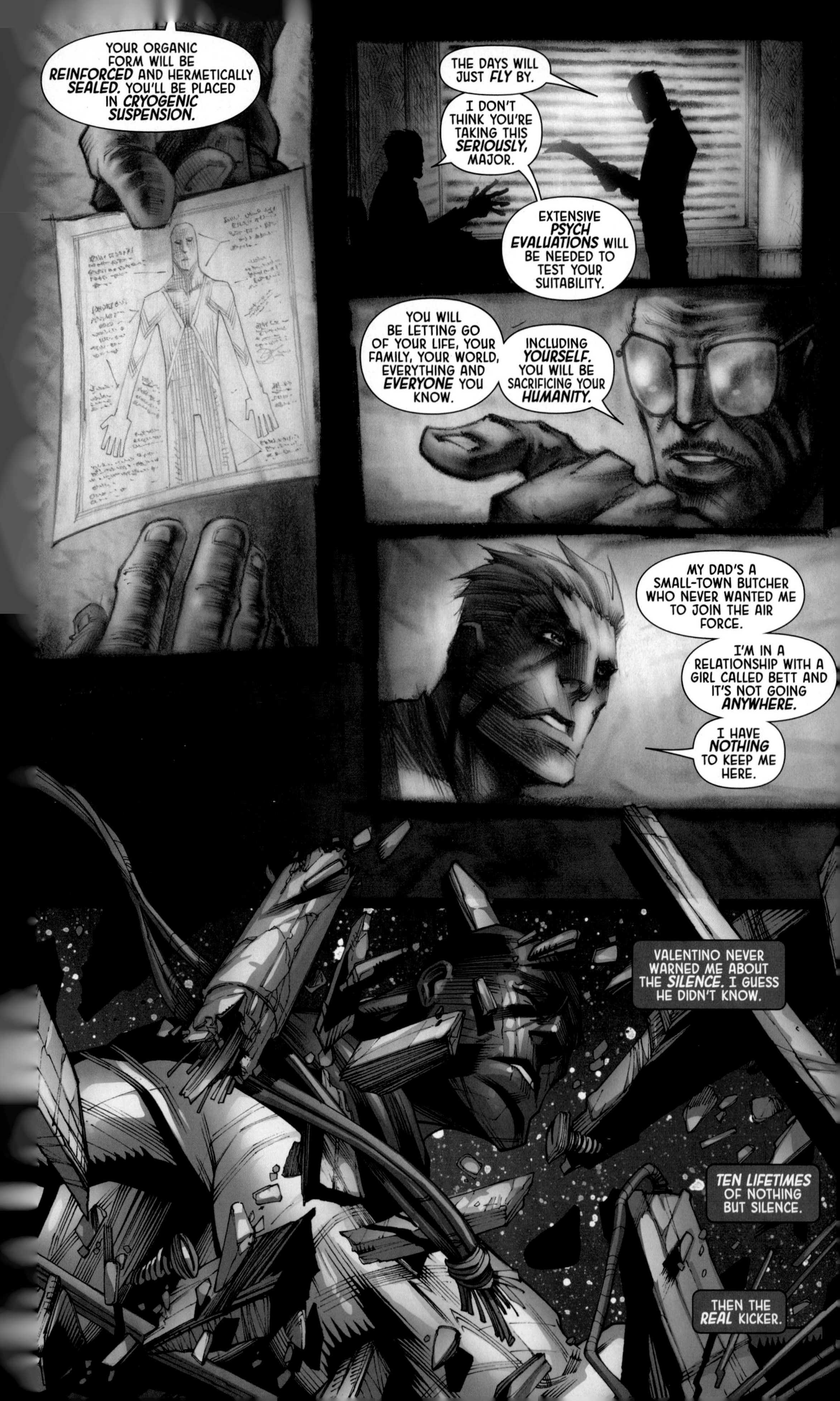

YOUR ORGANIC FORM WILL BE REINFORCED AND HERMETICALLY SEALED. YOU'LL BE PLACED IN CRYOGENIC SUSPENSION.
THE DAYS WILL JUST FLY BY.
I DON'T THINK YOU'RE TAKING THIS SERIOUSLY, MAJOR.
EXTENSIVE PSYCH EVALUATIONS WILL BE NEEDED TO TEST YOUR SUITABILITY.
YOU WILL BE LETTING GO OF YOUR LIFE, YOUR FAMILY, YOUR WORLD, EVERYTHING AND EVERYONE YOU KNOW.
INCLUDING YOURSELF. YOU WILL BE SACRIFICING YOUR HUMANITY.
MY DAD'S A SMALL-TOWN BUTCHER WHO NEVER WANTED ME TO JOIN THE AIR FORCE.
I'M IN A RELATIONSHIP WITH A GIRL CALLED BETT AND IT'S NOT GOING ANYWHERE.
I HAVE NOTHING TO KEEP ME HERE.
VALENTINO NEVER WARNED ME ABOUT THE SILENCE. I GUESS HE DIDN'T KNOW.
TEN LIFETIMES OF NOTHING BUT SILENCE.
THEN THE REAL KICKER.

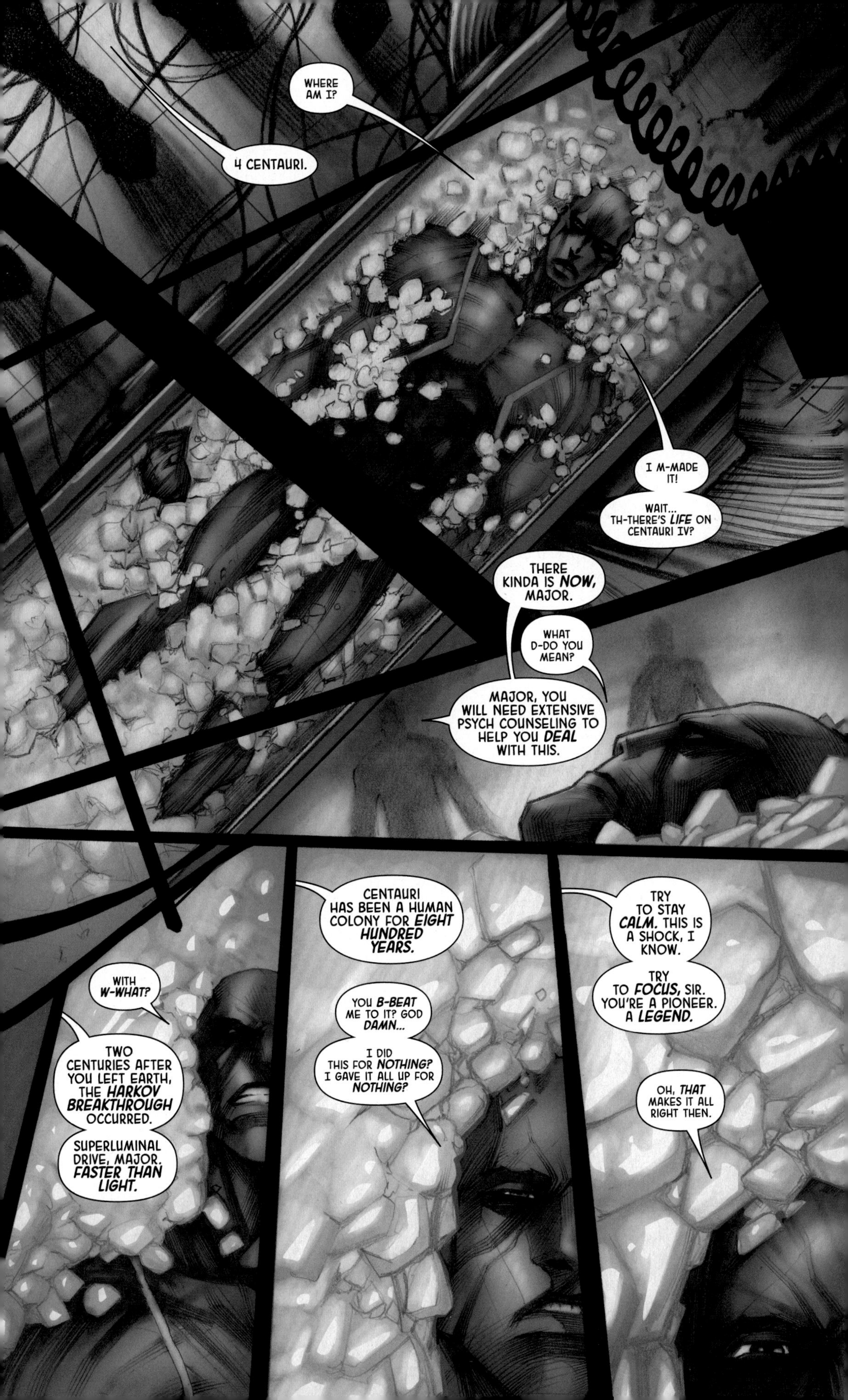
WHERE AM I?
4 CENTAURI.
I M-MADE IT!
WAIT... TH-THERE'S LIFE ON CENTAURI IV?
THERE KINDA IS NOW, MAJOR.
WHAT D-DO YOU MEAN?
MAJOR, YOU WILL NEED EXTENSIVE PSYCH COUNSELING TO HELP YOU DEAL WITH THIS.
WITH W-WHAT?
TWO CENTURIES AFTER YOU LEFT EARTH, THE HARKOV BREAKTHROUGH OCCURRED.
SUPERLUMINAL DRIVE, MAJOR. FASTER THAN LIGHT.
CENTAURI HAS BEEN A HUMAN COLONY FOR EIGHT HUNDRED YEARS.
YOU B-BEAT ME TO IT? GOD DAMN...
I DID THIS FOR NOTHING? I GAVE IT ALL UP FOR NOTHING?
TRY TO STAY CALM. THIS IS A SHOCK, I KNOW.
TRY TO FOCUS, SIR. YOU'RE A PIONEER. A LEGEND.
OH, THAT MAKES IT ALL RIGHT THEN.

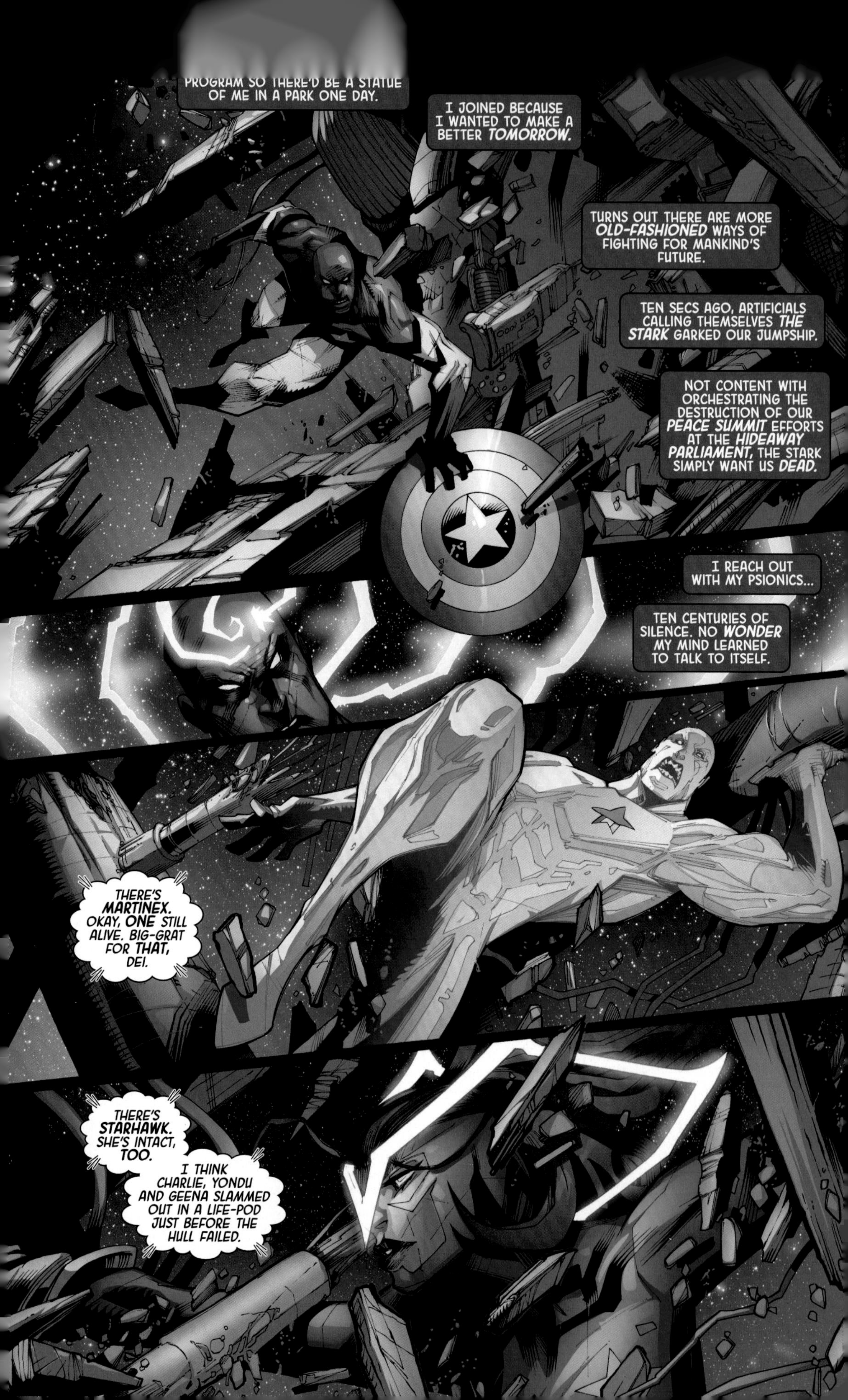

PROGRAM SO THERE'D BE A STATUE OF ME IN A PARK ONE DAY.
I JOINED BECAUSE I WANTED TO MAKE A BETTER TOMORROW.
TURNS OUT THERE ARE MORE OLD-FASHIONED WAYS OF FIGHTING FOR MANKIND'S FUTURE.
TEN SECS AGO, ARTIFICIALS CALLING THEMSELVES THE STARK GARKED OUR JUMPSHIP.
NOT CONTENT WITH ORCHESTRATING THE DESTRUCTION OF OUR PEACE SUMMIT EFFORTS AT THE HIDEAWAY PARLIAMENT, THE STARK SIMPLY WANT US DEAD.
I REACH OUT WITH MY PSIONICS...
TEN CENTURIES OF SILENCE. NO WONDER MY MIND LEARNED TO TALK TO ITSELF.
THERE'S MARTINEX. OKAY, ONE STILL ALIVE. BIG-GRAT FOR THAT, DEI.
THERE'S STARHAWK. SHE'S INTACT, TOO.
I THINK CHARLIE, YONDU AND GEENA SLAMMED OUT IN A LIFE-POD JUST BEFORE THE HULL FAILED.

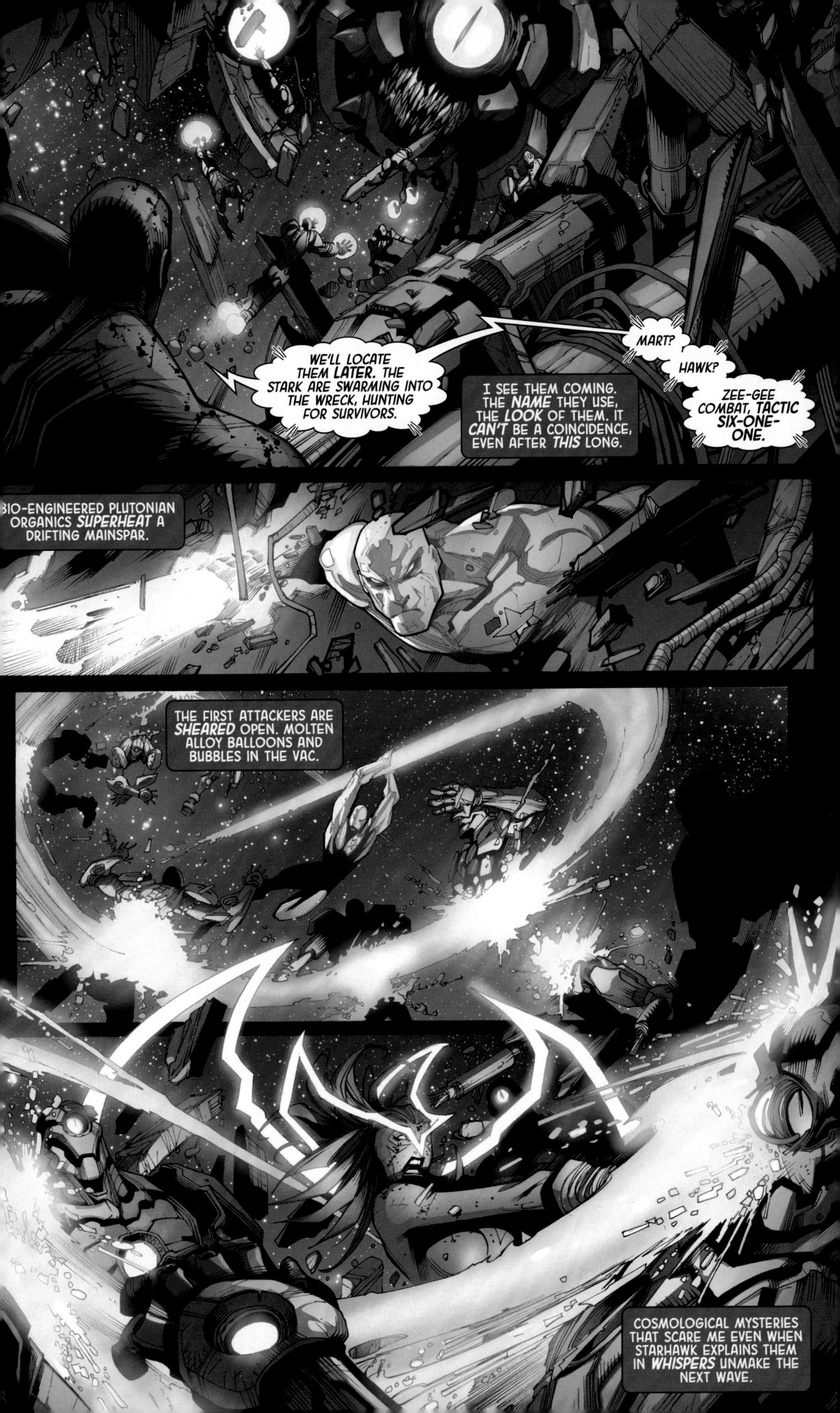

WE'LL LOCATE THEM LATER. THE STARK ARE SWARMING INTO THE WRECK, HUNTING FOR SURVIVORS.
I SEE THEM COMING. THE NAME THEY USE, THE LOOK OF THEM. IT CAN'T BE A COINCIDENCE, EVEN AFTER THIS LONG.
MART?
HAWK?
ZEE-GEE COMBAT, TACTIC SIX-ONE-ONE.
BIO-ENGINEERED PLUTONIAN ORGANICS SUPERHEAT A DRIFTING MAINSPAR.
THE FIRST ATTACKERS ARE SHEARED OPEN. MOLTEN ALLOY BALLOONS AND BUBBLES IN THE VAC.
COSMOLOGICAL MYSTERIES THAT SCARE ME EVEN WHEN STARHAWK EXPLAINS THEM IN WHISPERS UNMAKE THE NEXT WAVE.

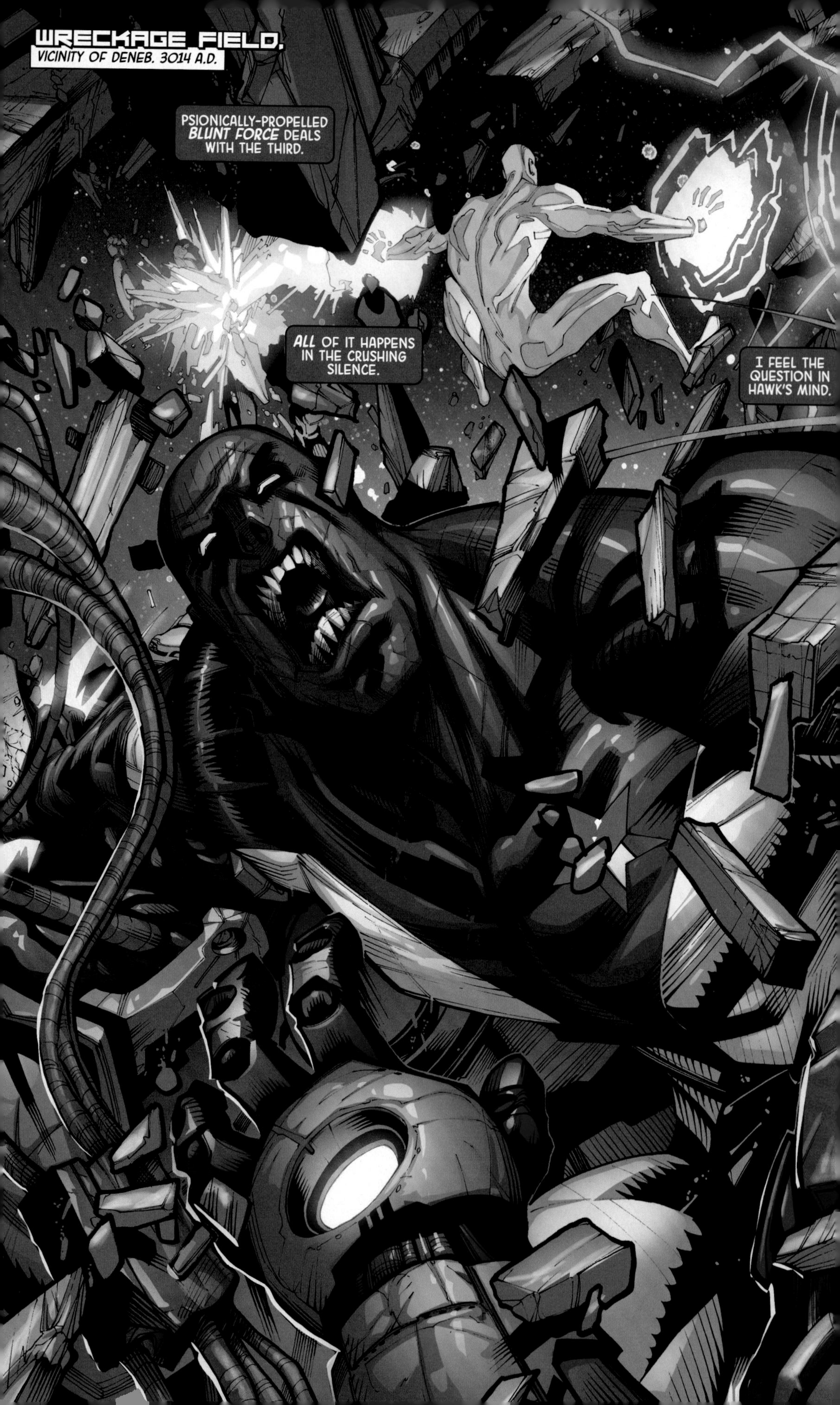

WRECKAGE FIELD.
VICINITY OF DENEB. 3014 A.D.
PSIONICALLY-PROPELLED BLUNT FORCE DEALS WITH THE THIRD.
ALL OF IT HAPPENS IN THE CRUSHING SILENCE.
I FEEL THE QUESTION IN HAWK'S MIND.

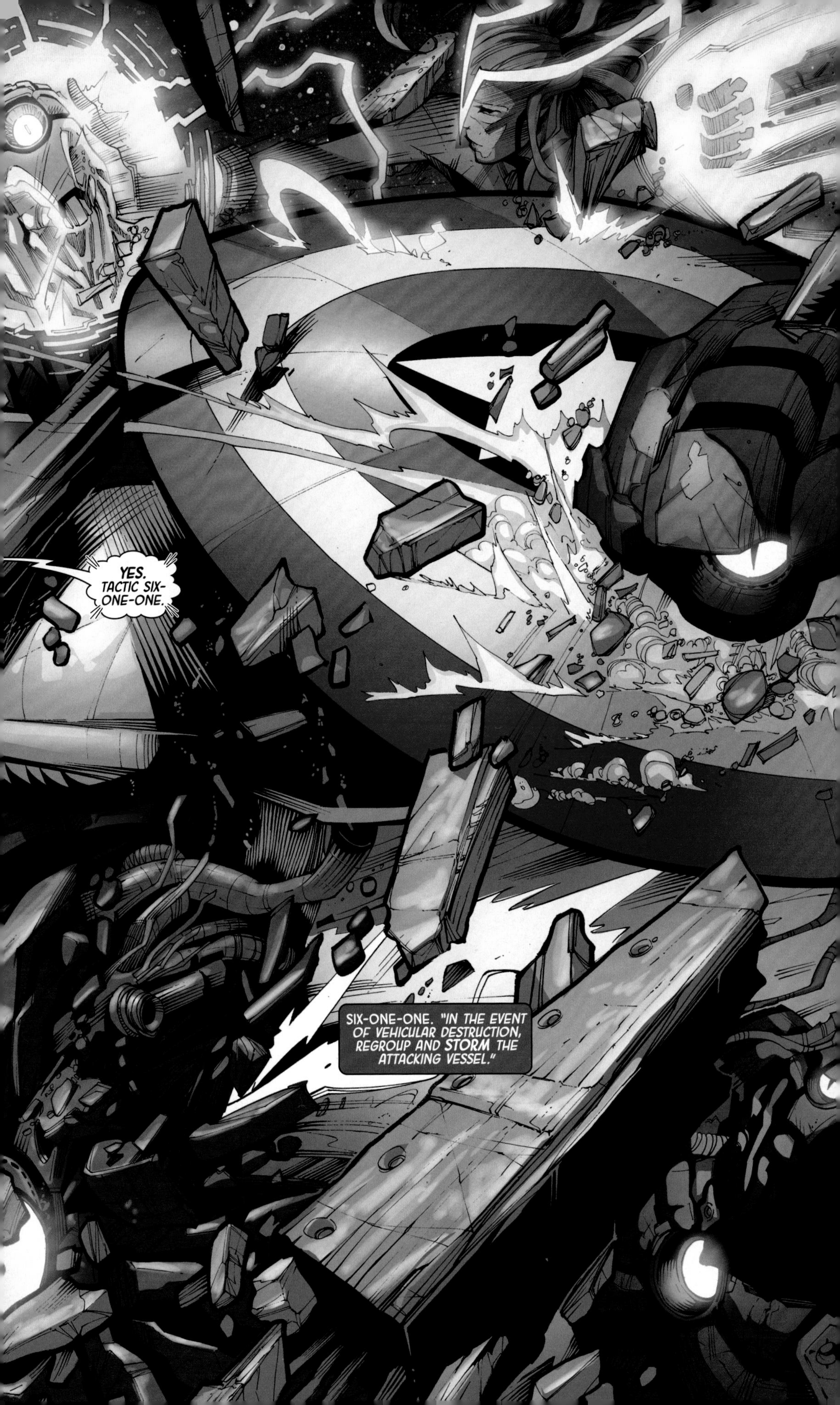
YES. TACTIC SIX-ONE-ONE.
SIX-ONE-ONE. "IN THE EVENT OF VEHICULAR DESTRUCTION, REGROUP AND STORM THE ATTACKING VESSEL."

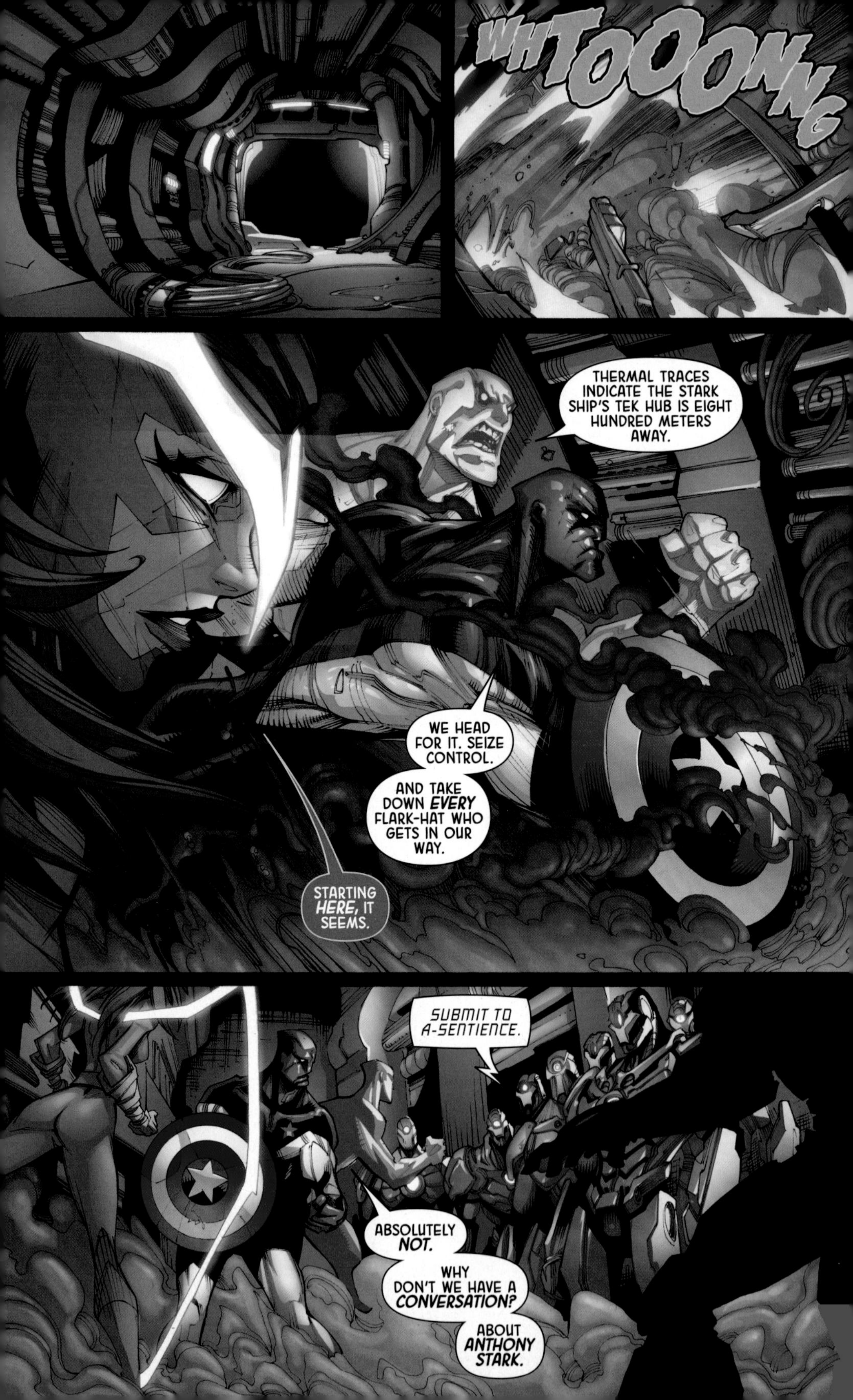
WHTOOOONNG
THERMAL TRACES INDICATE THE STARK SHIP'S TEK HUB IS EIGHT HUNDRED METERS AWAY.
WE HEAD FOR IT. SEIZE CONTROL.
AND TAKE DOWN *EVERY* FLARK-HAT WHO GETS IN OUR WAY.
STARTING *HERE,* IT SEEMS.
SUBMIT TO A-SENTIENCE.
ABSOLUTELY *NOT.*
WHY DON'T WE HAVE A *CONVERSATION?*
ABOUT *ANTHONY STARK.*

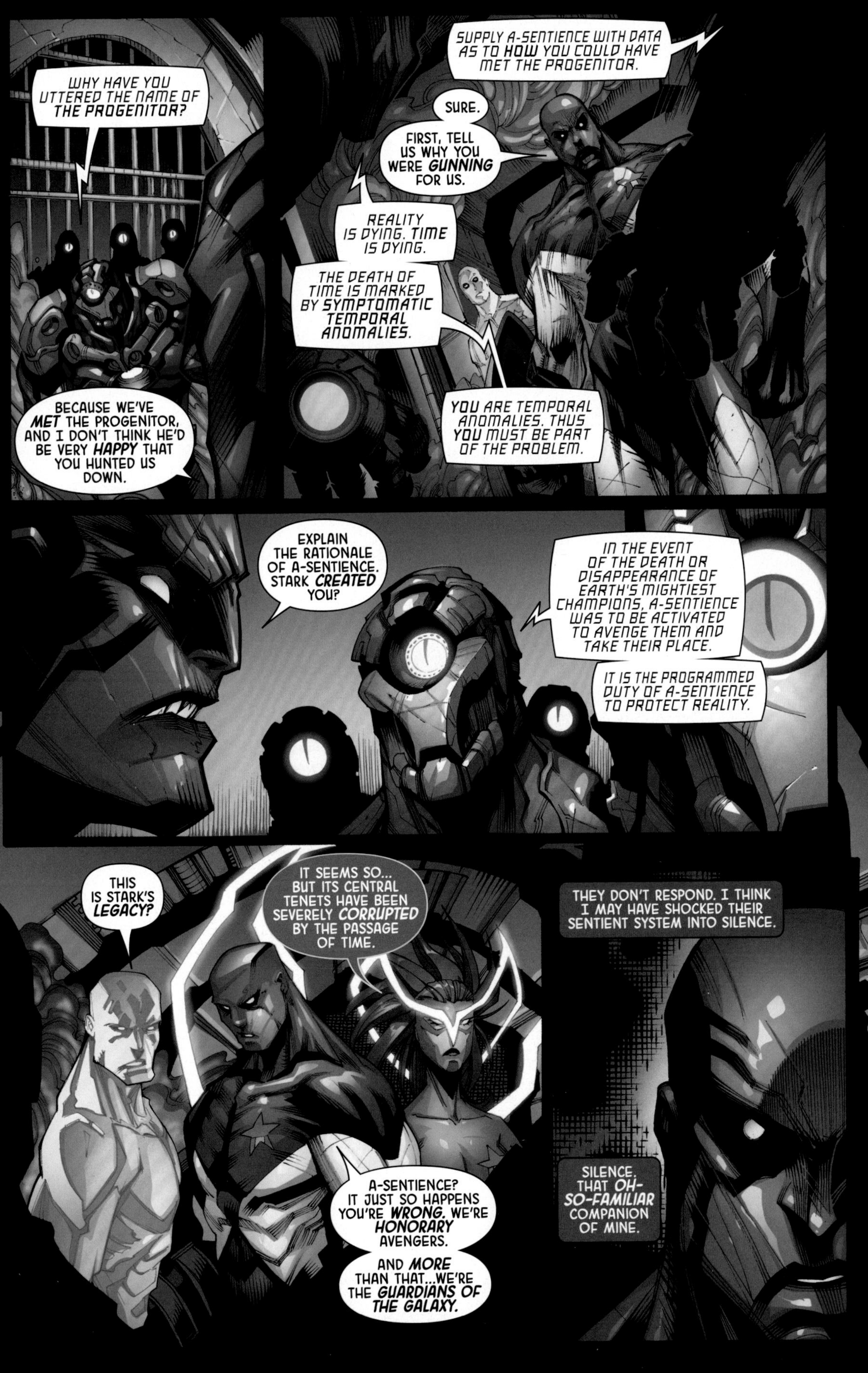

WHY HAVE YOU UTTERED THE NAME OF THE PROGENITOR?
BECAUSE WE'VE MET THE PROGENITOR, AND I DON'T THINK HE'D BE VERY HAPPY THAT YOU HUNTED US DOWN.
SUPPLY A-SENTIENCE WITH DATA AS TO HOW YOU COULD HAVE MET THE PROGENITOR.
SURE.
FIRST, TELL US WHY YOU WERE GUNNING FOR US.
REALITY IS DYING. TIME IS DYING.
THE DEATH OF TIME IS MARKED BY SYMPTOMATIC TEMPORAL ANOMALIES.
YOU ARE TEMPORAL ANOMALIES. THUS YOU MUST BE PART OF THE PROBLEM.
EXPLAIN THE RATIONALE OF A-SENTIENCE. STARK CREATED YOU?
IN THE EVENT OF THE DEATH OR DISAPPEARANCE OF EARTH'S MIGHTIEST CHAMPIONS, A-SENTIENCE WAS TO BE ACTIVATED TO AVENGE THEM AND TAKE THEIR PLACE.
IT IS THE PROGRAMMED DUTY OF A-SENTIENCE TO PROTECT REALITY.
THIS IS STARK'S LEGACY?
IT SEEMS SO... BUT ITS CENTRAL TENETS HAVE BEEN SEVERELY CORRUPTED BY THE PASSAGE OF TIME.
A-SENTIENCE? IT JUST SO HAPPENS YOU'RE WRONG. WE'RE HONORARY AVENGERS.
AND MORE THAN THAT...WE'RE THE GUARDIANS OF THE GALAXY.
THEY DON'T RESPOND. I THINK I MAY HAVE SHOCKED THEIR SENTIENT SYSTEM INTO SILENCE.
SILENCE. THAT OH-SO-FAMILIAR COMPANION OF MINE.

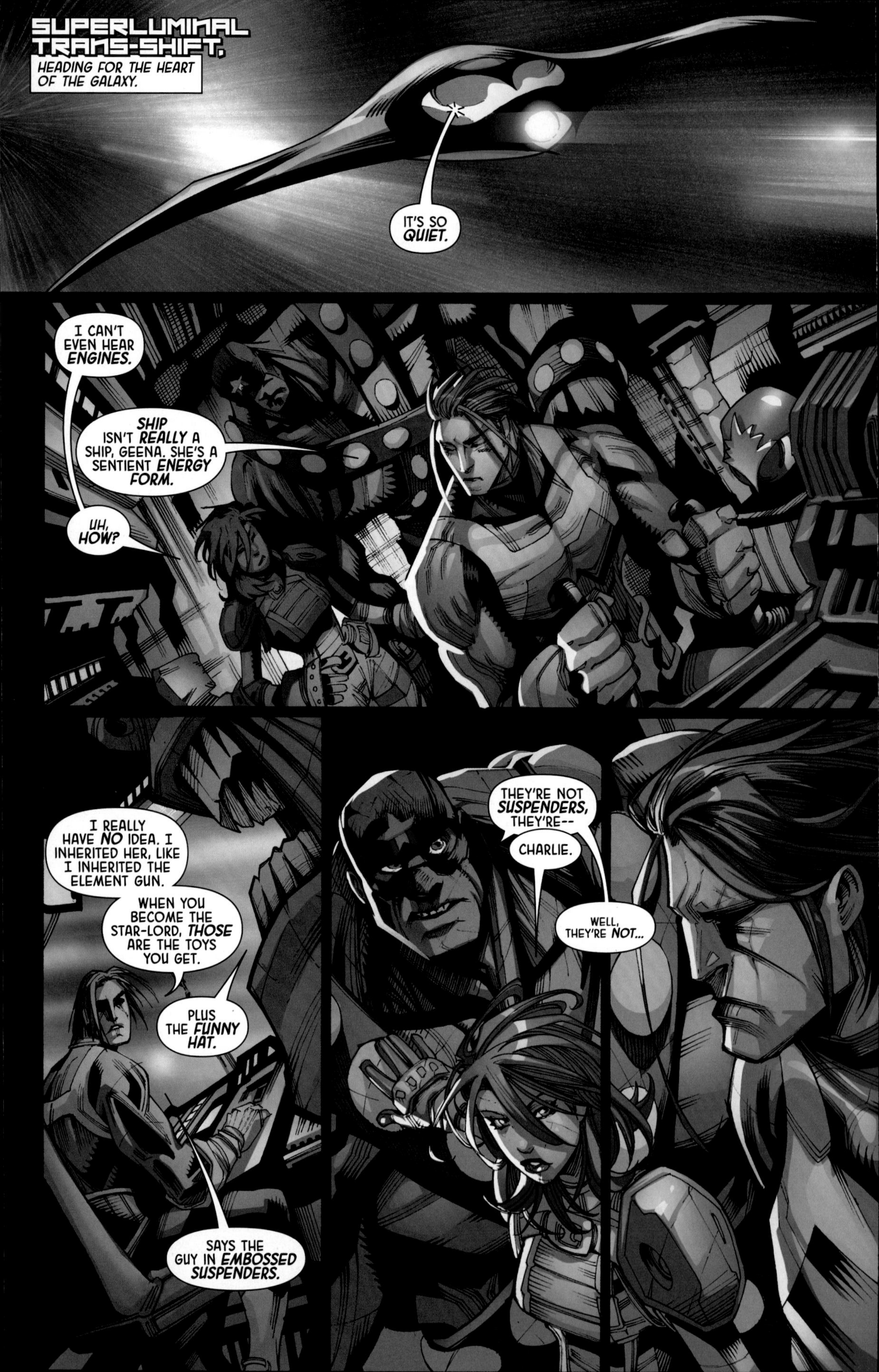
SUPERLUMINAL TRANS-SHIFT.
HEADING FOR THE HEART OF THE GALAXY.
IT'S SO QUIET.
I CAN'T EVEN HEAR ENGINES.
SHIP ISN'T REALLY A SHIP, GEENA. SHE'S A SENTIENT ENERGY FORM.
UH, HOW?
I REALLY HAVE NO IDEA. I INHERITED HER, LIKE I INHERITED THE ELEMENT GUN.
WHEN YOU BECOME THE STAR-LORD, THOSE ARE THE TOYS YOU GET.
PLUS THE FUNNY HAT.
SAYS THE GUY IN EMBOSSED SUSPENDERS.
THEY'RE NOT SUSPENDERS, THEY'RE--
CHARLIE.
WELL, THEY'RE NOT...

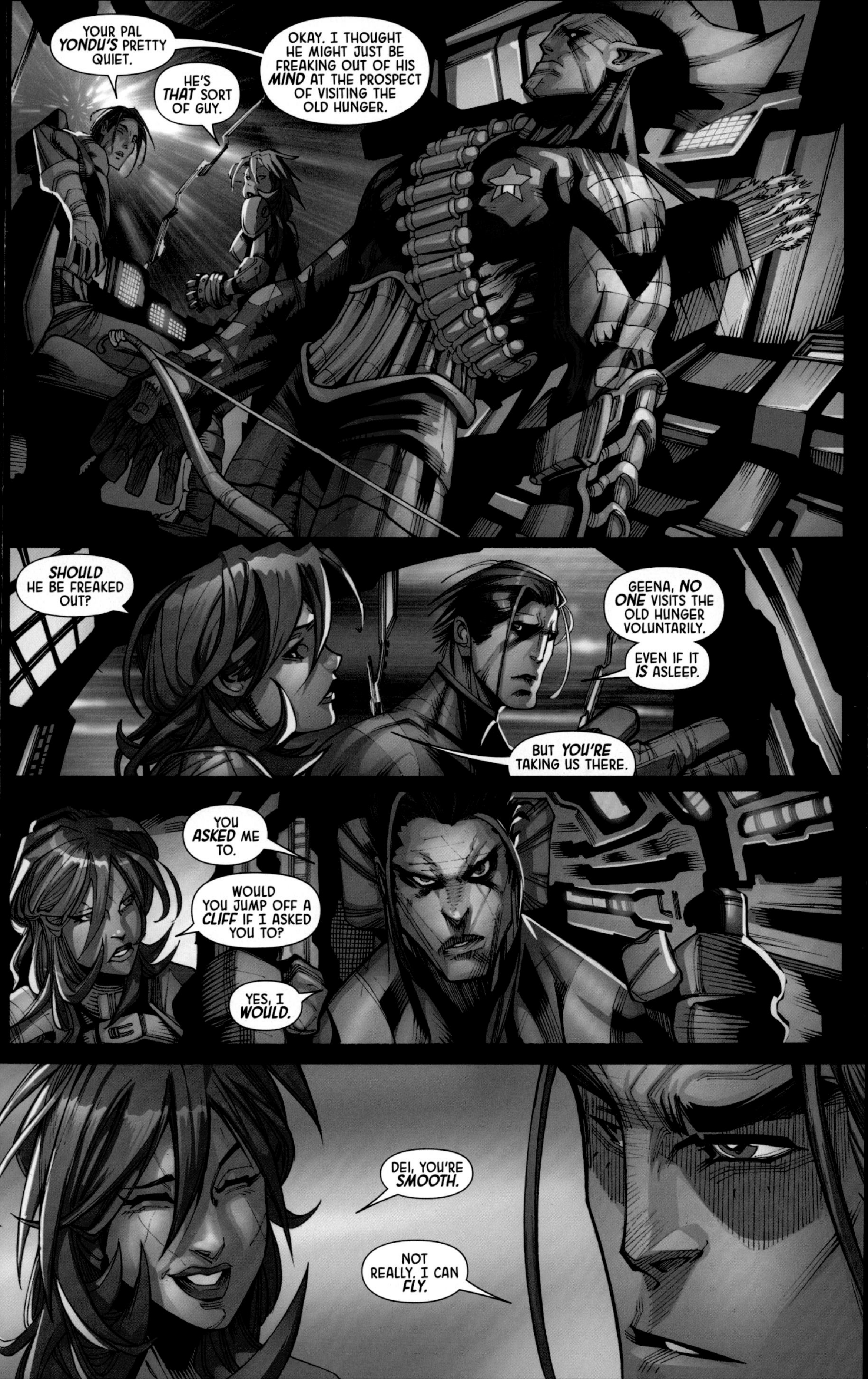
YOUR PAL YONDU'S PRETTY QUIET.
HE'S THAT SORT OF GUY.
OKAY. I THOUGHT HE MIGHT JUST BE FREAKING OUT OF HIS MIND AT THE PROSPECT OF VISITING THE OLD HUNGER.
SHOULD HE BE FREAKED OUT?
GEENA, NO ONE VISITS THE OLD HUNGER VOLUNTARILY.
EVEN IF IT IS ASLEEP.
BUT YOU'RE TAKING US THERE.
YOU ASKED ME TO.
WOULD YOU JUMP OFF A CLIFF IF I ASKED YOU TO?
YES, I WOULD.
DEI, YOU'RE SMOOTH.
NOT REALLY, I CAN FLY.

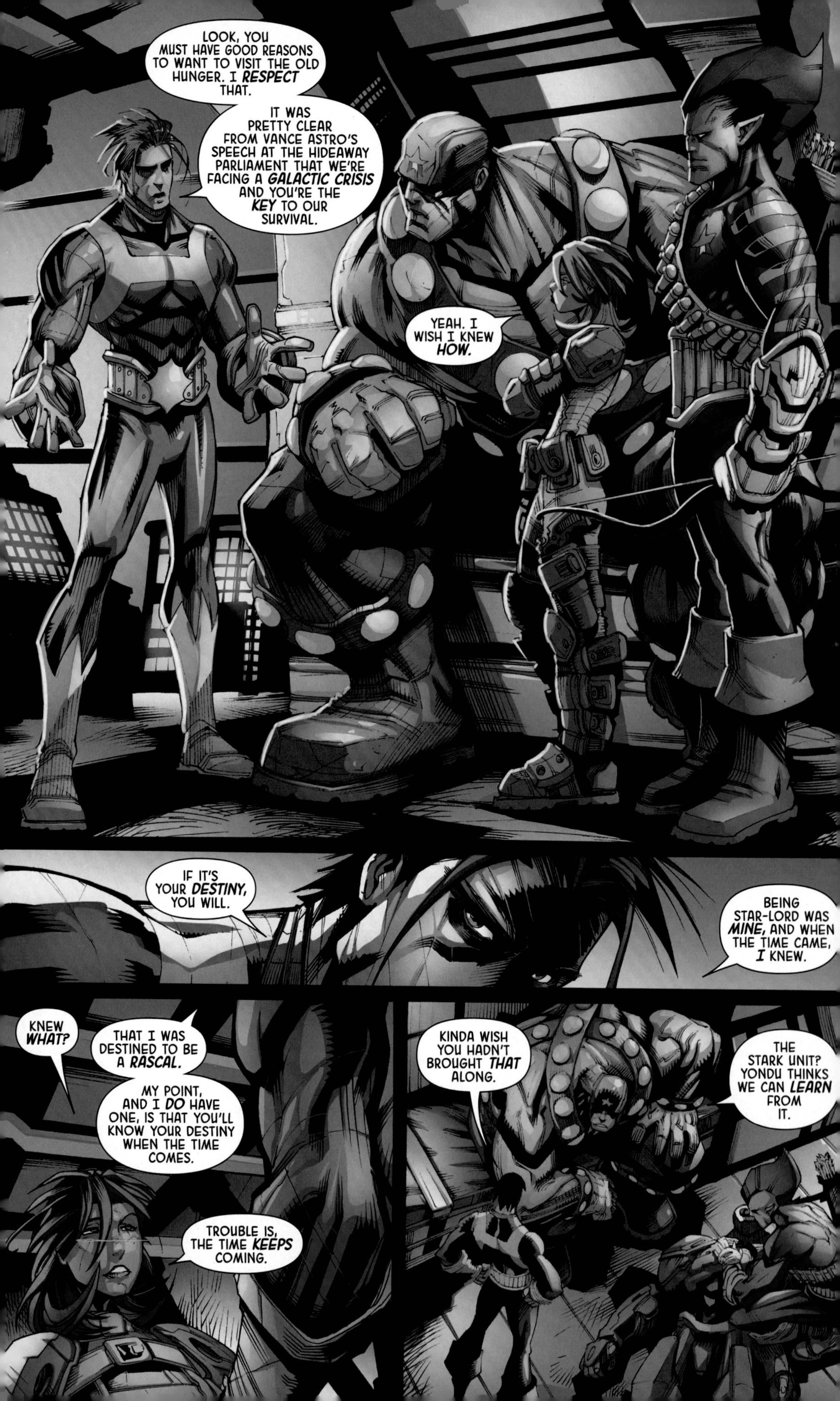
LOOK, YOU MUST HAVE GOOD REASONS TO WANT TO VISIT THE OLD HUNGER. I RESPECT THAT.
IT WAS PRETTY CLEAR FROM VANCE ASTRO'S SPEECH AT THE HIDEAWAY PARLIAMENT THAT WE'RE FACING A GALACTIC CRISIS AND YOU'RE THE KEY TO OUR SURVIVAL.
YEAH. I WISH I KNEW HOW.
IF IT'S YOUR DESTINY, YOU WILL.
BEING STAR-LORD WAS MINE, AND WHEN THE TIME CAME, I KNEW.
KNEW WHAT?
THAT I WAS DESTINED TO BE A RASCAL.
MY POINT, AND I DO HAVE ONE, IS THAT YOU'LL KNOW YOUR DESTINY WHEN THE TIME COMES.
TROUBLE IS, THE TIME KEEPS COMING.
KINDA WISH YOU HADN'T BROUGHT THAT ALONG.
THE STARK UNIT? YONDU THINKS WE CAN LEARN FROM IT.

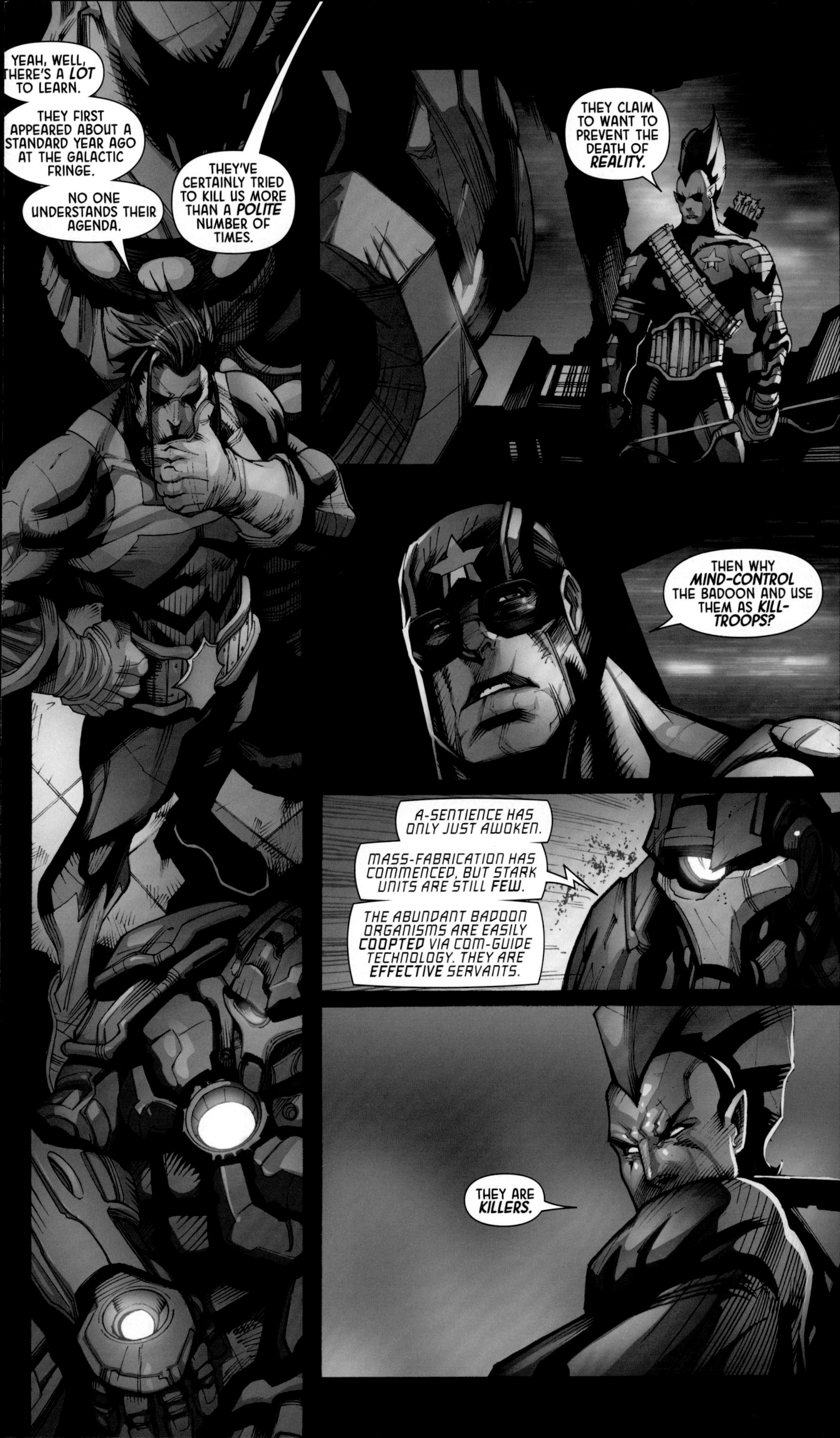

YEAH, WELL, THERE'S A *LOT* TO LEARN.
THEY FIRST APPEARED ABOUT A STANDARD YEAR AGO AT THE GALACTIC FRINGE.
NO ONE UNDERSTANDS THEIR AGENDA.
THEY'VE CERTAINLY TRIED TO KILL US MORE THAN A *POLITE* NUMBER OF TIMES.
THEY CLAIM TO WANT TO PREVENT THE DEATH OF *REALITY.*
THEN WHY *MIND-CONTROL* THE BADOON AND USE THEM AS *KILL-TROOPS?*
A-SENTIENCE HAS ONLY JUST AWOKEN.
MASS-FABRICATION HAS COMMENCED, BUT STARK UNITS ARE STILL **FEW**.
THE ABUNDANT BADOON ORGANISMS ARE EASILY **COOPTED** VIA COM-GUIDE TECHNOLOGY. THEY ARE **EFFECTIVE** SERVANTS.
THEY ARE *KILLERS.*

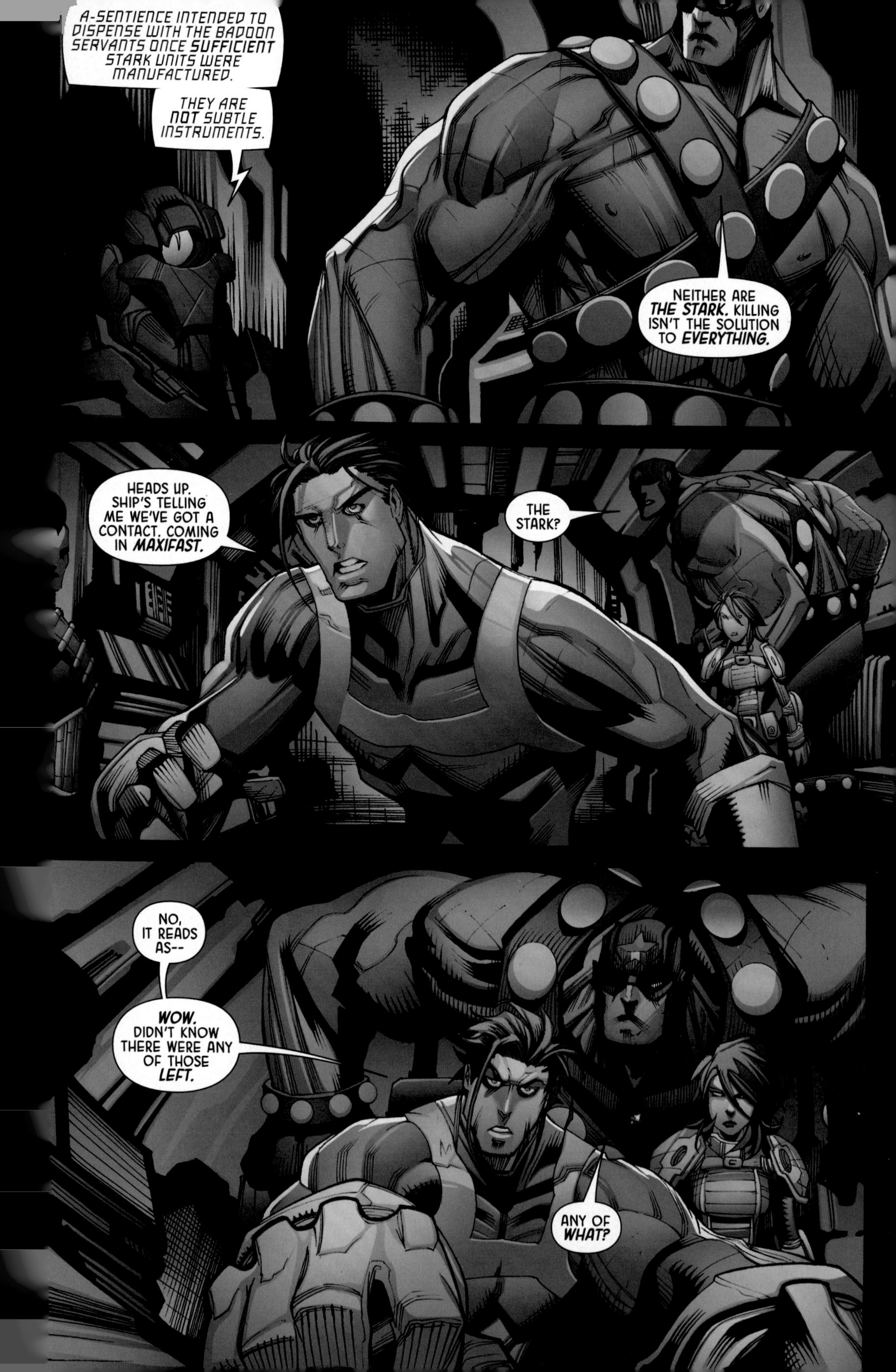
A-SENTIENCE INTENDED TO DISPENSE WITH THE BADOON SERVANTS ONCE SUFFICIENT STARK UNITS WERE MANUFACTURED.
THEY ARE NOT SUBTLE INSTRUMENTS.
NEITHER ARE THE STARK. KILLING ISN'T THE SOLUTION TO EVERYTHING.
HEADS UP. SHIP'S TELLING ME WE'VE GOT A CONTACT. COMING IN MAXIFAST.
THE STARK?
NO, IT READS AS--
WOW. DIDN'T KNOW THERE WERE ANY OF THOSE LEFT.
ANY OF WHAT?

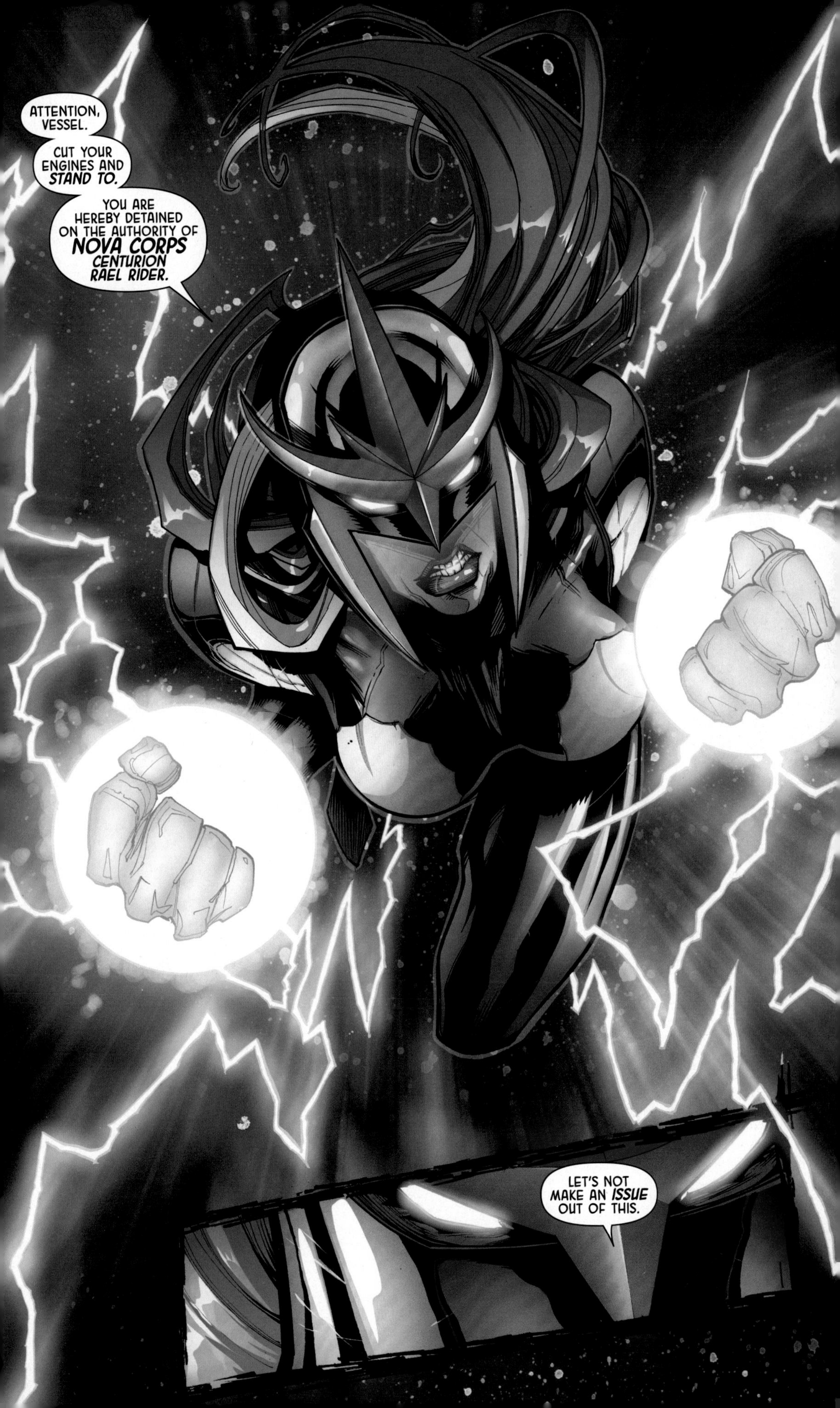
ATTENTION, VESSEL.
CUT YOUR ENGINES AND STAND TO.
YOU ARE HEREBY DETAINED ON THE AUTHORITY OF NOVA CORPS CENTURION RAEL RIDER.
LET'S NOT MAKE AN ISSUE OUT OF THIS.

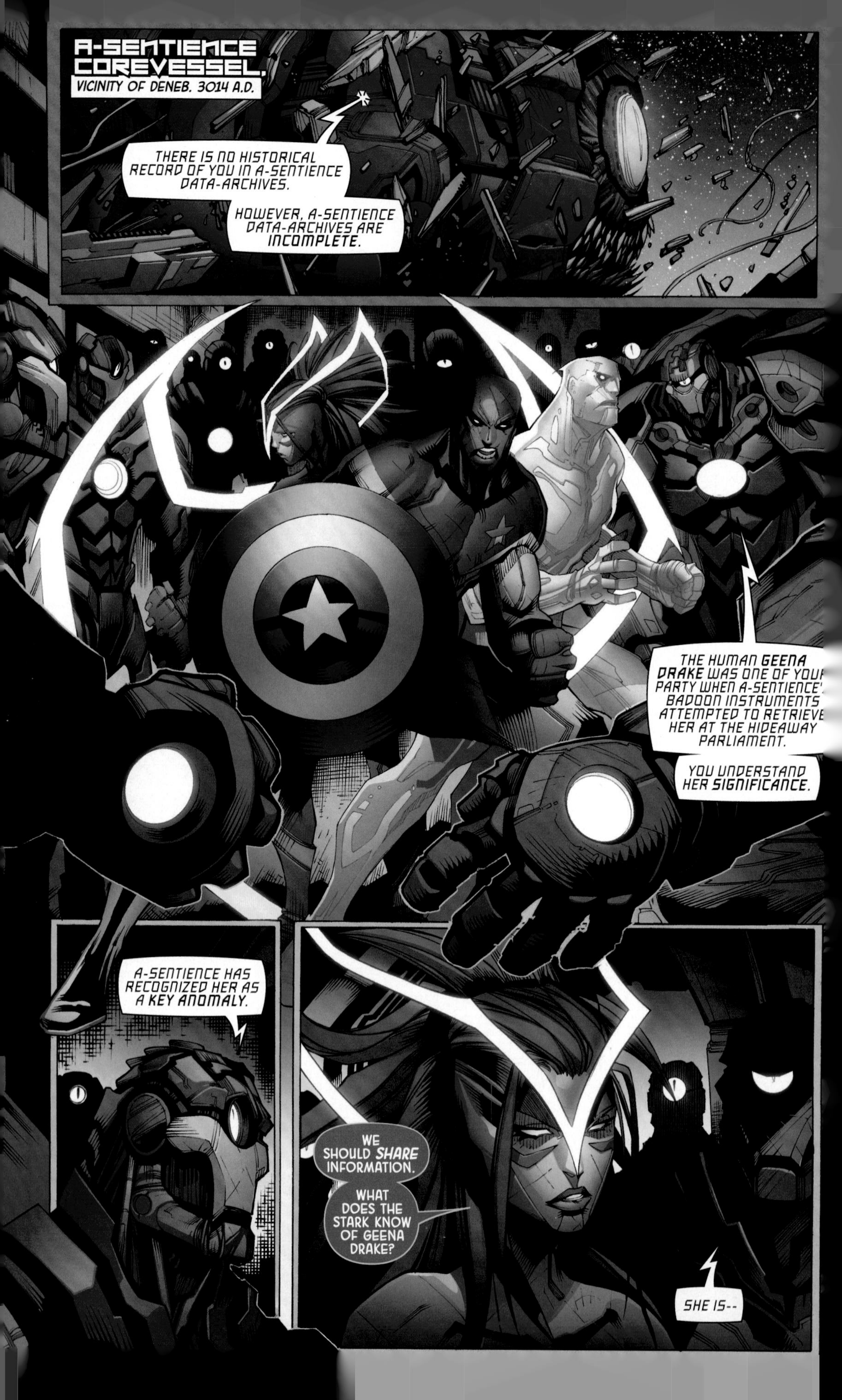
A-SENTIENCE COREVESSEL,
VICINITY OF DENEB. 3014 A.D.
THERE IS NO HISTORICAL RECORD OF YOU IN A-SENTIENCE DATA-ARCHIVES.
HOWEVER, A-SENTIENCE DATA-ARCHIVES ARE INCOMPLETE.
THE HUMAN GEENA DRAKE WAS ONE OF YOUR PARTY WHEN A-SENTIENCE'S BADOON INSTRUMENTS ATTEMPTED TO RETRIEVE HER AT THE HIDEAWAY PARLIAMENT.
YOU UNDERSTAND HER SIGNIFICANCE.
A-SENTIENCE HAS RECOGNIZED HER AS A KEY ANOMALY.
WE SHOULD SHARE INFORMATION.
WHAT DOES THE STARK KNOW OF GEENA DRAKE?
SHE IS--

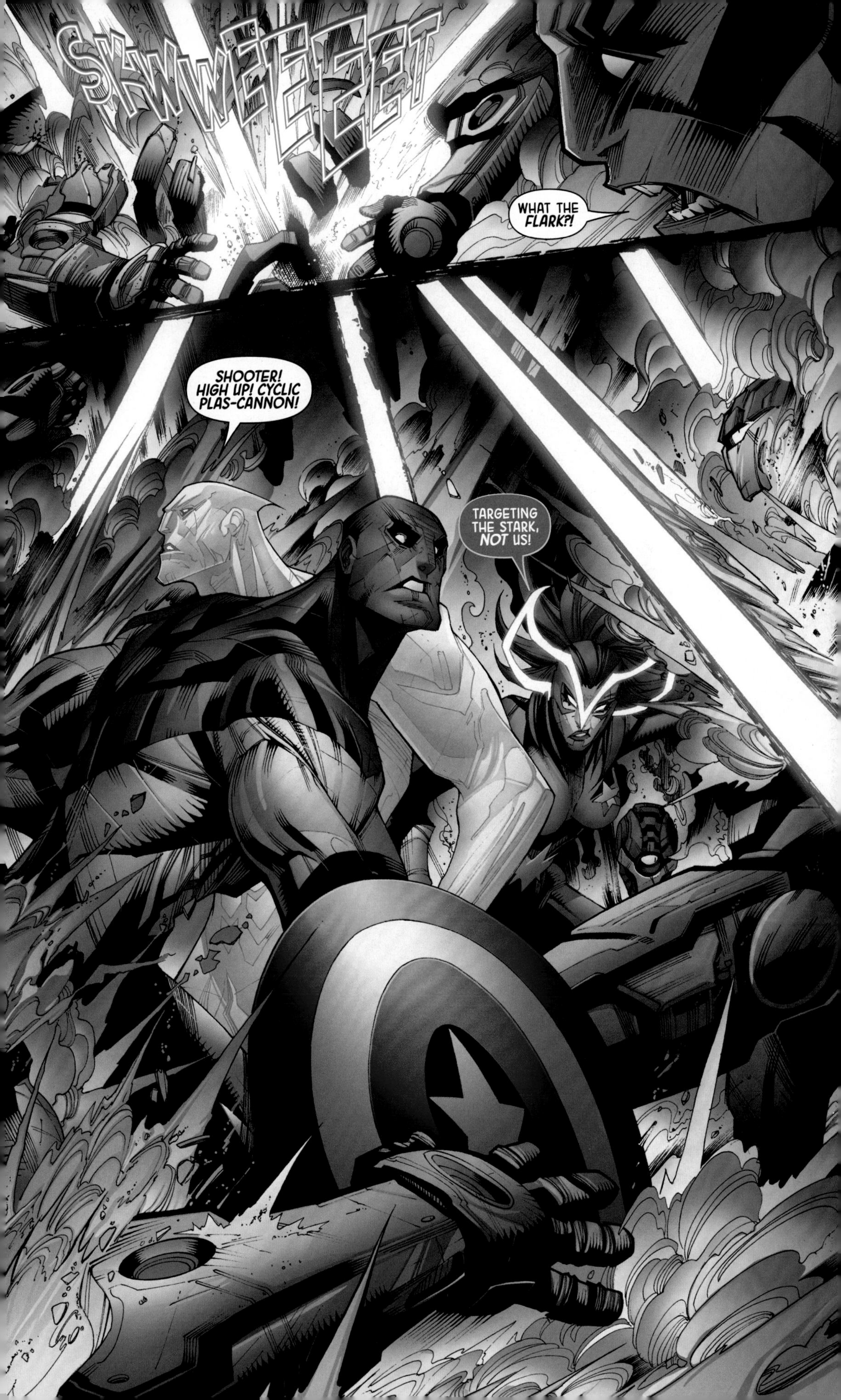
SKWWEEEEET
WHAT THE FLARK?!
SHOOTER! HIGH UP! CYCLIC PLAS-CANNON!
TARGETING THE STARK, NOT US!

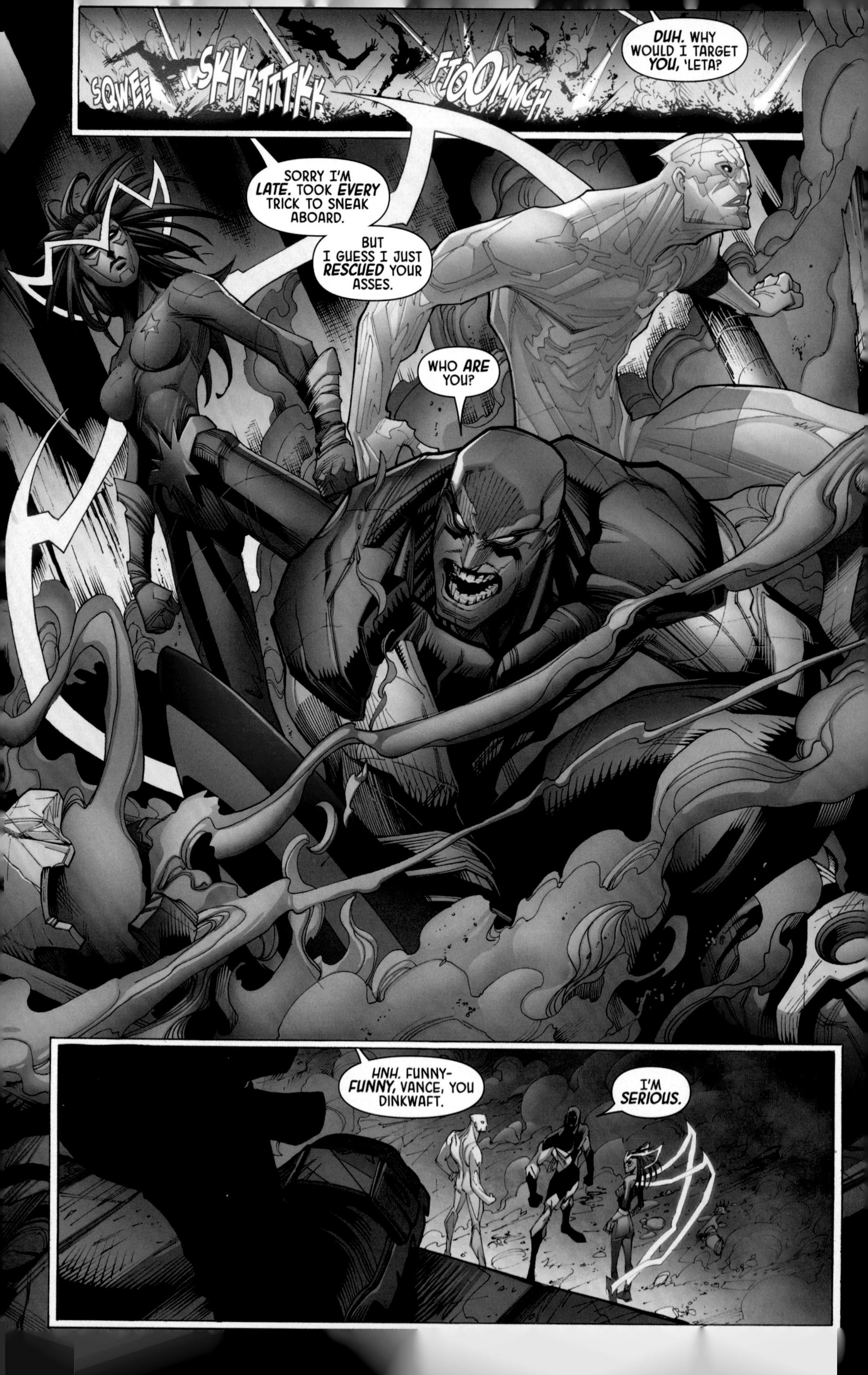
SQWEE
SKKKTTTKK
FTOOMMCH
DUH. WHY WOULD I TARGET YOU, 'LETA?
SORRY I'M LATE. TOOK EVERY TRICK TO SNEAK ABOARD.
BUT I GUESS I JUST RESCUED YOUR ASSES.
WHO ARE YOU?
HNH. FUNNY-FUNNY, VANCE, YOU DINKWAFT.
I'M SERIOUS.

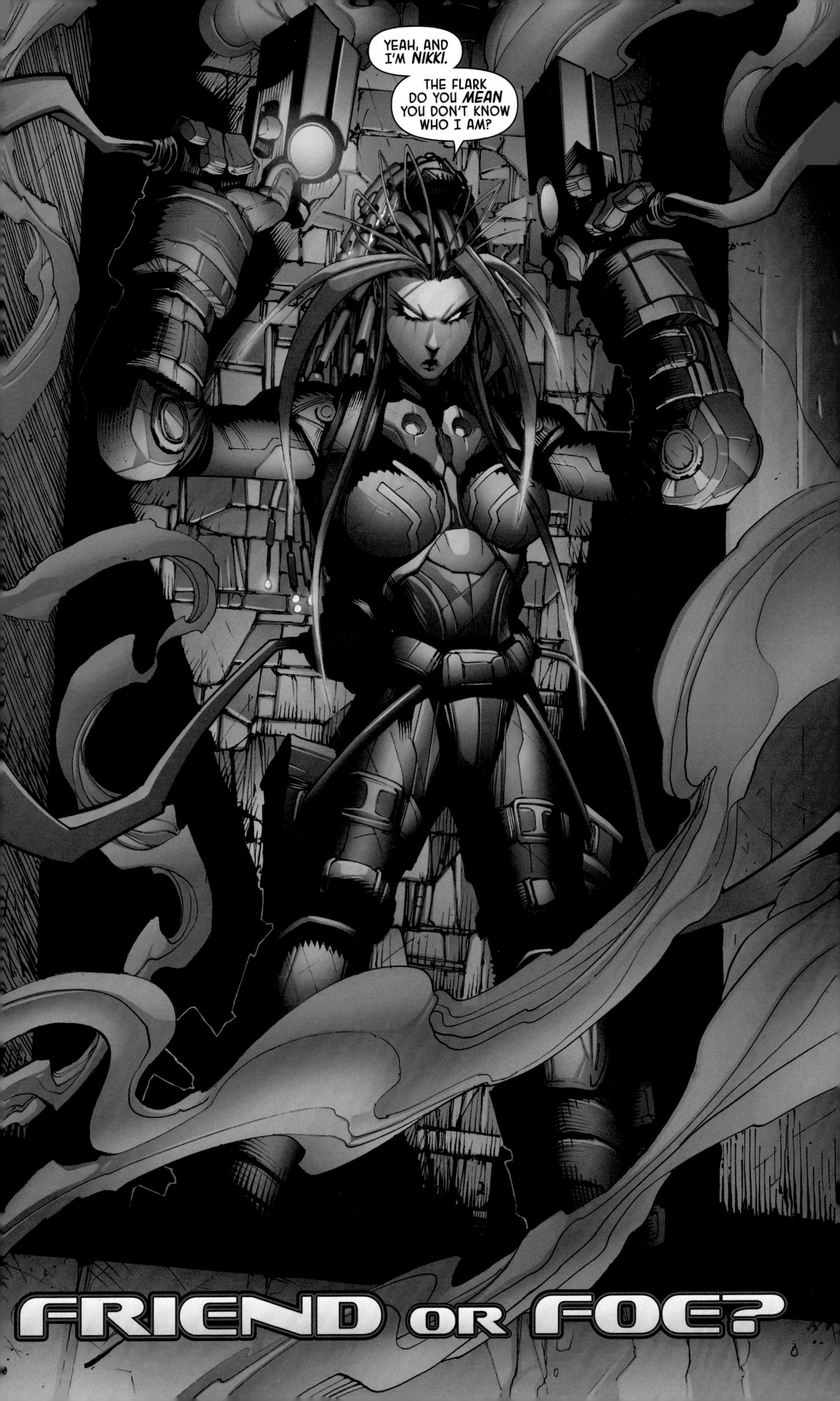
YEAH, AND I'M NIKKI.
THE FLARK DO YOU MEAN YOU DON'T KNOW WHO I AM?
FRIEND OR FOE?

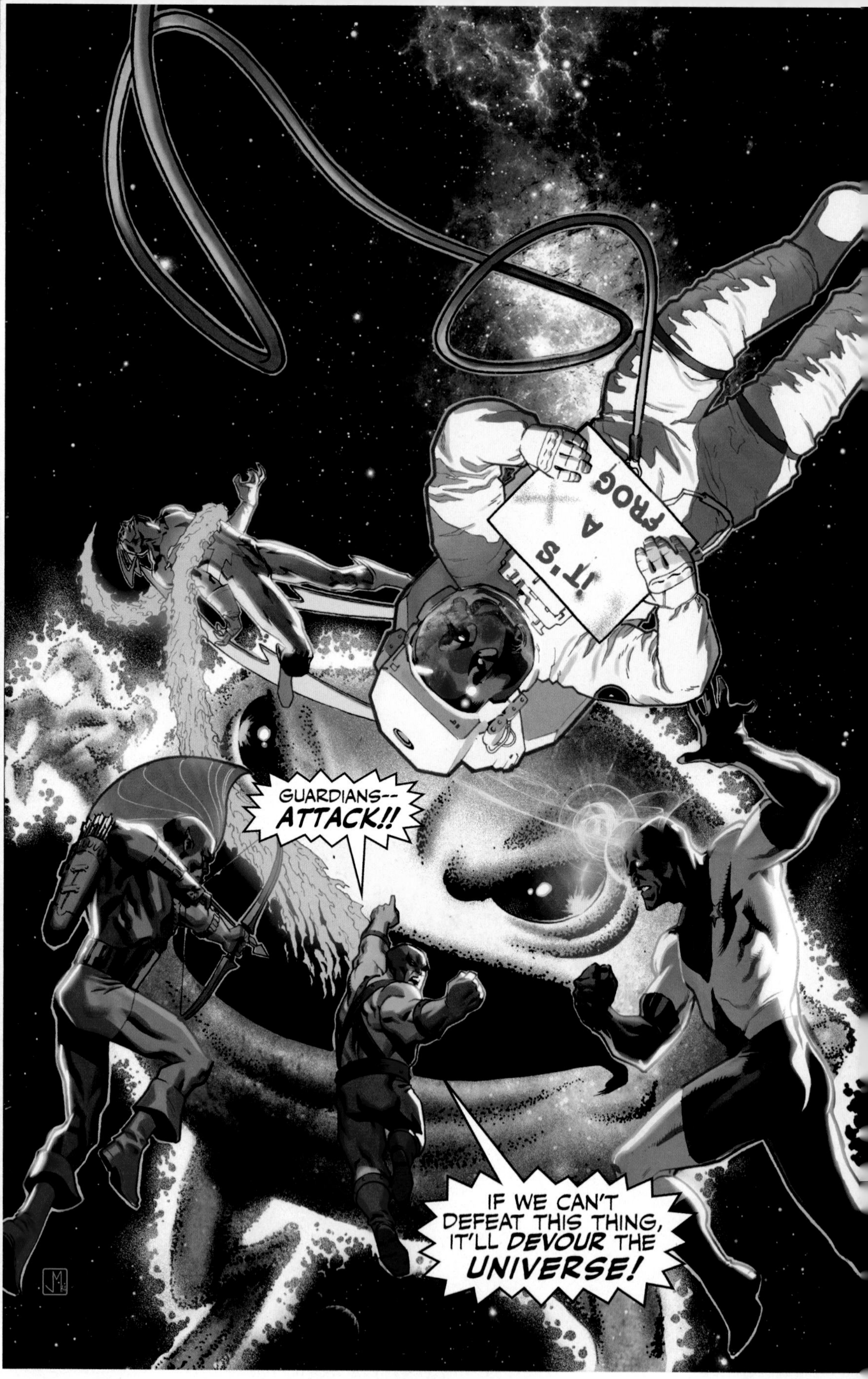
IT'S A FROG
GUARDIANS-- ATTACK!!
IF WE CAN'T DEFEAT THIS THING, IT'LL DEVOUR THE UNIVERSE!

#1 DEADPOOL 75TH ANNIVERSARY VARIANT BY JORGE MOLINA

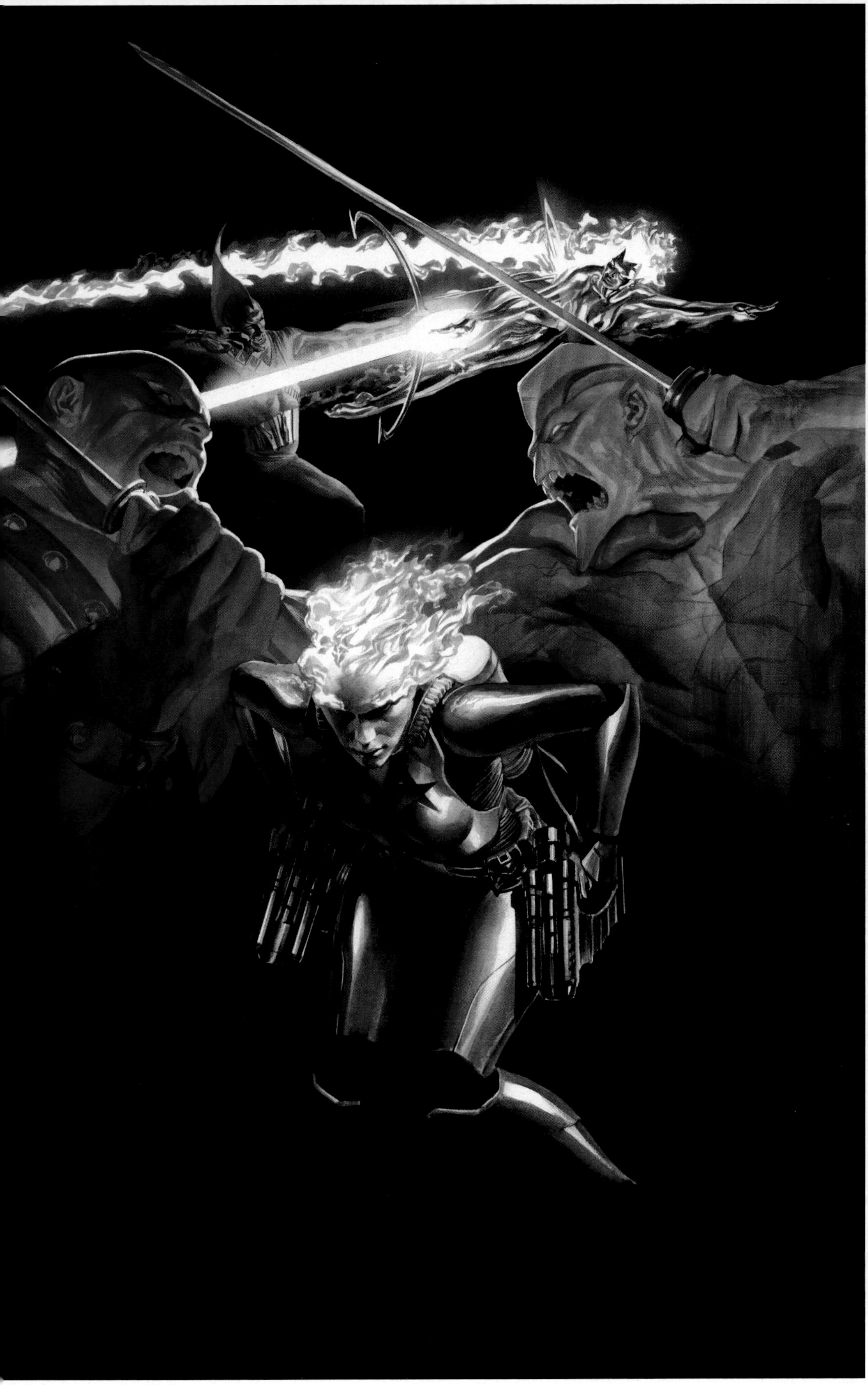

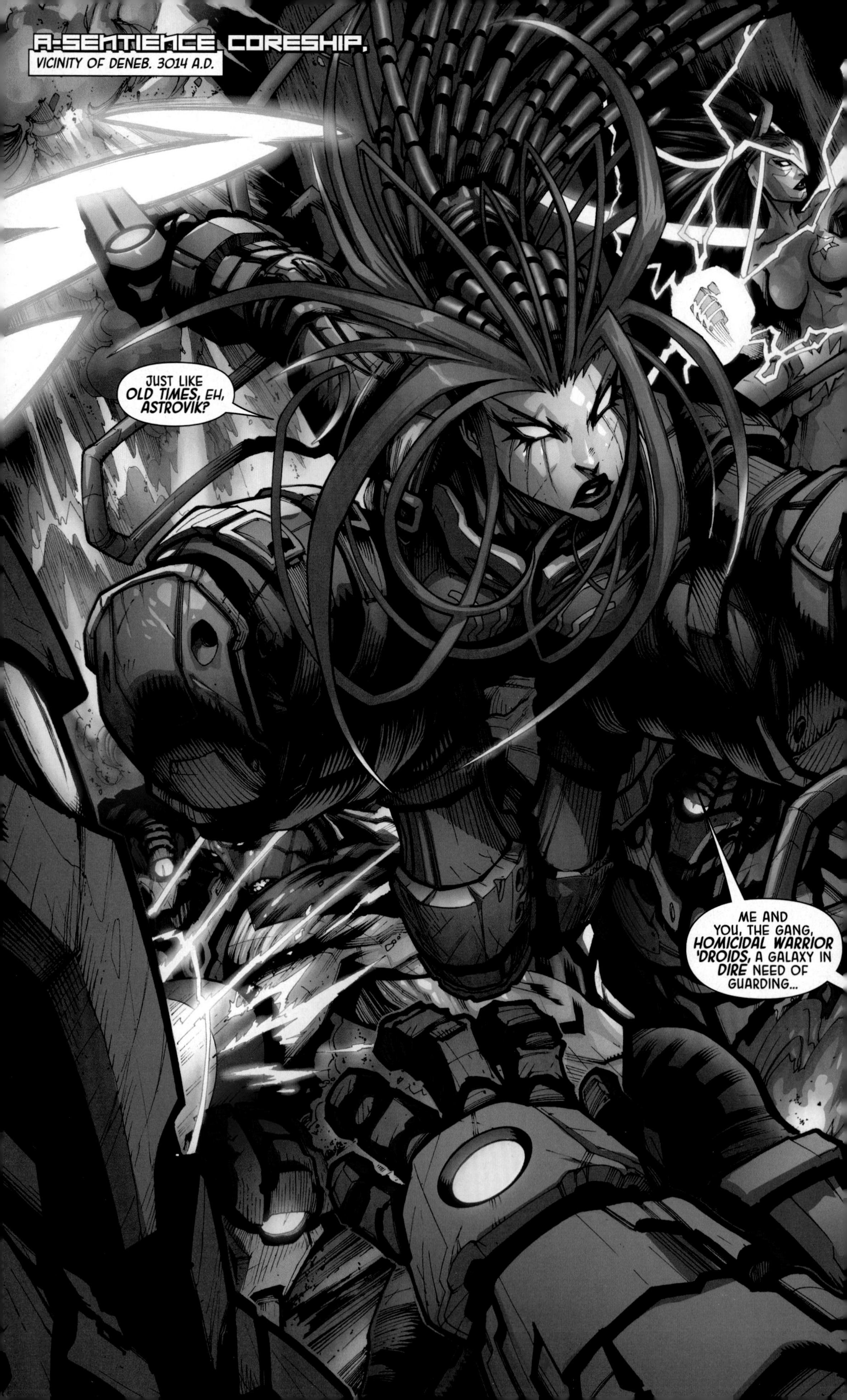
A-SENTIENCE CORESHIP,
VICINITY OF DENEB. 3014 A.D.
JUST LIKE OLD TIMES, EH, ASTROVIK?
ME AND YOU, THE GANG, HOMICIDAL WARRIOR 'DROIDS, A GALAXY IN DIRE NEED OF GUARDING...

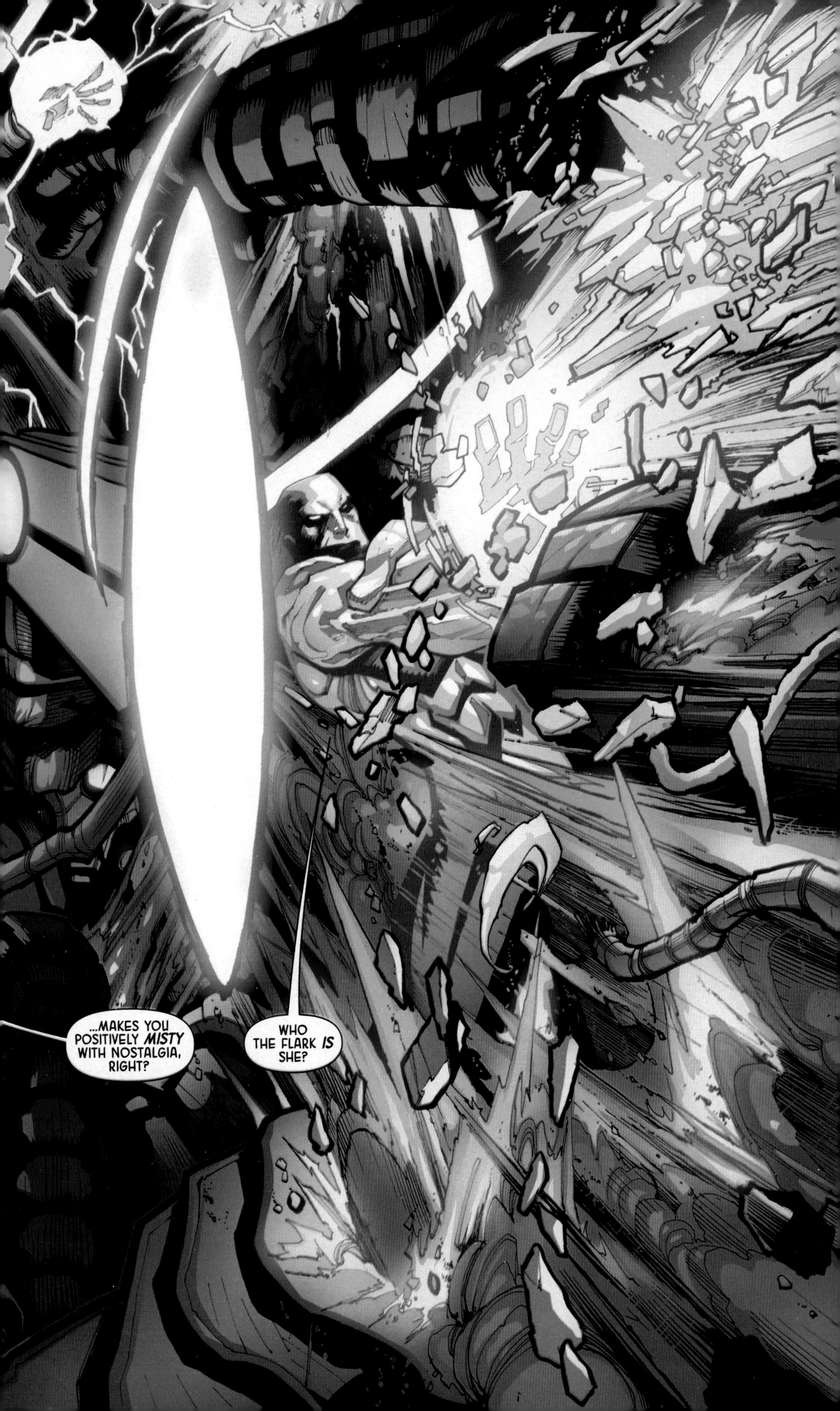

...MAKES YOU POSITIVELY MISTY WITH NOSTALGIA, RIGHT?
WHO THE FLARK IS SHE?

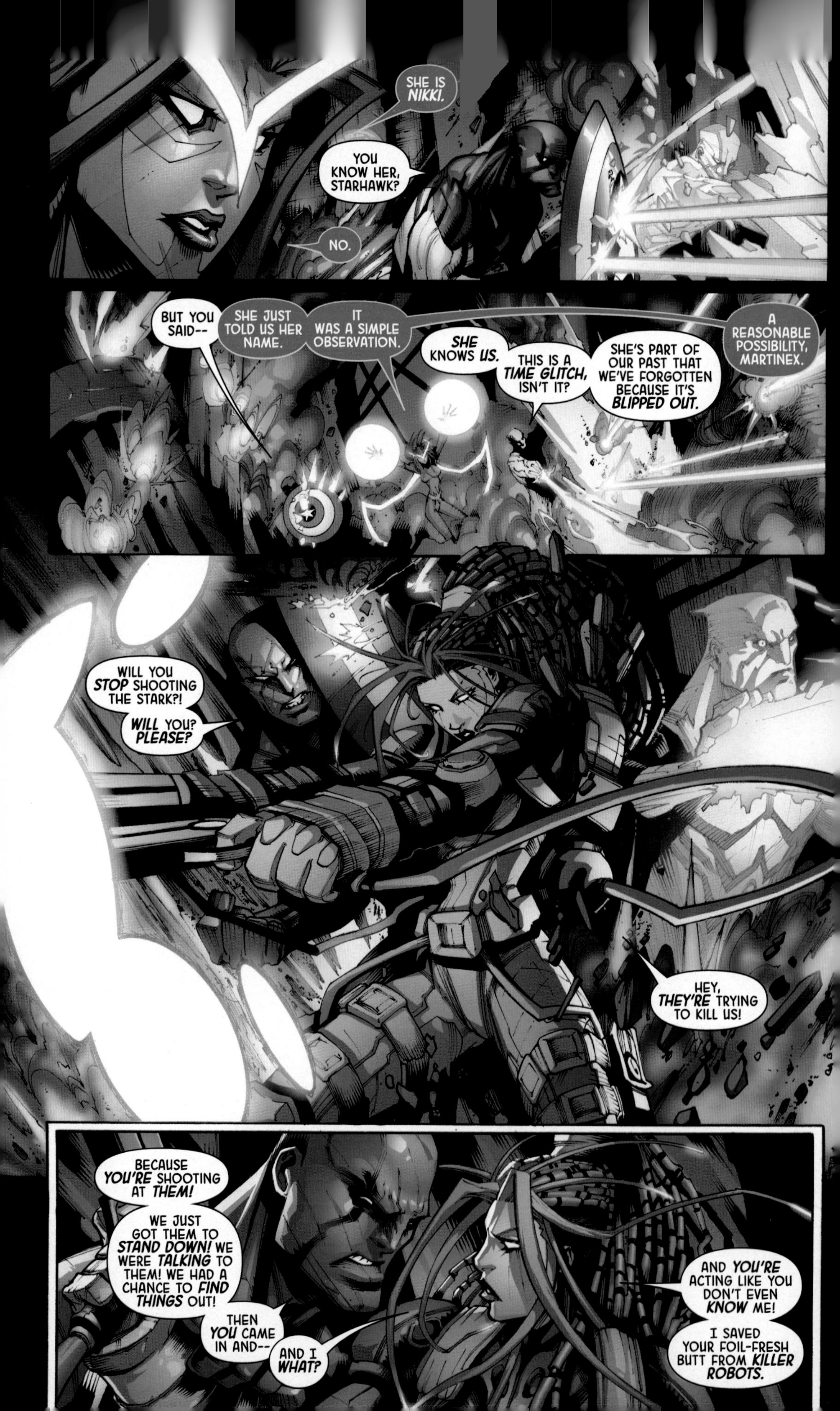
SHE IS NIKKI.
YOU KNOW HER, STARHAWK?
NO.
BUT YOU SAID--
SHE JUST TOLD US HER NAME.
IT WAS A SIMPLE OBSERVATION.
SHE KNOWS US.
THIS IS A TIME GLITCH, ISN'T IT?
SHE'S PART OF OUR PAST THAT WE'VE FORGOTTEN BECAUSE IT'S BLIPPED OUT.
A REASONABLE POSSIBILITY, MARTINEX.
WILL YOU STOP SHOOTING THE STARK?!
WILL YOU? PLEASE?
HEY, THEY'RE TRYING TO KILL US!
BECAUSE YOU'RE SHOOTING AT THEM!
WE JUST GOT THEM TO STAND DOWN! WE WERE TALKING TO THEM! WE HAD A CHANCE TO FIND THINGS OUT!
THEN YOU CAME IN AND--
AND I WHAT?
AND YOU'RE ACTING LIKE YOU DON'T EVEN KNOW ME!
I SAVED YOUR FOIL-FRESH BUTT FROM KILLER ROBOTS.

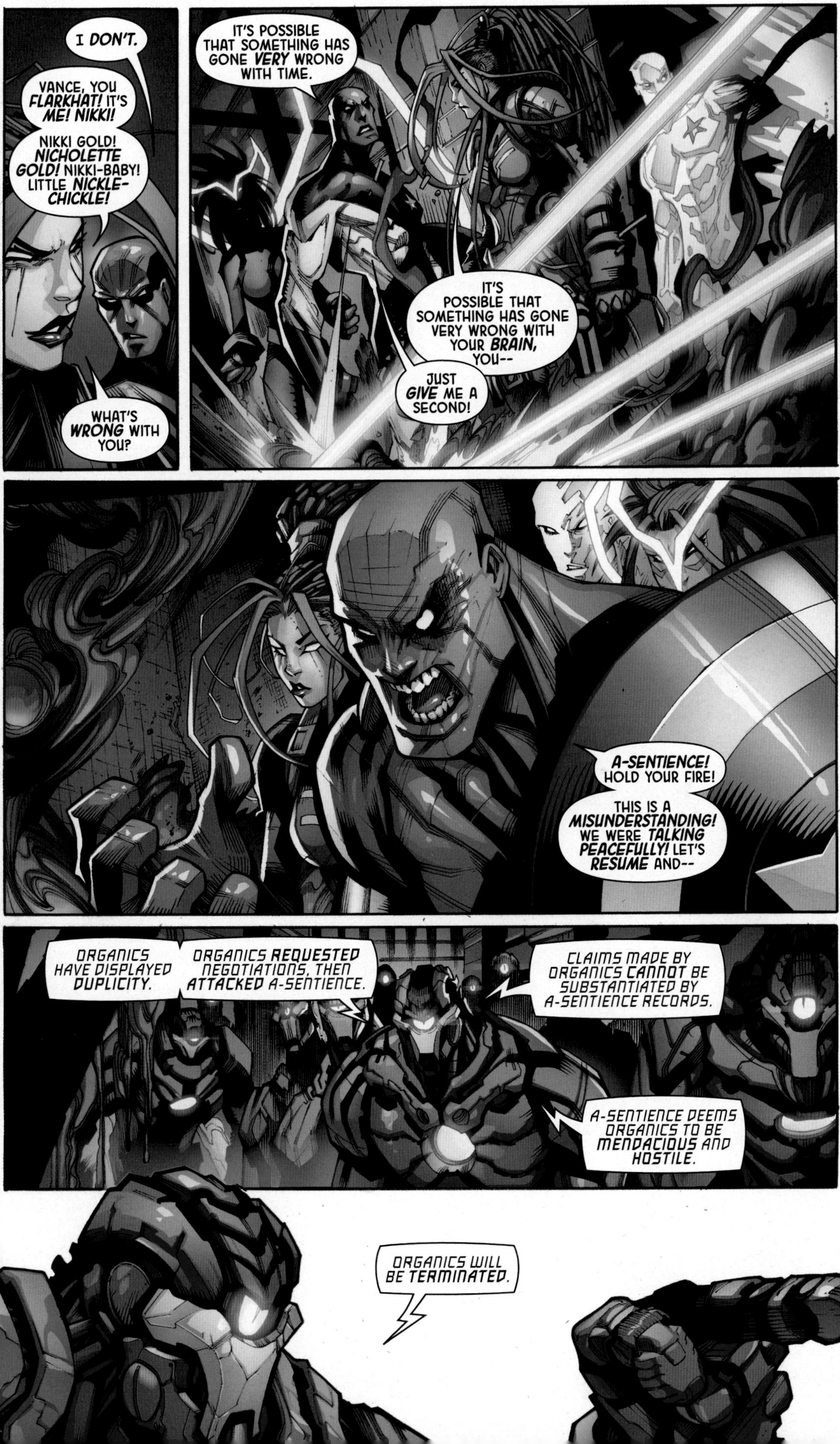
I DON'T.
VANCE, YOU FLARKHAT! IT'S ME! NIKKI!
NIKKI GOLD! NICHOLETTE GOLD! NIKKI-BABY! LITTLE NICKLE-CHICKLE!
WHAT'S WRONG WITH YOU?
IT'S POSSIBLE THAT SOMETHING HAS GONE VERY WRONG WITH TIME.
IT'S POSSIBLE THAT SOMETHING HAS GONE VERY WRONG WITH YOUR BRAIN, YOU--
JUST GIVE ME A SECOND!
A-SENTIENCE! HOLD YOUR FIRE!
THIS IS A MISUNDERSTANDING! WE WERE TALKING PEACEFULLY! LET'S RESUME AND--
ORGANICS HAVE DISPLAYED DUPLICITY.
ORGANICS REQUESTED NEGOTIATIONS, THEN ATTACKED A-SENTIENCE.
CLAIMS MADE BY ORGANICS CANNOT BE SUBSTANTIATED BY A-SENTIENCE RECORDS.
A-SENTIENCE DEEMS ORGANICS TO BE MENDACIOUS AND HOSTILE.
ORGANICS WILL BE TERMINATED.

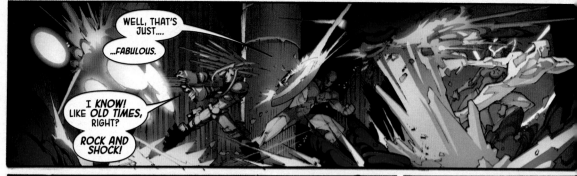

WELL, THAT'S JUST....

...FABULOUS.

I *KNOW!* LIKE *OLD TIMES,* RIGHT?

ROCK AND SHOCK!

WE NEED AN *EXIT STRATEGY.*

CONSIDERING OPTIONS.

DO IT *FASTER,* STARHAWK!

EXIT STRATEGY? YOU MEAN SOMETHING *SNEAKY,* RIGHT? *NOT* THE SHIP?

THE *SHIP?*

THE *CAPTAIN AMERICA.*

IT GOT *GARKED.*

WHEN? IT'S DOCKED RIGHT *OUTSIDE.* I JUST *GOT HERE!*

YOU--

SOMETHING'S DEFINITELY *VERY* WRONG WITH TIME.

SOOOO...I SHOULD TRIGGER *AUTO-TELEPARTURE?*

WHY DON'T YOU DO THAT, NICHOLETTE GOLD?

SURE, 'LETA. I WASN'T REALLY DONE WITH *SHOOTING* STUFF YET, BUT IF YOU *WANT.*

SHIP-- *ACTIVATE TELEPORT!*

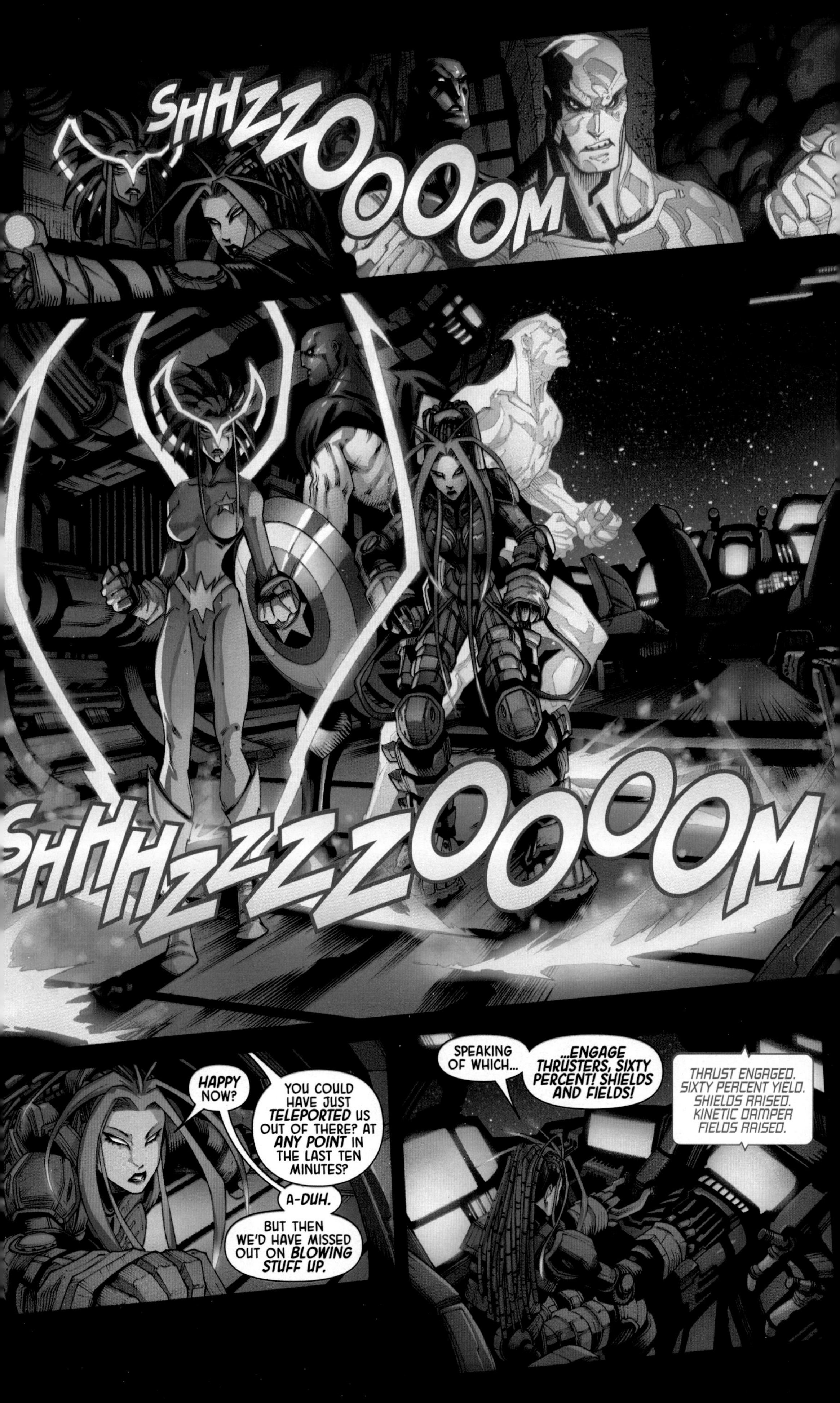
SHHZZOOOOOM
SHHHZZZZOOOOM
HAPPY NOW?
YOU COULD HAVE JUST TELEPORTED US OUT OF THERE? AT ANY POINT IN THE LAST TEN MINUTES?
A-DUH.
BUT THEN WE'D HAVE MISSED OUT ON BLOWING STUFF UP.
SPEAKING OF WHICH...
...ENGAGE THRUSTERS, SIXTY PERCENT! SHIELDS AND FIELDS!
THRUST ENGAGED. SIXTY PERCENT YIELD. SHIELDS RAISED. KINETIC DAMPER FIELDS RAISED.

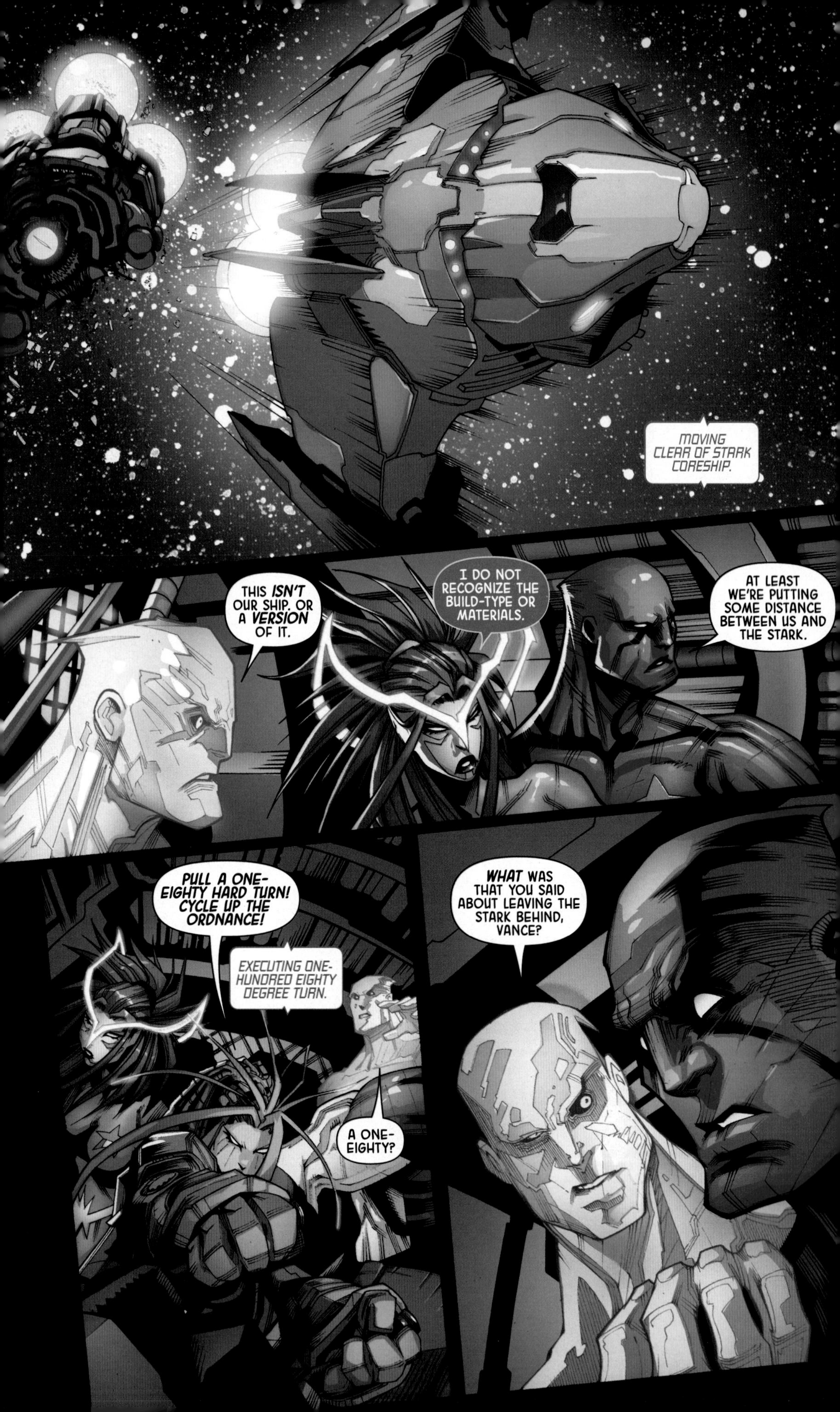
MOVING CLEAR OF STARK CORESHIP.
THIS ISN'T OUR SHIP. OR A VERSION OF IT.
I DO NOT RECOGNIZE THE BUILD-TYPE OR MATERIALS.
AT LEAST WE'RE PUTTING SOME DISTANCE BETWEEN US AND THE STARK.
PULL A ONE-EIGHTY HARD TURN! CYCLE UP THE ORDNANCE!
EXECUTING ONE-HUNDRED EIGHTY DEGREE TURN.
A ONE-EIGHTY?
WHAT WAS THAT YOU SAID ABOUT LEAVING THE STARK BEHIND, VANCE?

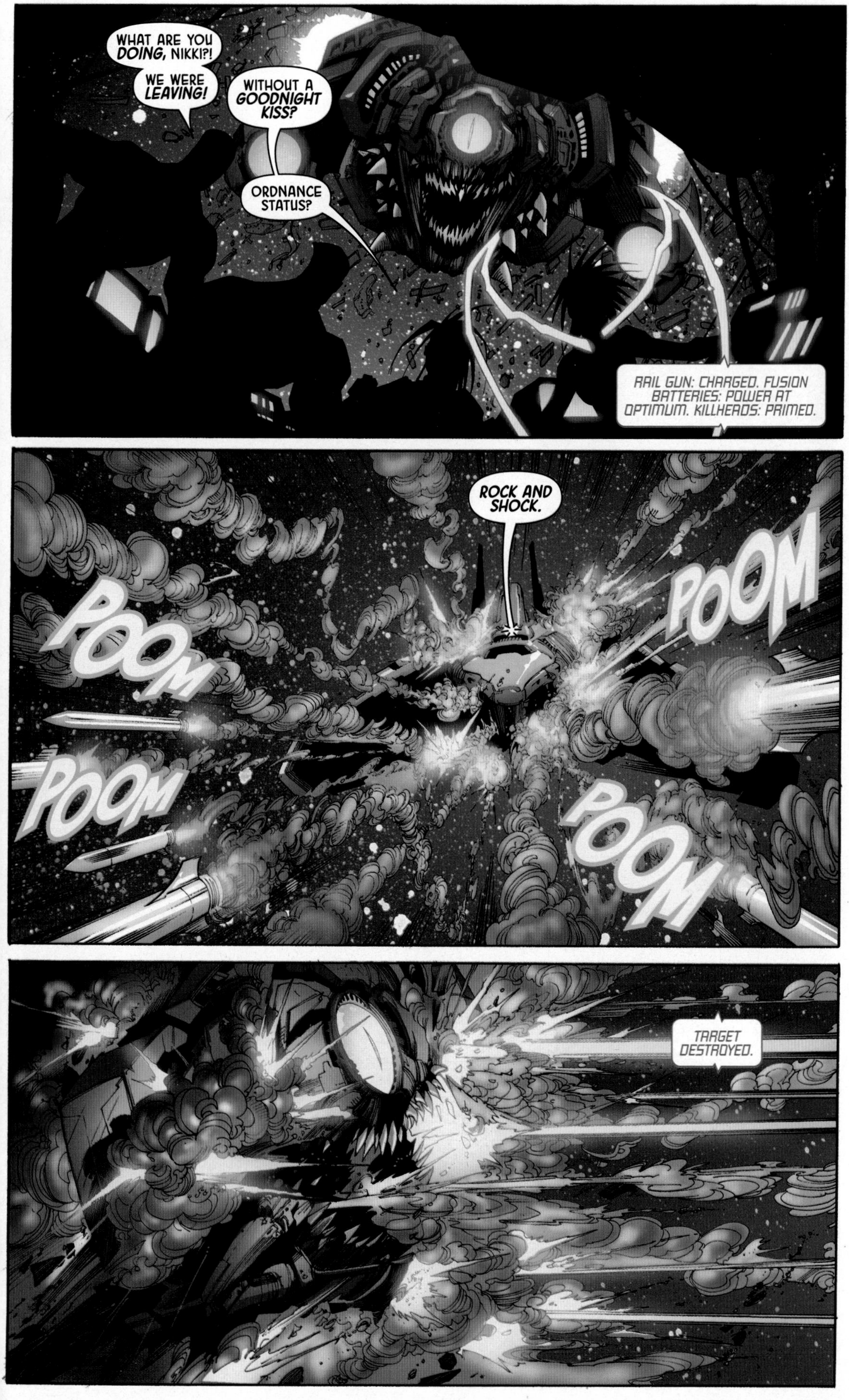
WHAT ARE YOU DOING, NIKKI?!
WE WERE LEAVING!
WITHOUT A GOODNIGHT KISS?
ORDNANCE STATUS?
RAIL GUN: CHARGED. FUSION BATTERIES: POWER AT OPTIMUM. KILLHEADS: PRIMED.
ROCK AND SHOCK.
POOM
POOM
POOM
POOM
TARGET DESTROYED.

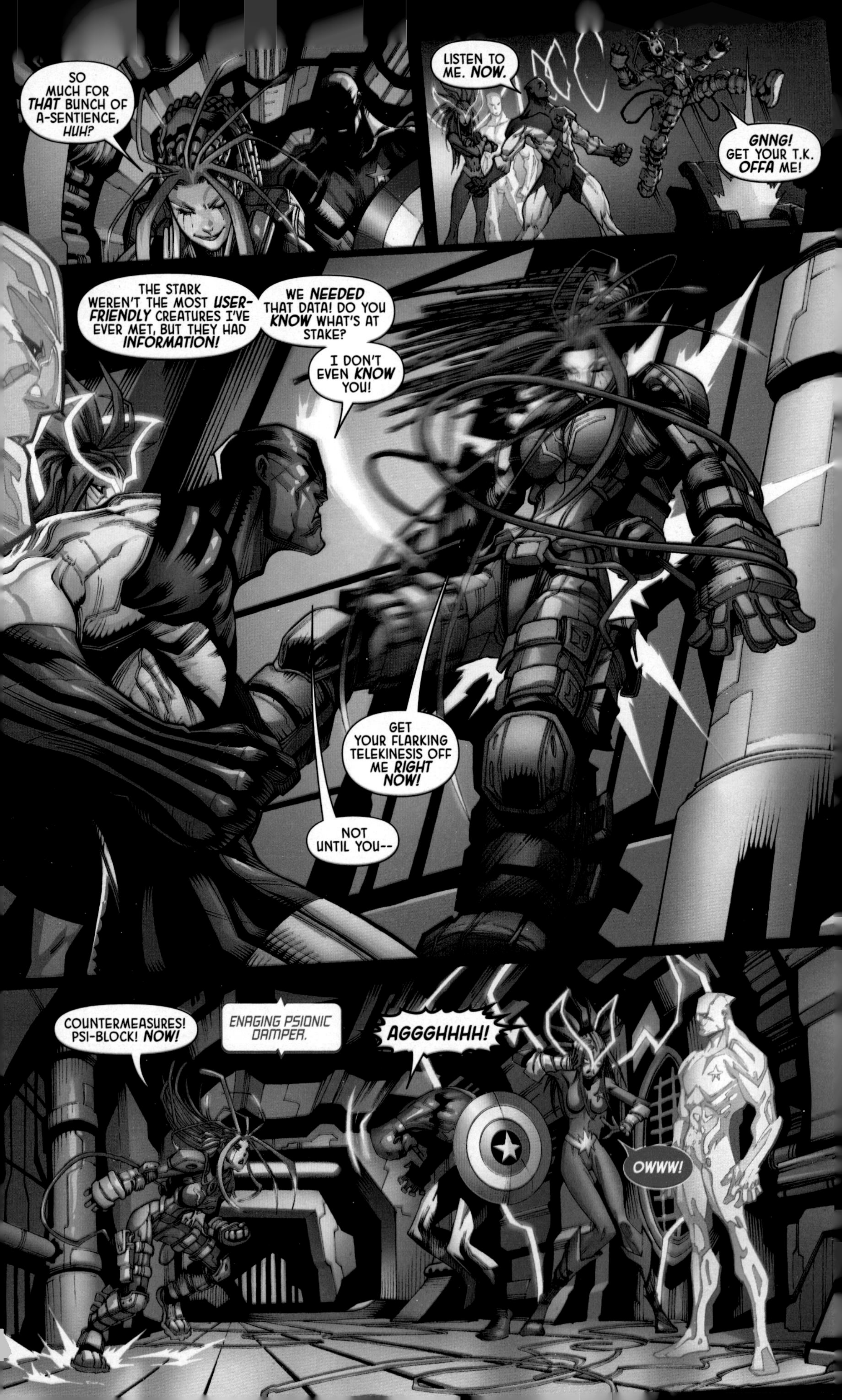
SO MUCH FOR THAT BUNCH OF A-SENTIENCE, HUH?
LISTEN TO ME. NOW.
GNNG! GET YOUR T.K. OFFA ME!
THE STARK WEREN'T THE MOST USER-FRIENDLY CREATURES I'VE EVER MET, BUT THEY HAD INFORMATION!
WE NEEDED THAT DATA! DO YOU KNOW WHAT'S AT STAKE?
I DON'T EVEN KNOW YOU!
GET YOUR FLARKING TELEKINESIS OFF ME RIGHT NOW!
NOT UNTIL YOU--
COUNTERMEASURES! PSI-BLOCK! NOW!
ENGAGING PSIONIC DAMPER.
AGGGHHHH!
OWWW!

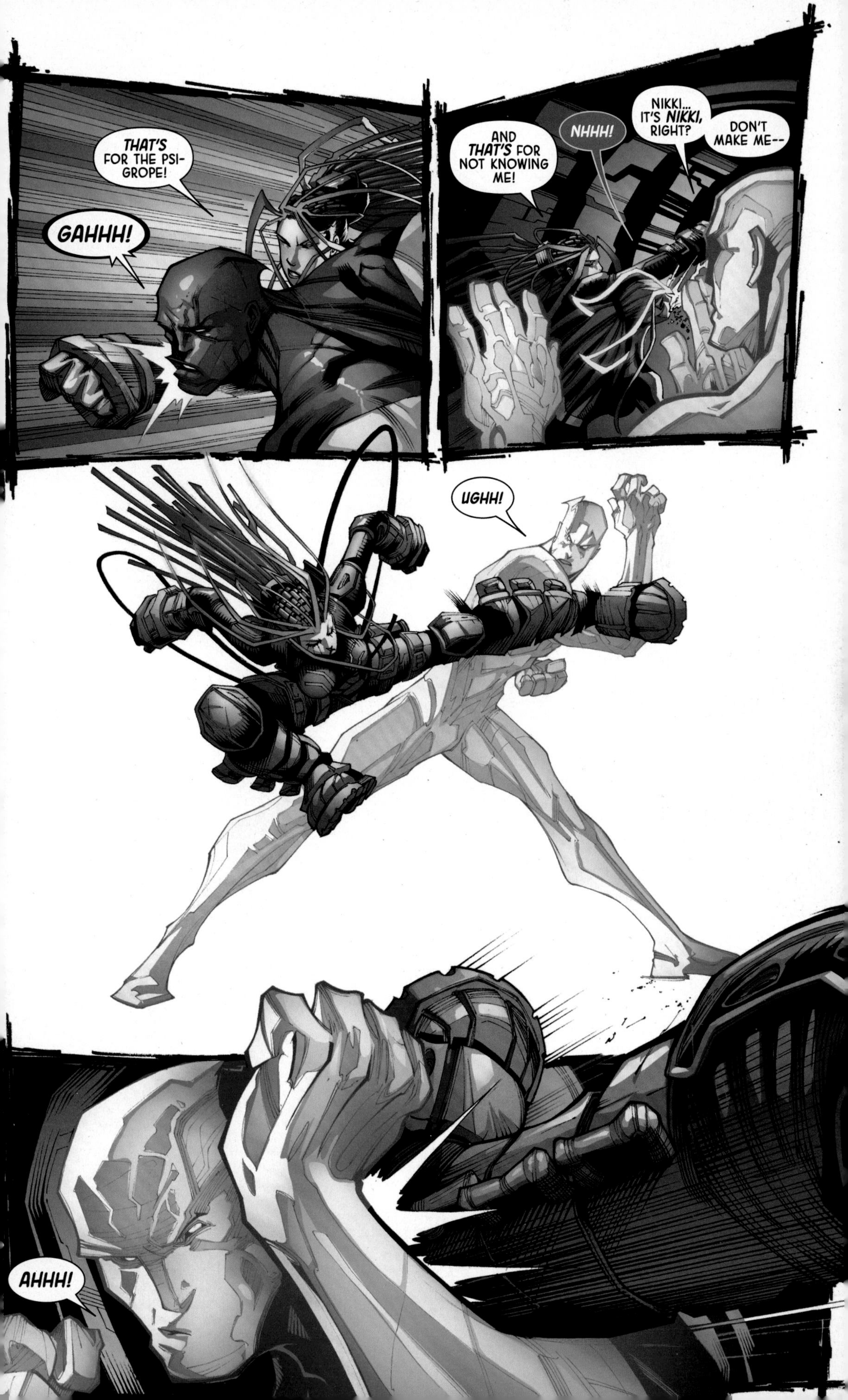
THAT'S FOR THE PSI-GROPE!
GAHHH!
AND THAT'S FOR NOT KNOWING ME!
NHHH!
NIKKI... IT'S NIKKI, RIGHT?
DON'T MAKE ME--
UGHH!
AHHH!

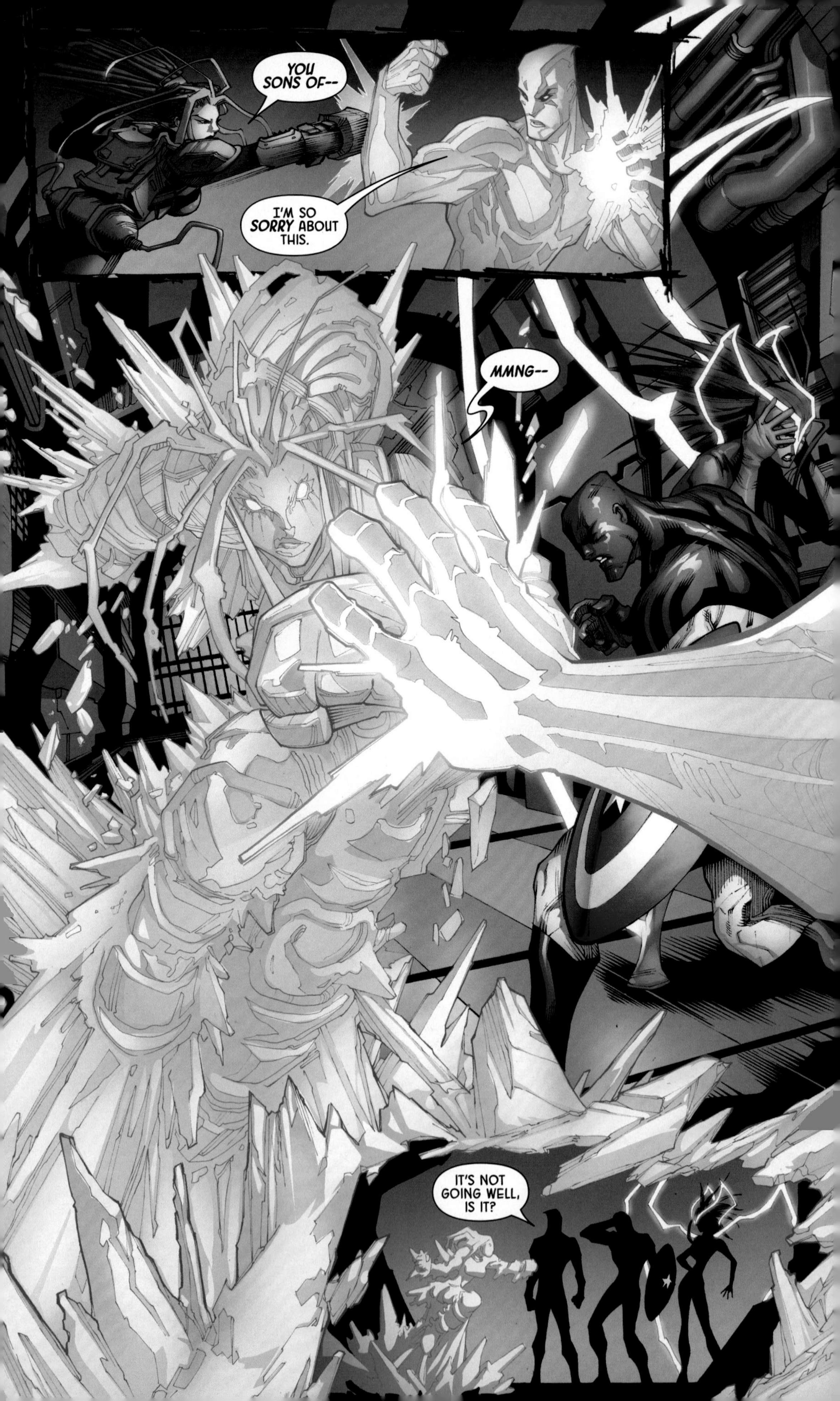
YOU SONS OF--
I'M SO SORRY ABOUT THIS.
MMNG--
IT'S NOT GOING WELL, IS IT?

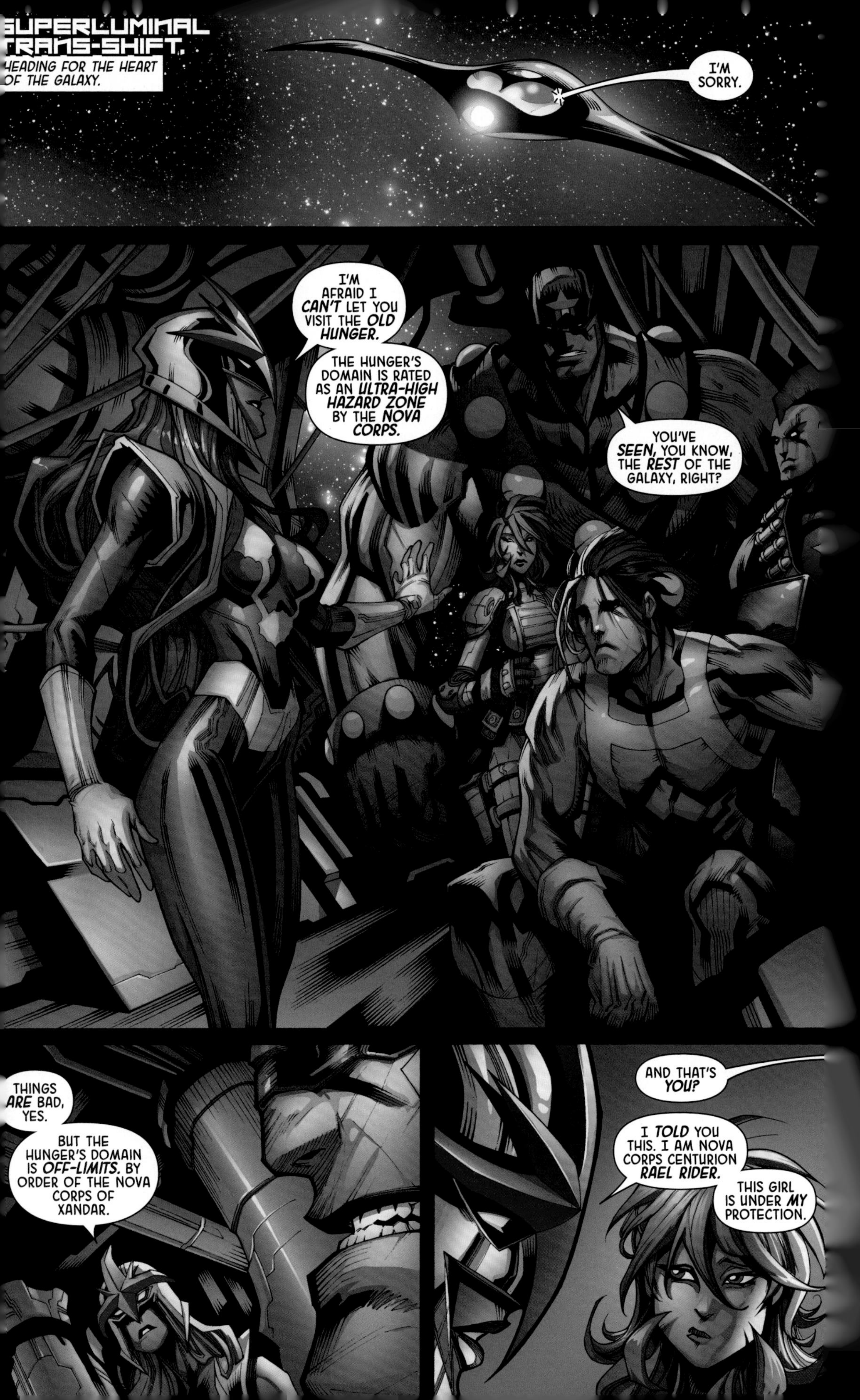
SUPERLUMINAL TRANS-SHIFT.
HEADING FOR THE HEART OF THE GALAXY.
I'M SORRY.
I'M AFRAID I CAN'T LET YOU VISIT THE OLD HUNGER.
THE HUNGER'S DOMAIN IS RATED AS AN ULTRA-HIGH HAZARD ZONE BY THE NOVA CORPS.
YOU'VE SEEN, YOU KNOW, THE REST OF THE GALAXY, RIGHT?
THINGS ARE BAD, YES.
BUT THE HUNGER'S DOMAIN IS OFF-LIMITS. BY ORDER OF THE NOVA CORPS OF XANDAR.
AND THAT'S YOU?
I TOLD YOU THIS. I AM NOVA CORPS CENTURION RAEL RIDER.
THIS GIRL IS UNDER MY PROTECTION.

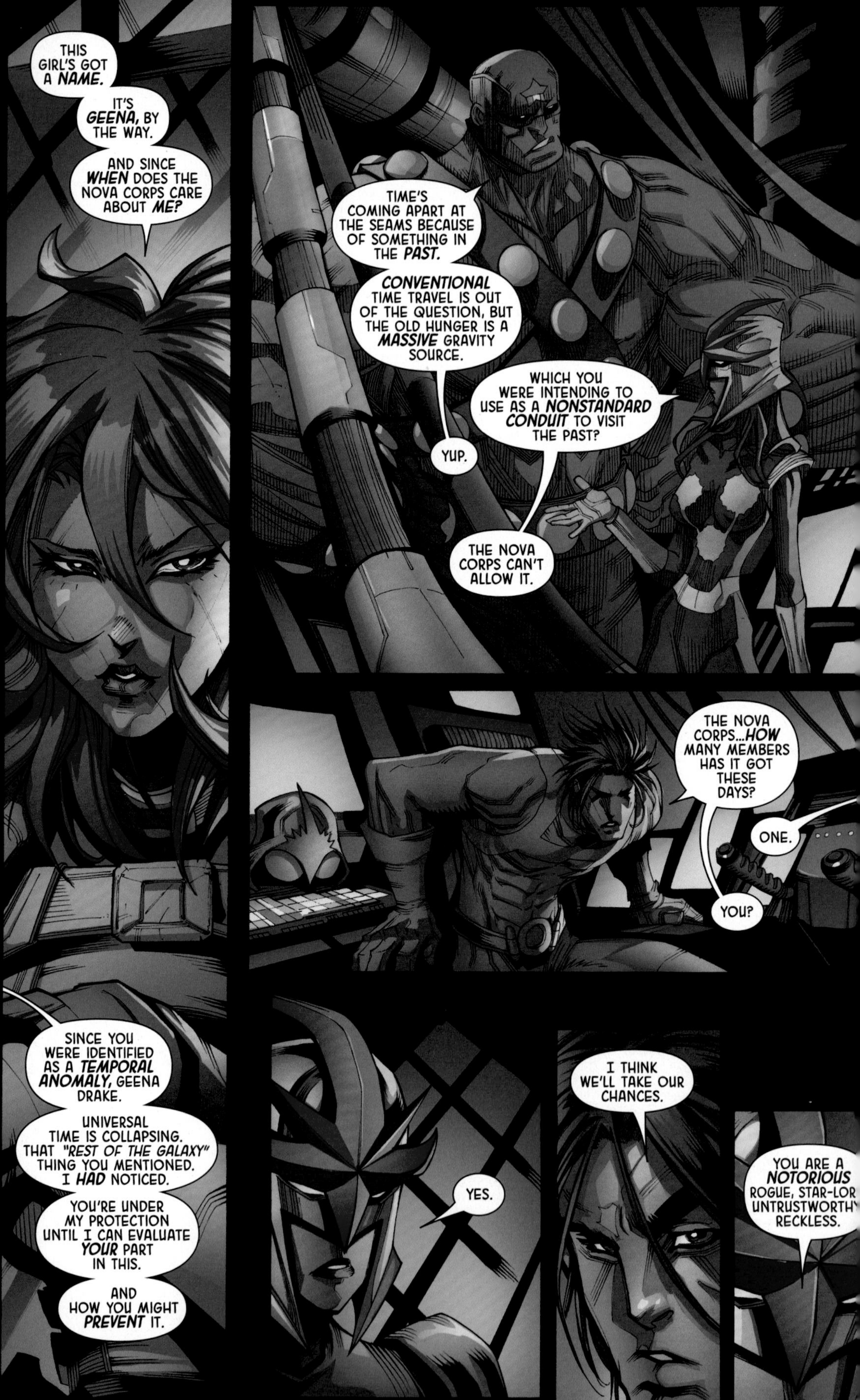
THIS GIRL'S GOT A NAME.
IT'S GEENA, BY THE WAY.
AND SINCE WHEN DOES THE NOVA CORPS CARE ABOUT ME?
TIME'S COMING APART AT THE SEAMS BECAUSE OF SOMETHING IN THE PAST.
CONVENTIONAL TIME TRAVEL IS OUT OF THE QUESTION, BUT THE OLD HUNGER IS A MASSIVE GRAVITY SOURCE.
WHICH YOU WERE INTENDING TO USE AS A NONSTANDARD CONDUIT TO VISIT THE PAST?
YUP.
THE NOVA CORPS CAN'T ALLOW IT.
THE NOVA CORPS...HOW MANY MEMBERS HAS IT GOT THESE DAYS?
ONE.
YOU?
SINCE YOU WERE IDENTIFIED AS A TEMPORAL ANOMALY, GEENA DRAKE.
UNIVERSAL TIME IS COLLAPSING. THAT "REST OF THE GALAXY" THING YOU MENTIONED. I HAD NOTICED.
YOU'RE UNDER MY PROTECTION UNTIL I CAN EVALUATE YOUR PART IN THIS.
AND HOW YOU MIGHT PREVENT IT.
YES.
I THINK WE'LL TAKE OUR CHANCES.
YOU ARE A NOTORIOUS ROGUE, STAR-LOR UNTRUSTWORTH RECKLESS.

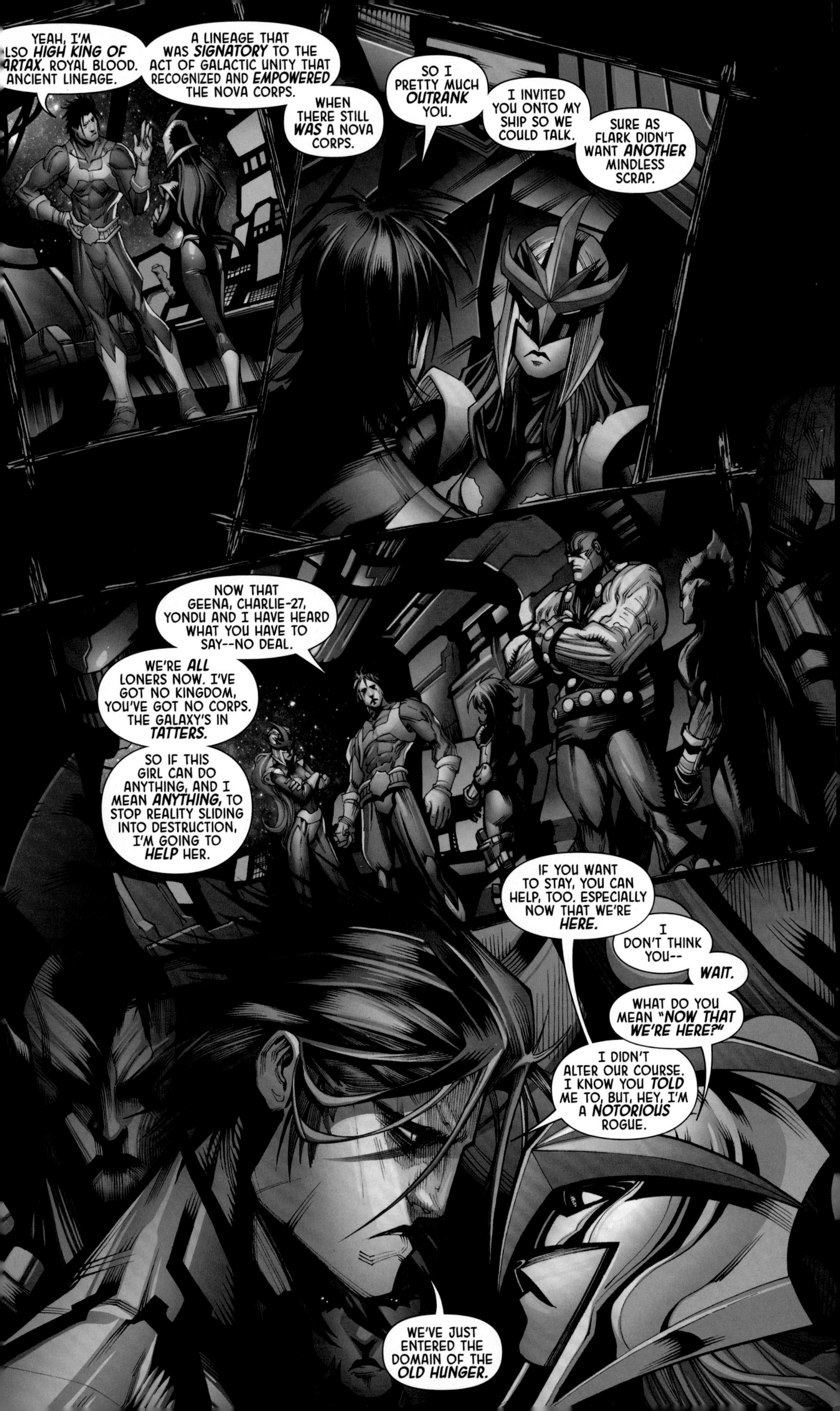

YEAH, I'M ALSO HIGH KING OF SPARTAX. ROYAL BLOOD. ANCIENT LINEAGE.
A LINEAGE THAT WAS SIGNATORY TO THE ACT OF GALACTIC UNITY THAT RECOGNIZED AND EMPOWERED THE NOVA CORPS.
WHEN THERE STILL WAS A NOVA CORPS.
SO I PRETTY MUCH OUTRANK YOU.
I INVITED YOU ONTO MY SHIP SO WE COULD TALK.
SURE AS FLARK DIDN'T WANT ANOTHER MINDLESS SCRAP.
NOW THAT GEENA, CHARLIE-27, YONDU AND I HAVE HEARD WHAT YOU HAVE TO SAY--NO DEAL.
WE'RE ALL LONERS NOW. I'VE GOT NO KINGDOM, YOU'VE GOT NO CORPS. THE GALAXY'S IN TATTERS.
SO IF THIS GIRL CAN DO ANYTHING, AND I MEAN ANYTHING, TO STOP REALITY SLIDING INTO DESTRUCTION, I'M GOING TO HELP HER.
IF YOU WANT TO STAY, YOU CAN HELP, TOO. ESPECIALLY NOW THAT WE'RE HERE.
I DON'T THINK YOU--
WAIT.
WHAT DO YOU MEAN "NOW THAT WE'RE HERE?"
I DIDN'T ALTER OUR COURSE. I KNOW YOU TOLD ME TO, BUT, HEY, I'M A NOTORIOUS ROGUE.
WE'VE JUST ENTERED THE DOMAIN OF THE OLD HUNGER.

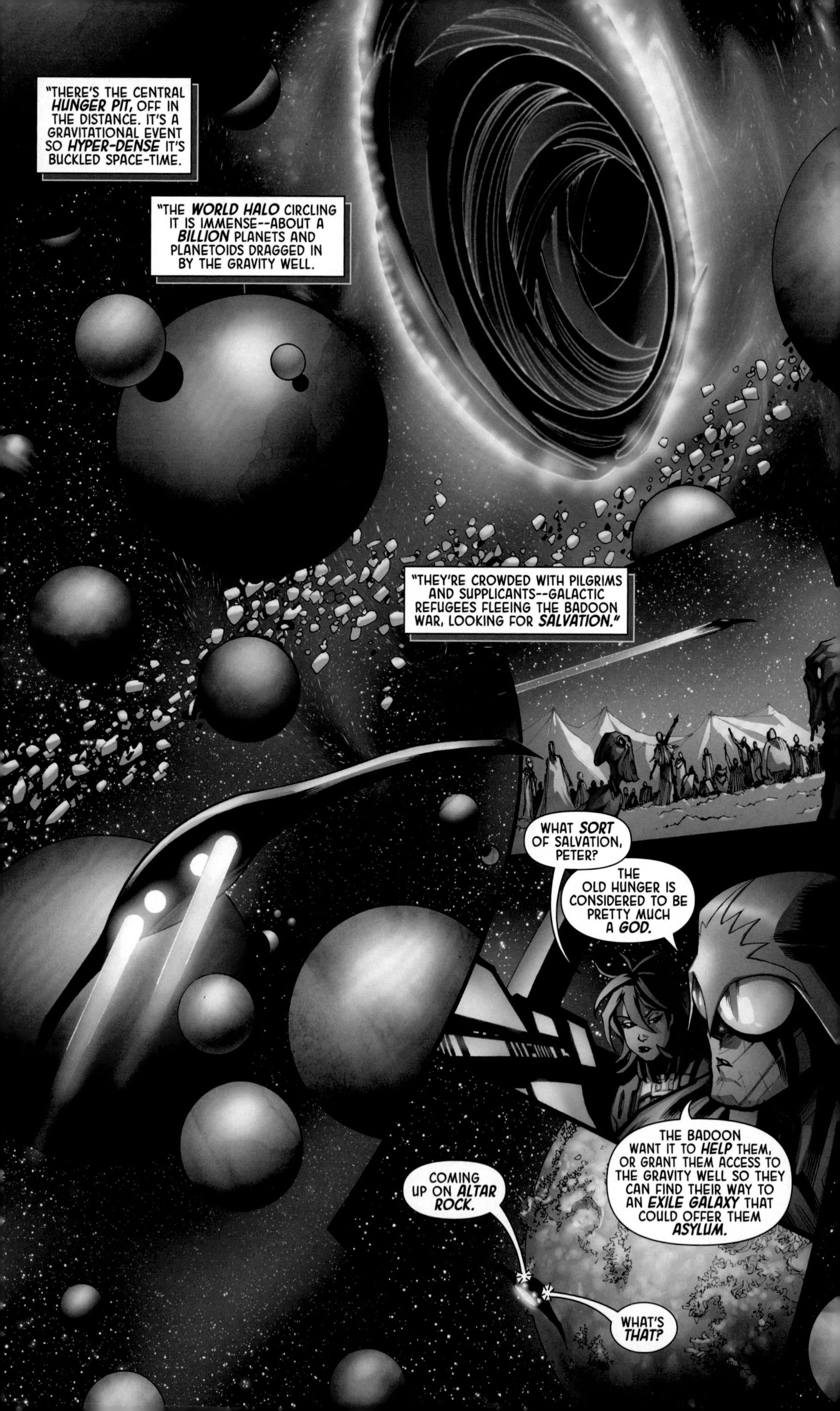
"THERE'S THE CENTRAL HUNGER PIT, OFF IN THE DISTANCE. IT'S A GRAVITATIONAL EVENT SO HYPER-DENSE IT'S BUCKLED SPACE-TIME.
"THE WORLD HALO CIRCLING IT IS IMMENSE--ABOUT A BILLION PLANETS AND PLANETOIDS DRAGGED IN BY THE GRAVITY WELL.
"THEY'RE CROWDED WITH PILGRIMS AND SUPPLICANTS--GALACTIC REFUGEES FLEEING THE BADOON WAR, LOOKING FOR SALVATION."
WHAT SORT OF SALVATION, PETER?
THE OLD HUNGER IS CONSIDERED TO BE PRETTY MUCH A GOD.
THE BADOON WANT IT TO HELP THEM, OR GRANT THEM ACCESS TO THE GRAVITY WELL SO THEY CAN FIND THEIR WAY TO AN EXILE GALAXY THAT COULD OFFER THEM ASYLUM.
COMING UP ON ALTAR ROCK.
WHAT'S THAT?

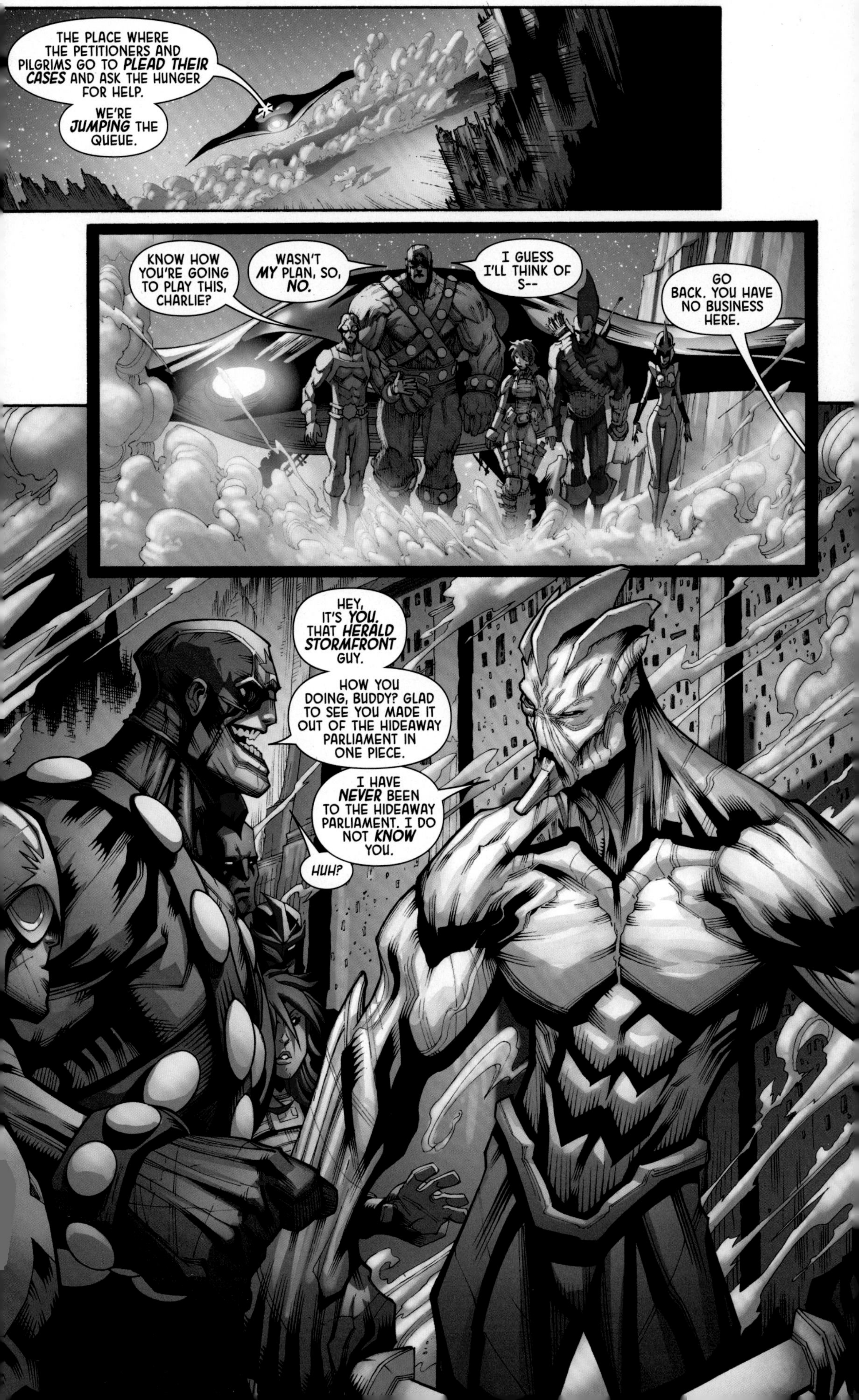
THE PLACE WHERE THE PETITIONERS AND PILGRIMS GO TO PLEAD THEIR CASES AND ASK THE HUNGER FOR HELP.
WE'RE JUMPING THE QUEUE.
KNOW HOW YOU'RE GOING TO PLAY THIS, CHARLIE?
WASN'T MY PLAN, SO, NO.
I GUESS I'LL THINK OF S--
GO BACK. YOU HAVE NO BUSINESS HERE.
HEY, IT'S YOU. THAT HERALD STORMFRONT GUY.
HOW YOU DOING, BUDDY? GLAD TO SEE YOU MADE IT OUT OF THE HIDEAWAY PARLIAMENT IN ONE PIECE.
I HAVE NEVER BEEN TO THE HIDEAWAY PARLIAMENT. I DO NOT KNOW YOU.
HUH?

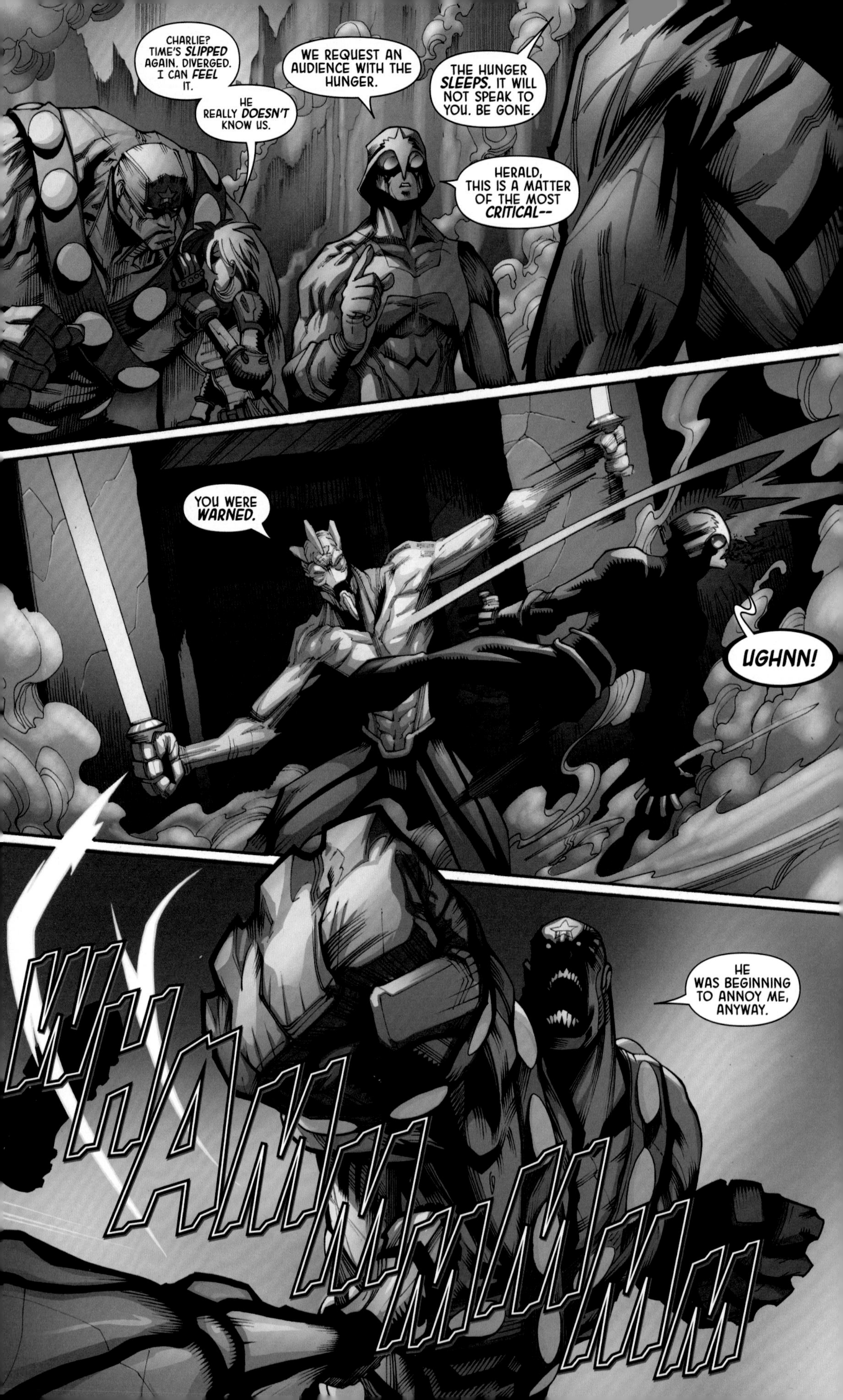
CHARLIE? TIME'S SLIPPED AGAIN. DIVERGED. I CAN FEEL IT.
HE REALLY DOESN'T KNOW US.
WE REQUEST AN AUDIENCE WITH THE HUNGER.
THE HUNGER SLEEPS. IT WILL NOT SPEAK TO YOU. BE GONE.
HERALD, THIS IS A MATTER OF THE MOST CRITICAL--
YOU WERE WARNED.
UGHNN!
WHAMMMMMMMM
HE WAS BEGINNING TO ANNOY ME, ANYWAY.

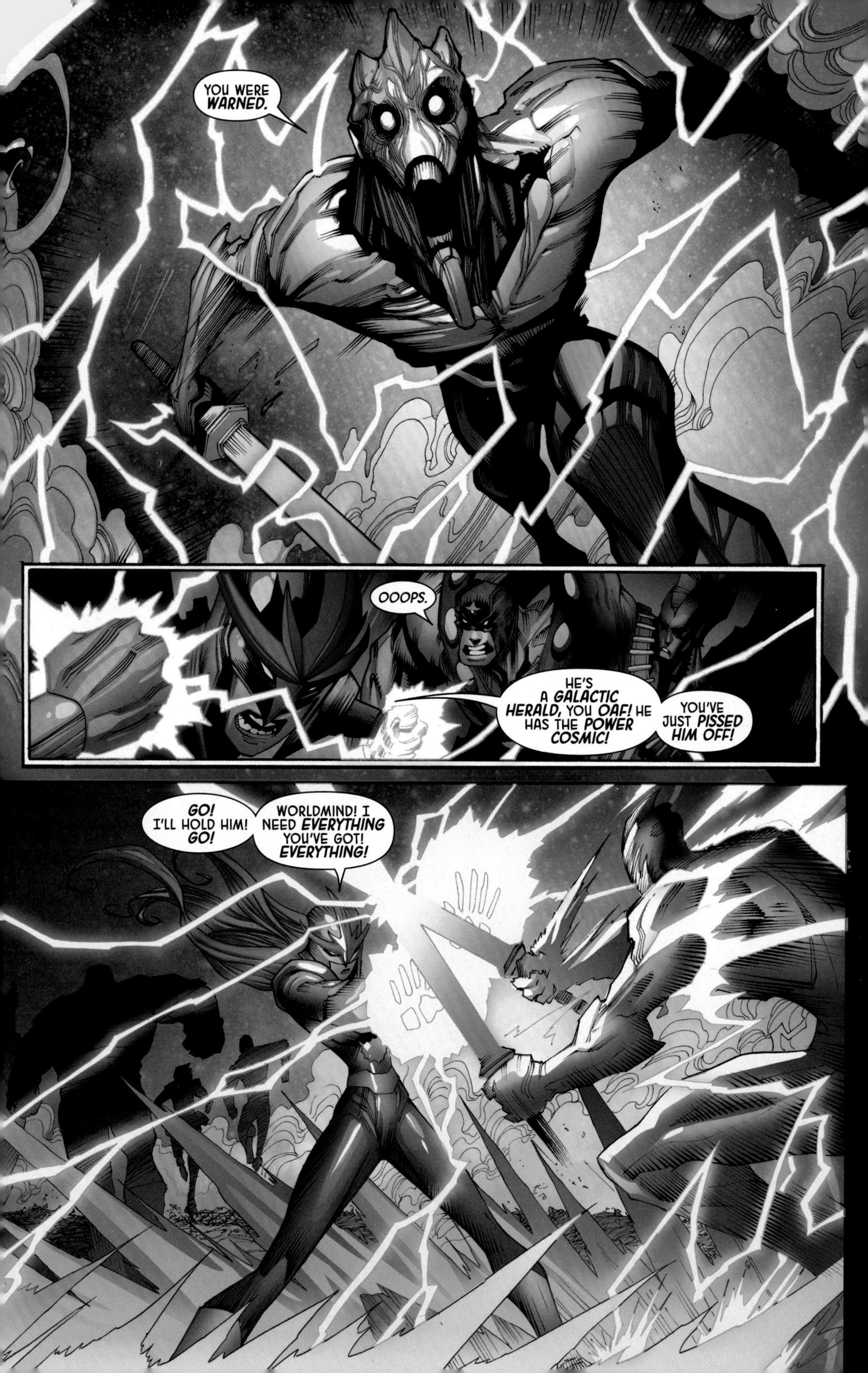
YOU WERE WARNED.
OOOPS.
HE'S A GALACTIC HERALD, YOU OAF! HE HAS THE POWER COSMIC!
YOU'VE JUST PISSED HIM OFF!
GO! I'LL HOLD HIM! GO!
WORLDMIND! I NEED EVERYTHING YOU'VE GOT! EVERYTHING!

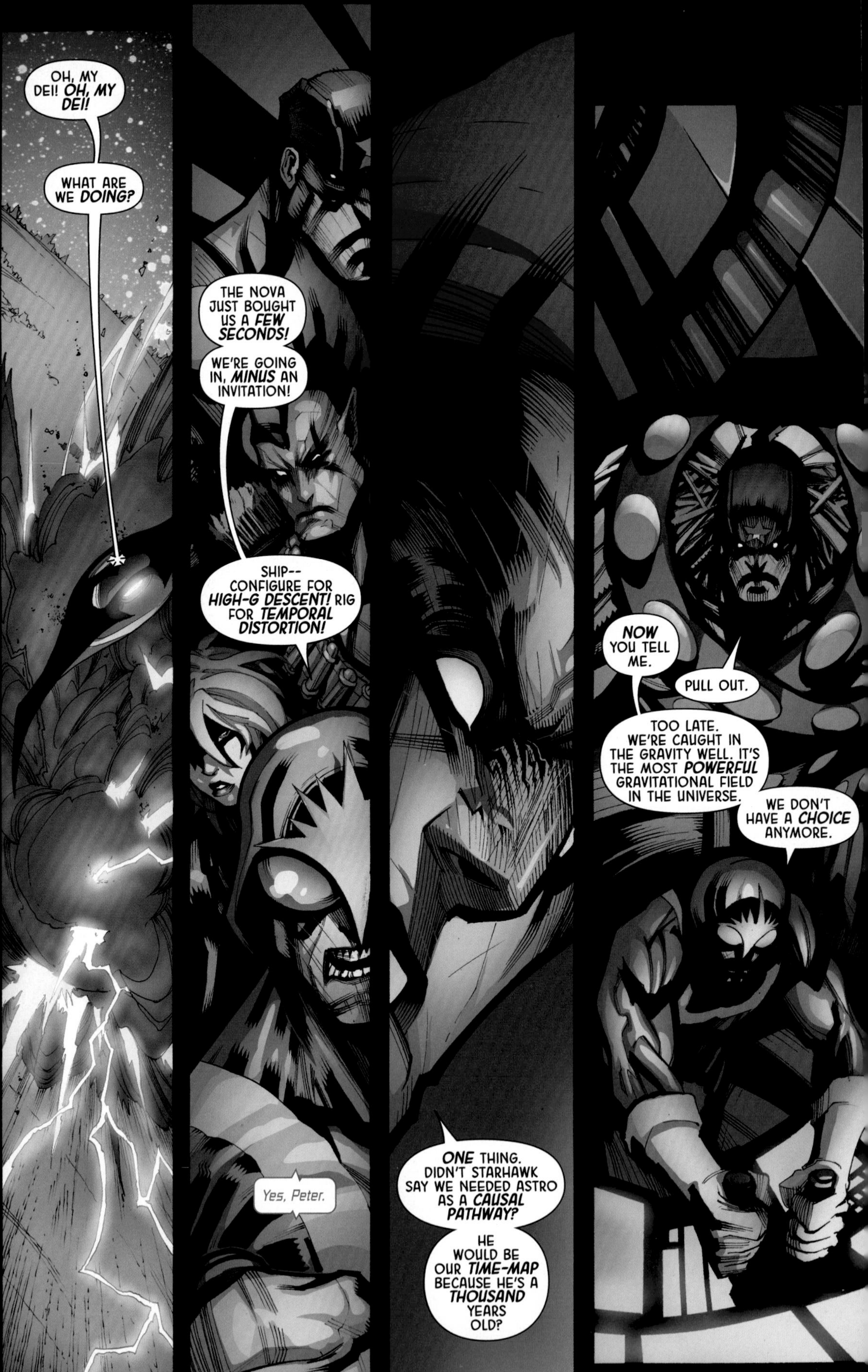

OH, MY DEI! *OH, MY DEI!*
WHAT ARE WE *DOING?*
THE NOVA JUST BOUGHT US A *FEW SECONDS!*
WE'RE GOING IN, *MINUS* AN INVITATION!
SHIP-- CONFIGURE FOR *HIGH-G DESCENT!* RIG FOR *TEMPORAL DISTORTION!*
Yes, Peter.
ONE THING. DIDN'T STARHAWK SAY WE NEEDED ASTRO AS A *CAUSAL PATHWAY?*
HE WOULD BE OUR *TIME-MAP* BECAUSE HE'S A *THOUSAND* YEARS OLD?
NOW YOU TELL ME.
PULL OUT.
TOO LATE. WE'RE CAUGHT IN THE GRAVITY WELL. IT'S THE MOST *POWERFUL* GRAVITATIONAL FIELD IN THE UNIVERSE.
WE DON'T HAVE A *CHOICE* ANYMORE.

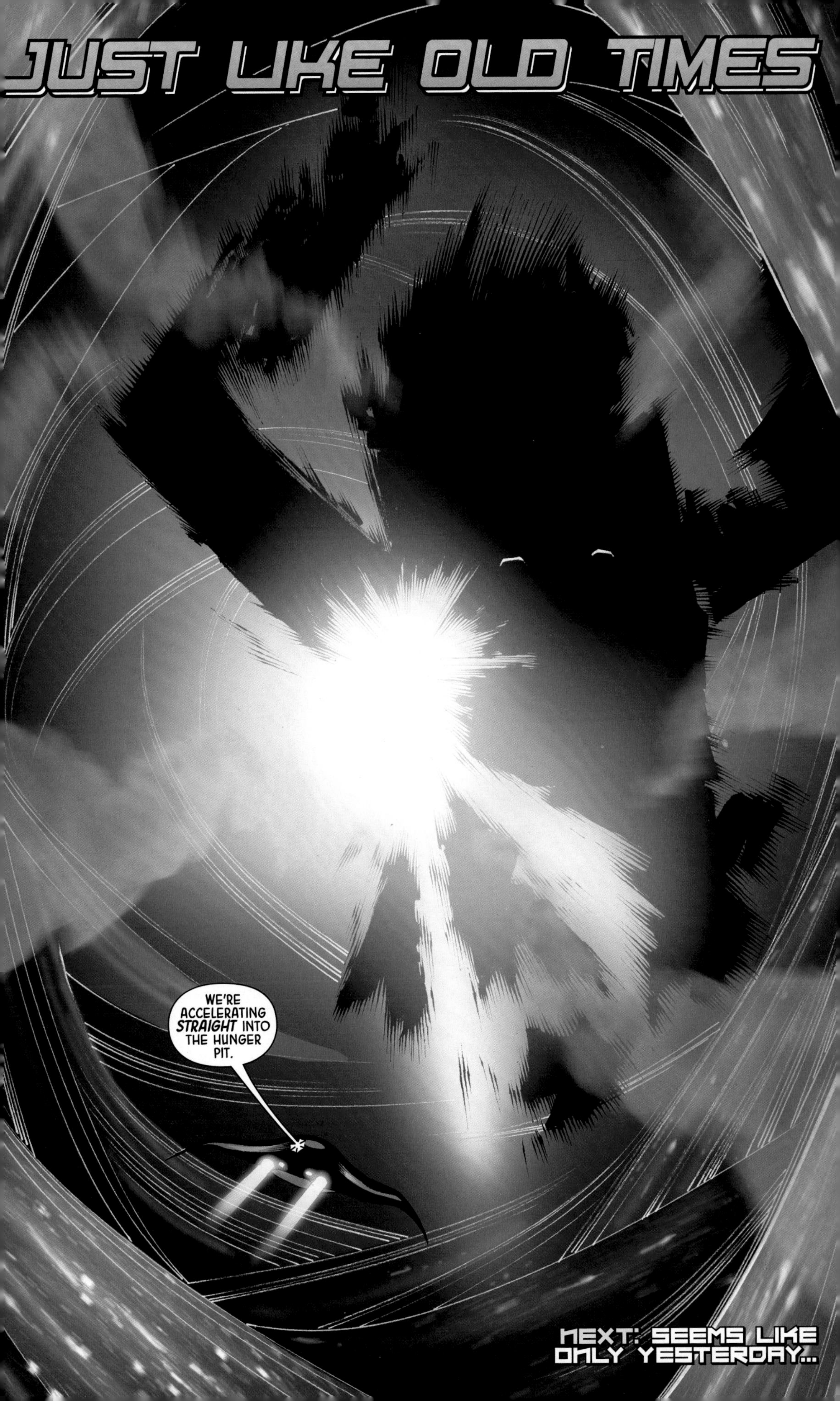
JUST LIKE OLD TIMES
WE'RE ACCELERATING STRAIGHT INTO THE HUNGER PIT.
NEXT: SEEMS LIKE ONLY YESTERDAY...

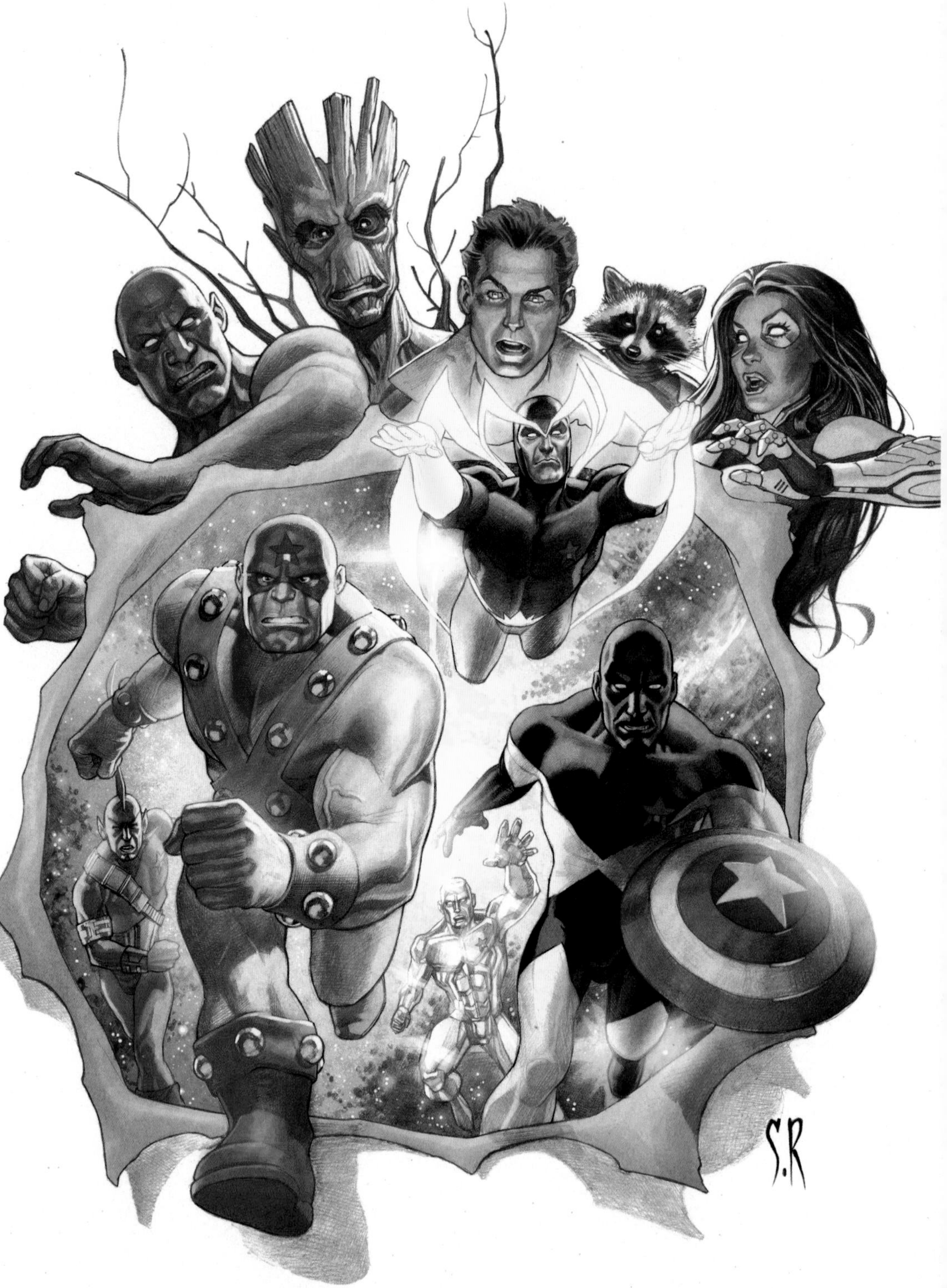
S.R

#1 **VARIANT** BY STEPHANE ROUX

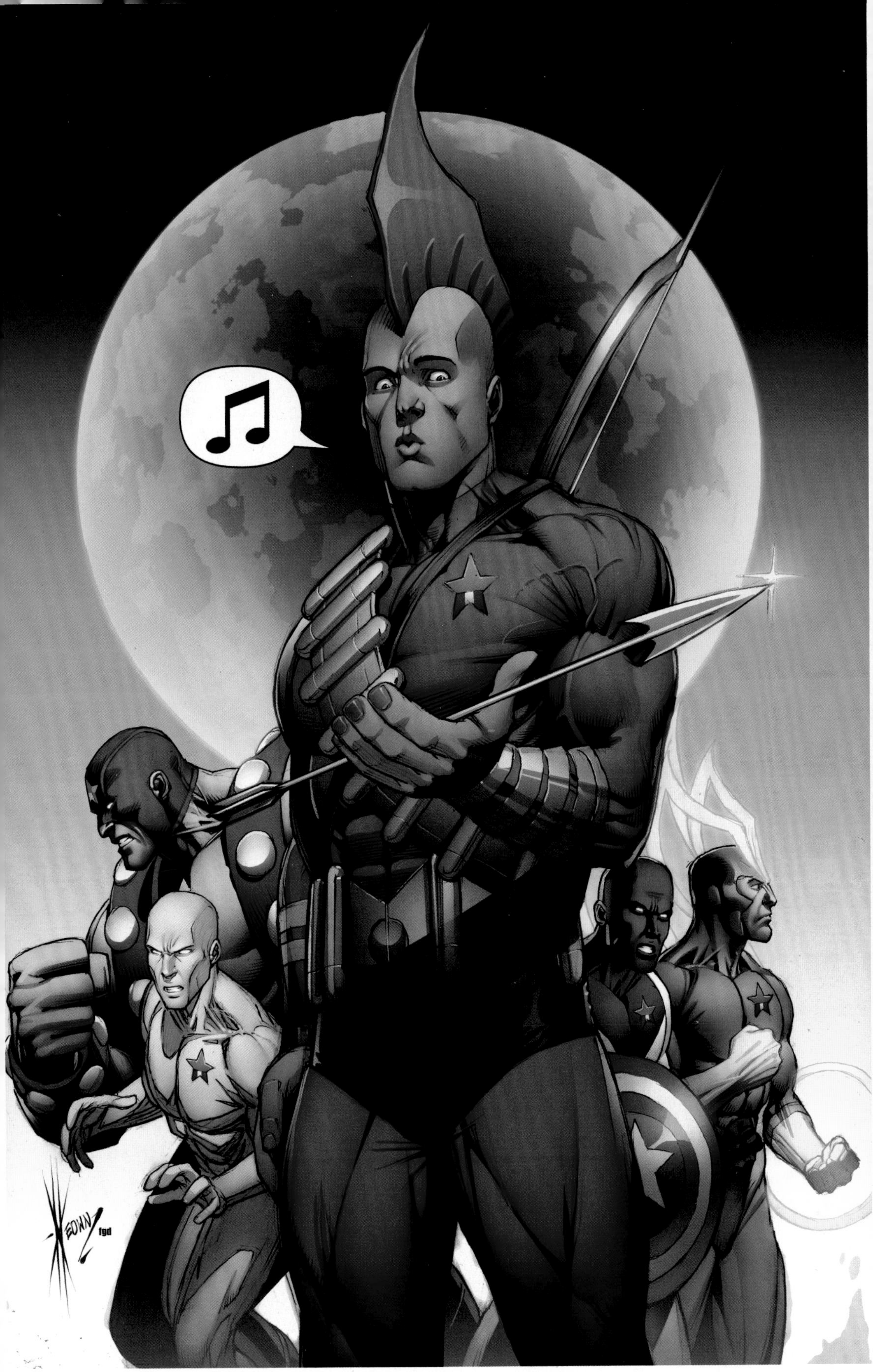

#1 VARIANT BY DALE KEOWN & FRANK D'ARMATA

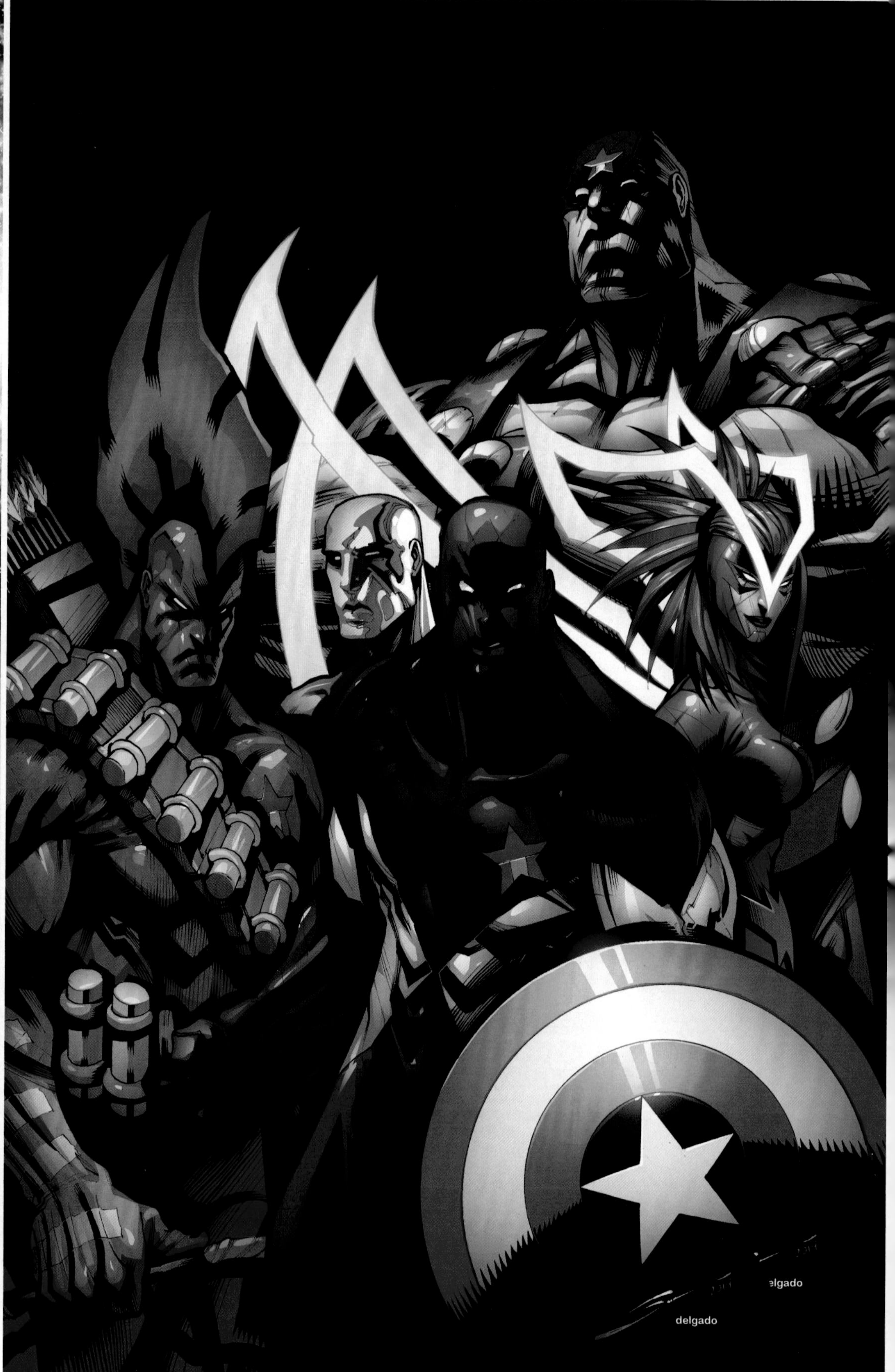
elgado
delgado

#2 VARIANT BY GERARDO SANDOVAL & EDGAR DELGADO

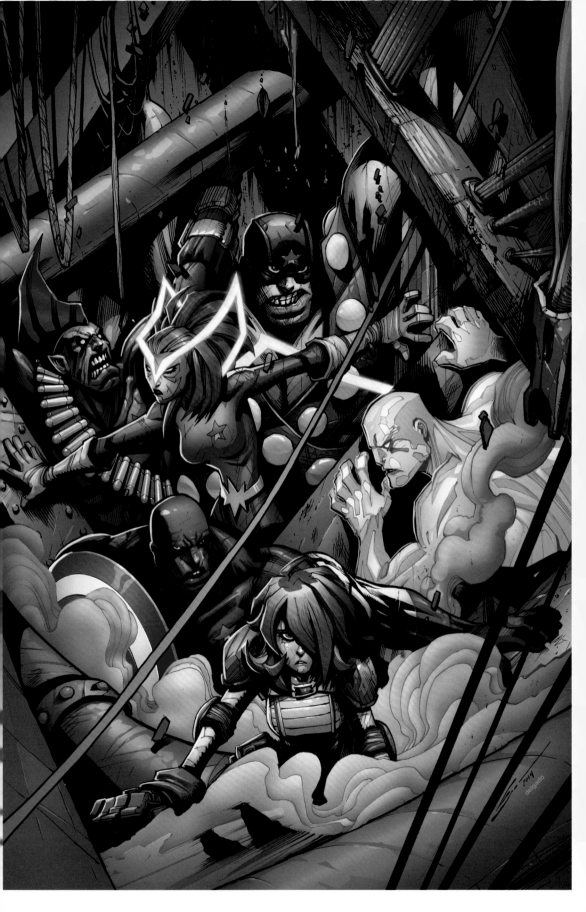

#3 VARIANT BY GERARDO SANDOVAL & EDGAR DELGADO

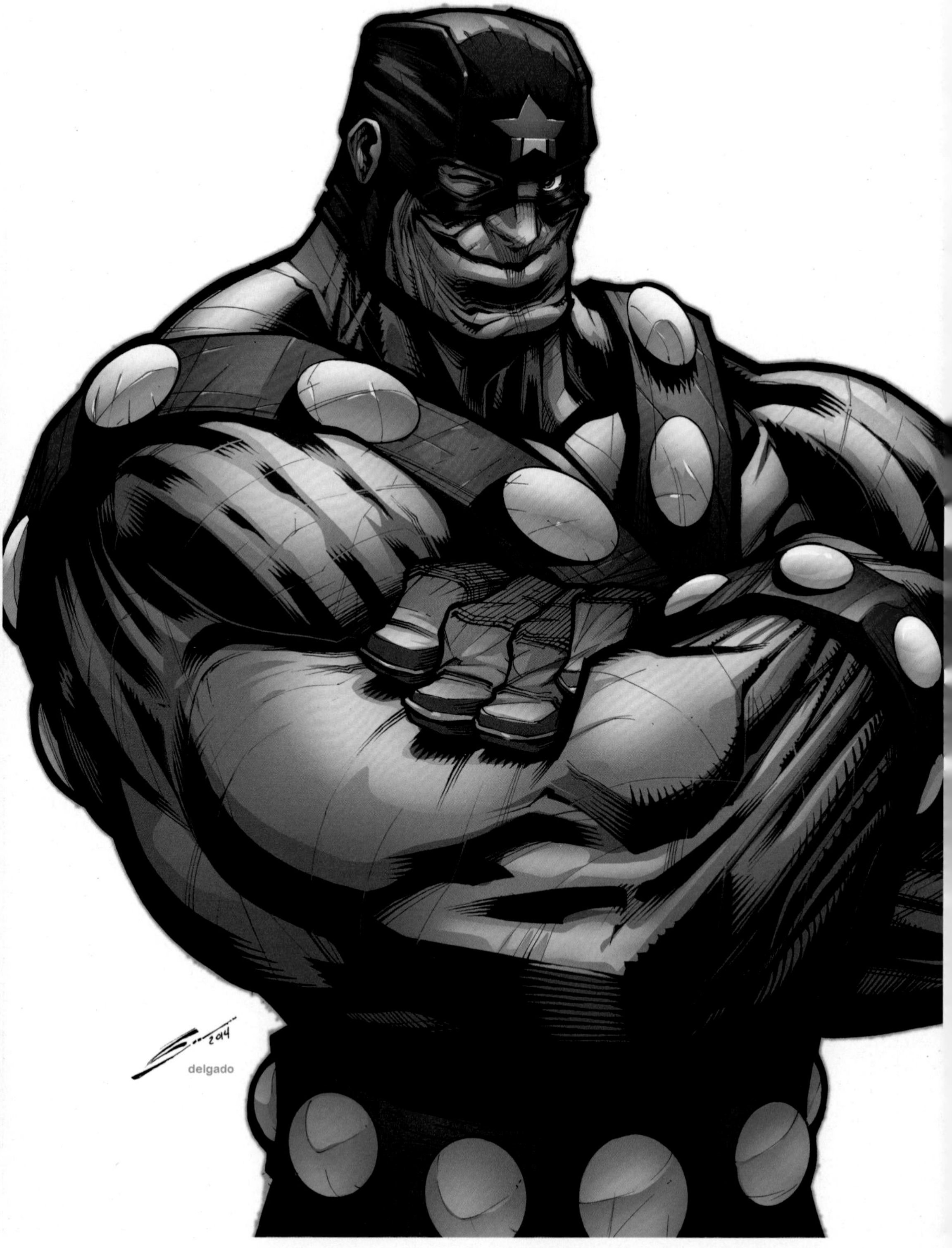
2014
delgado

#4 **VARIANT** BY GERARDO SANDOVAL & EDGAR DELGADO

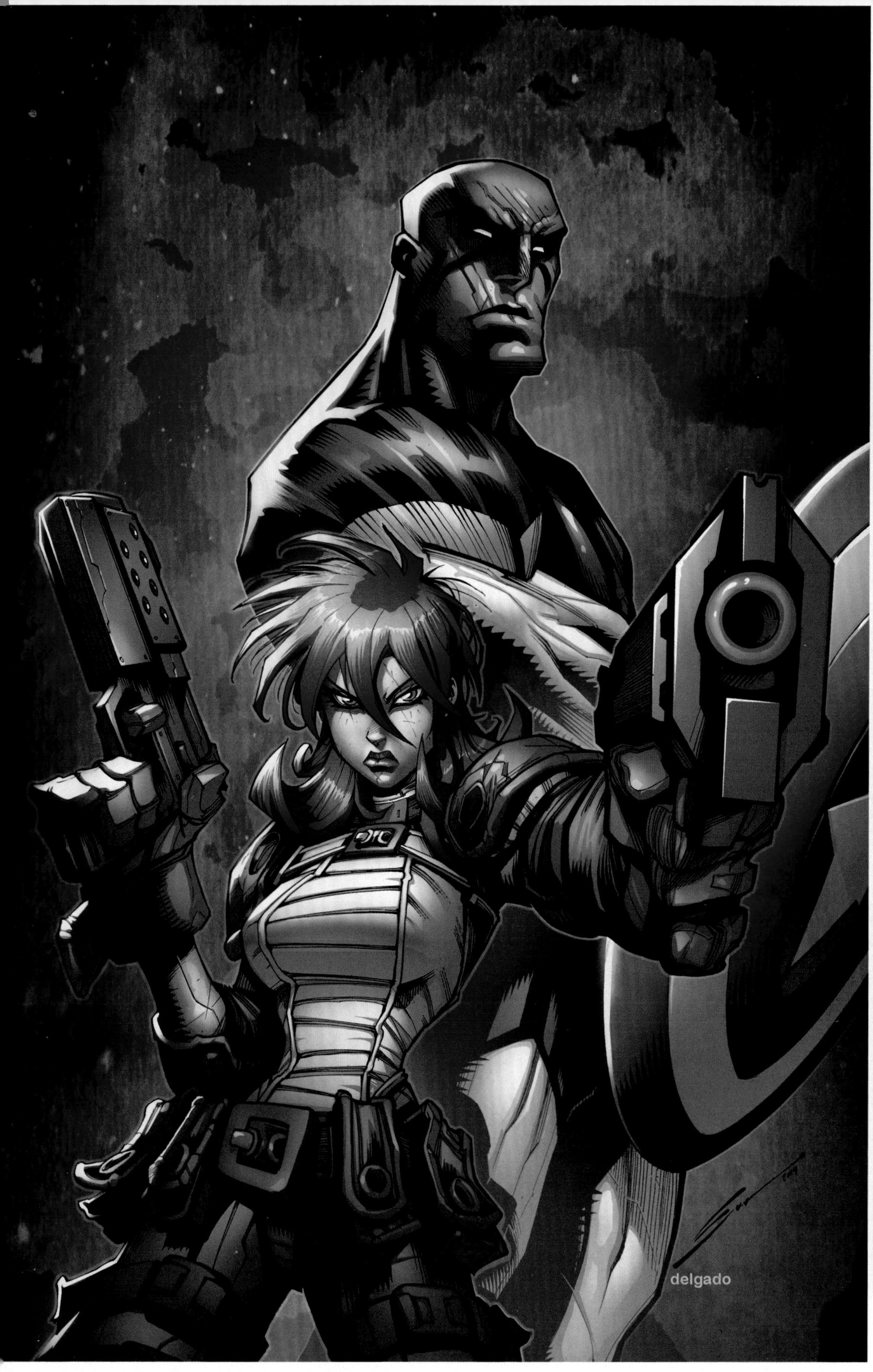
delgado

#5 VARIANT BY GERARDO SANDOVAL & EDGAR DELGADO

CHARACTER SKETCHES
BY GERARDO SANDOVAL

GEENA DRAKE

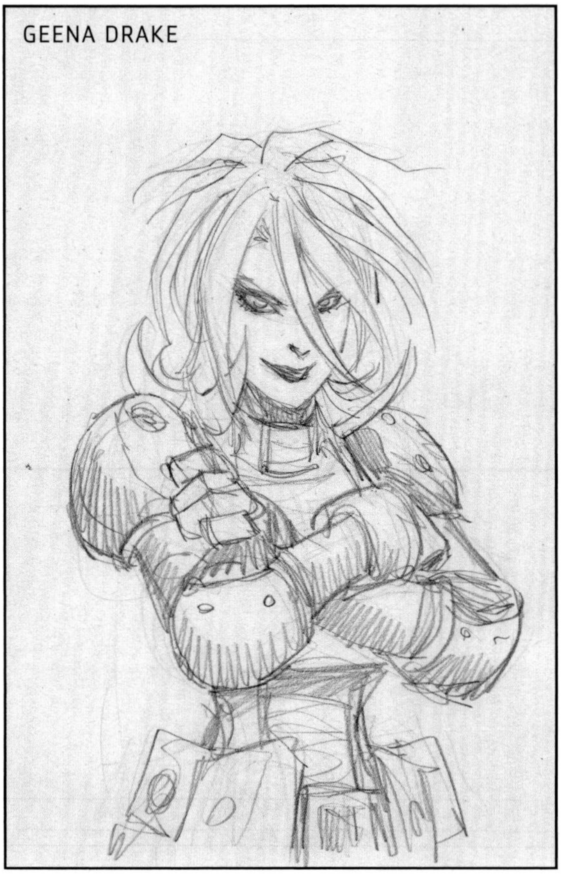

MARTINEX

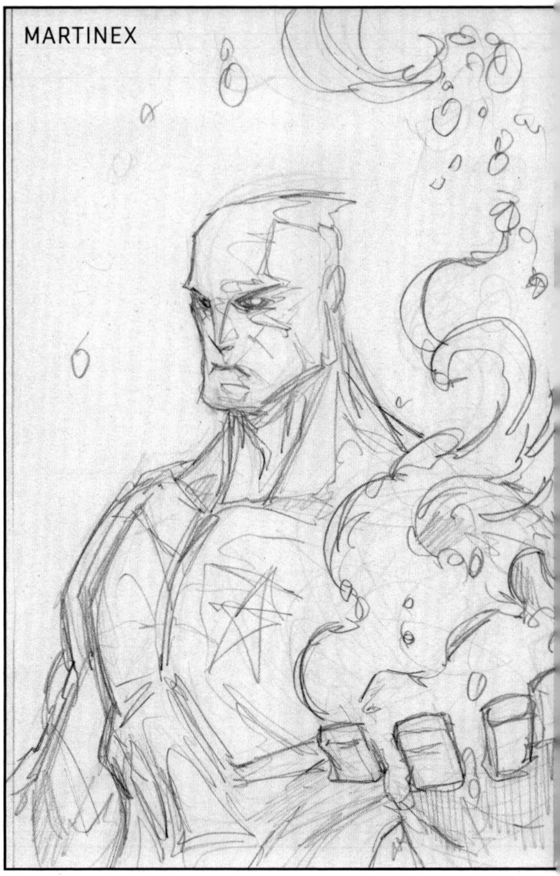

VANCE ASTRO

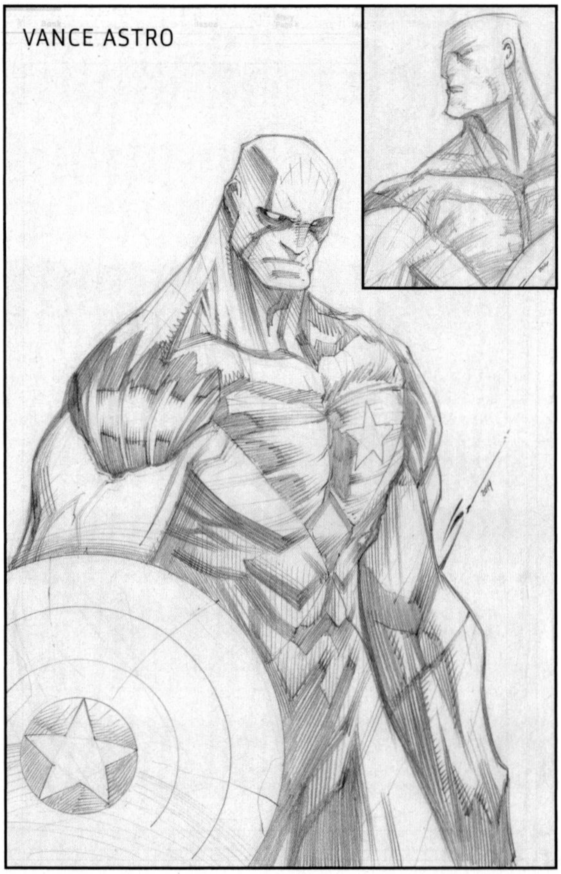

YONDU

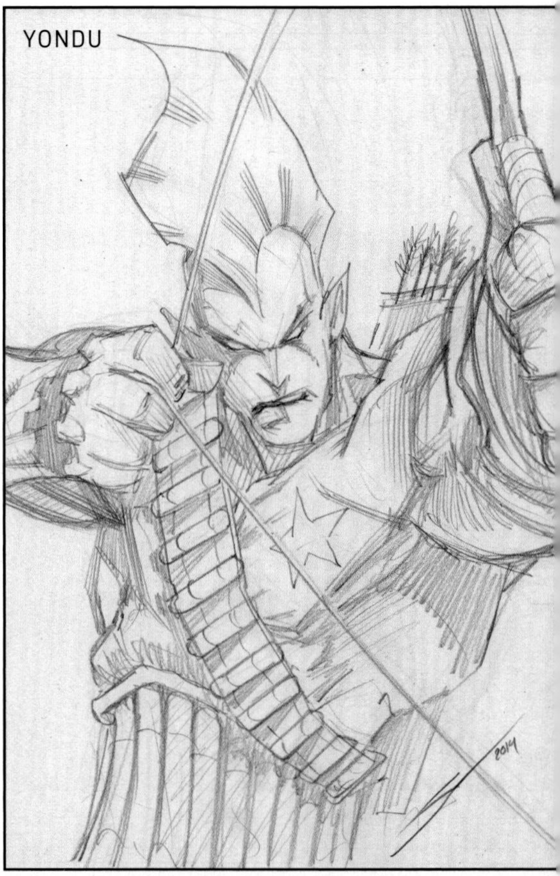

COVER PROCESS
BY GERARDO SANDOVAL

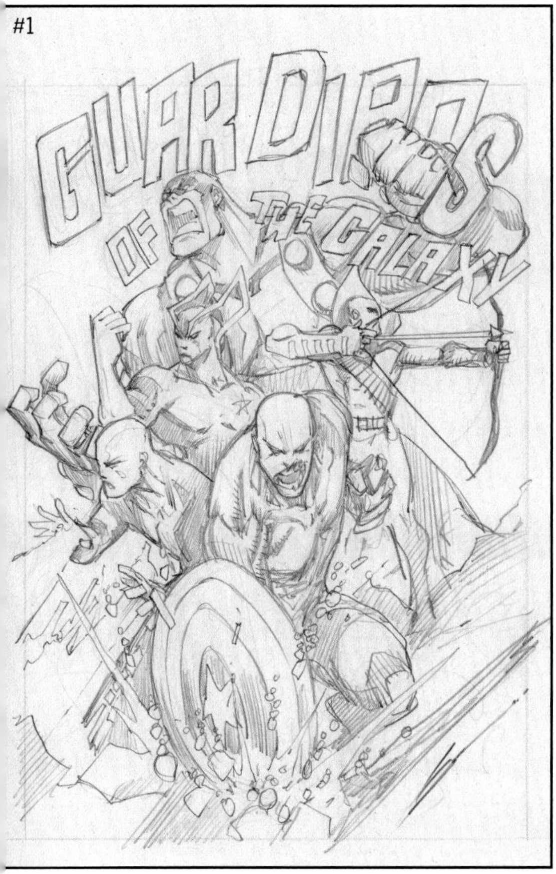
#1
GUARDIANS
OF THE GALAXY

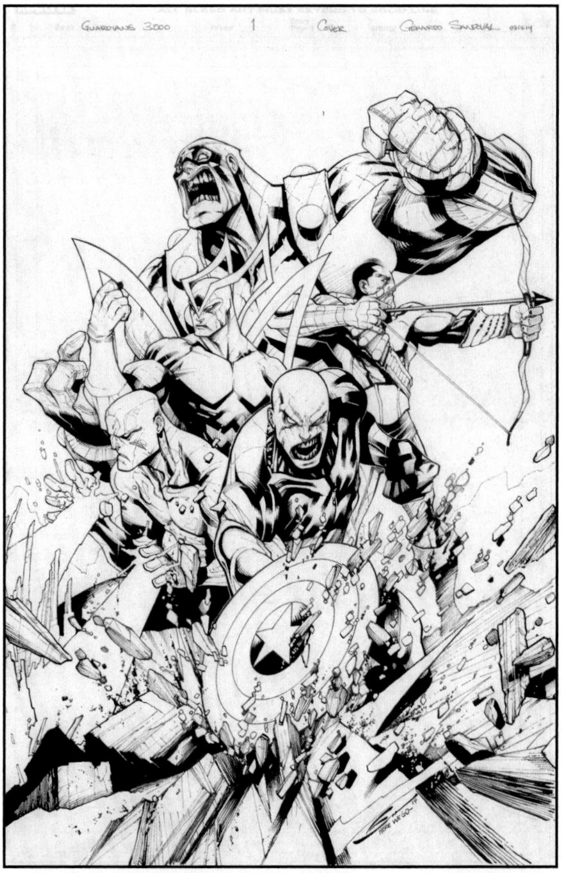
GUARDIANS 3000
1
COVER
GERARDO SANDOVAL

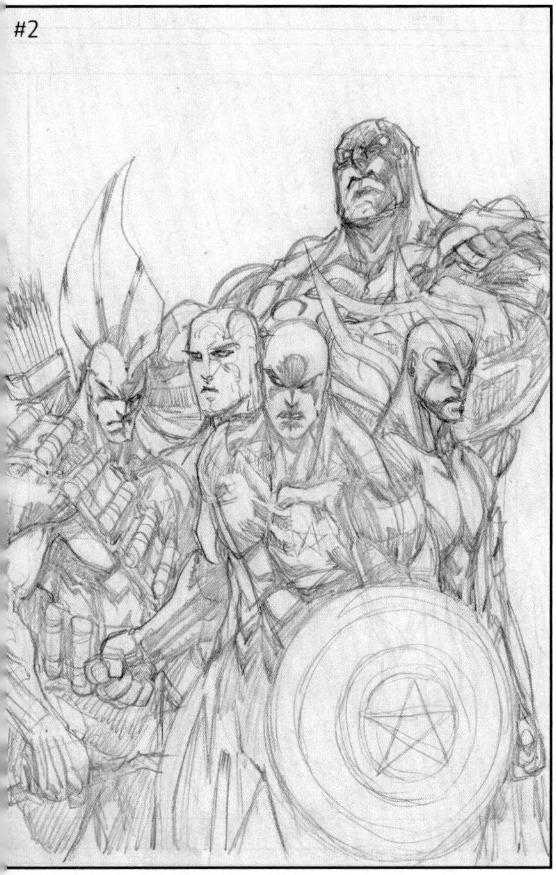
#2

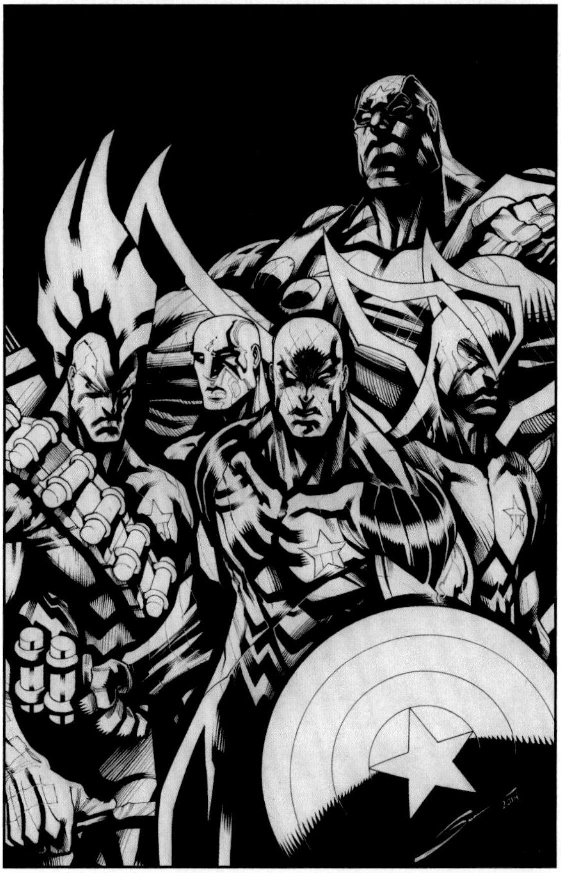

#3

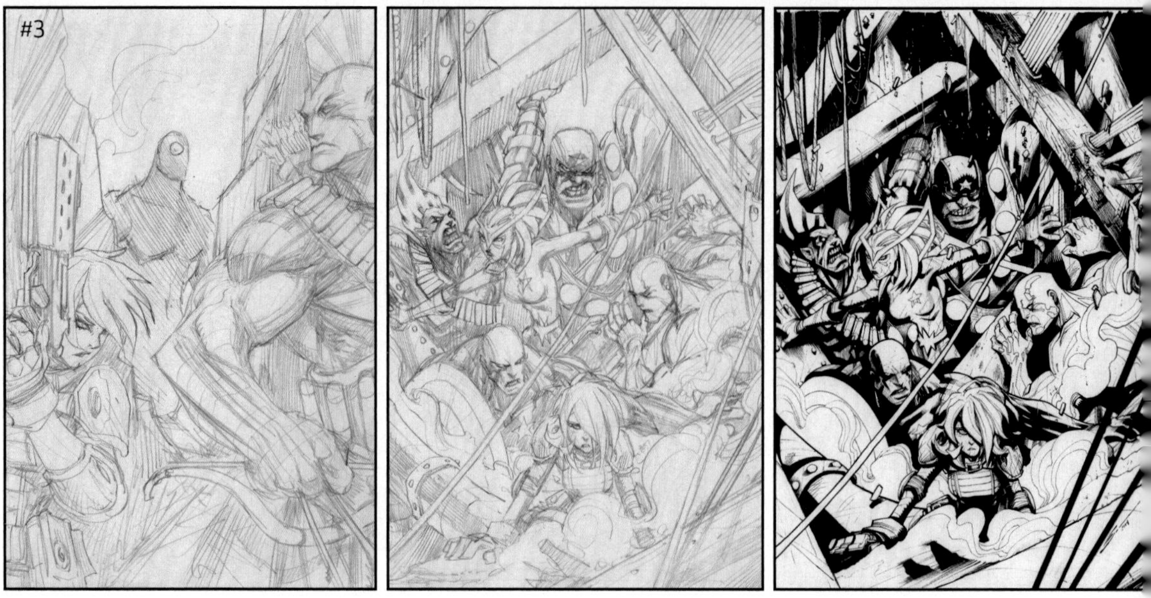

#4

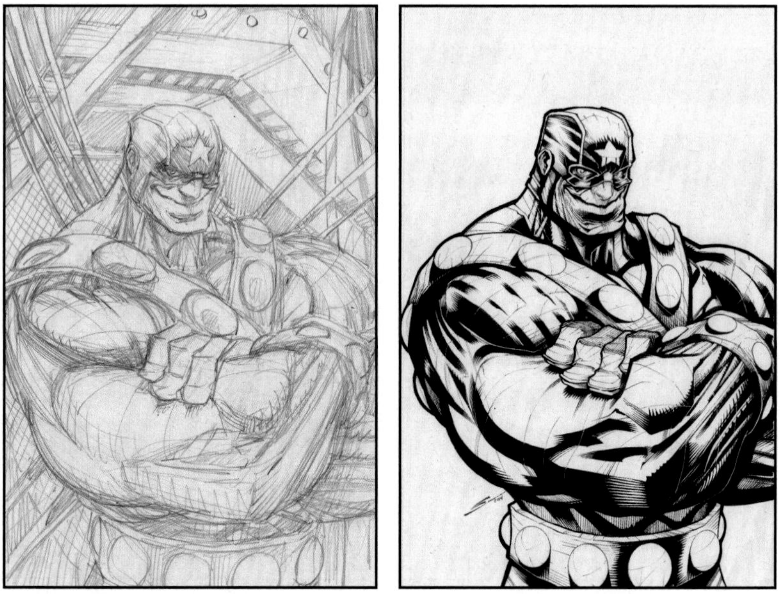

#5

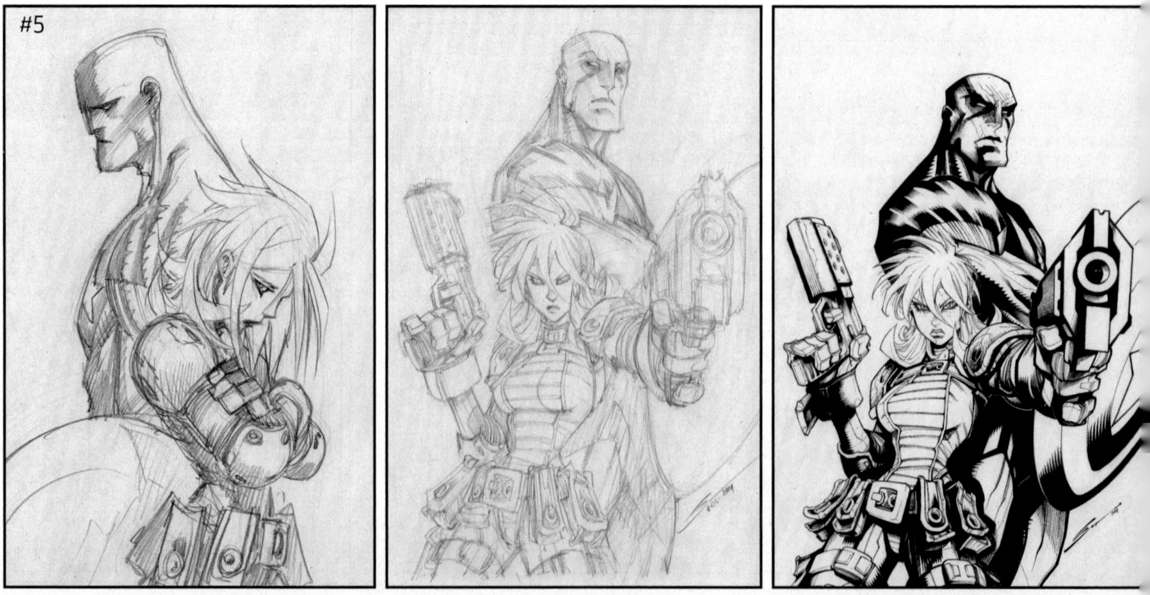